Clinical Handbook

of

Chinese Prepared Medicines

Clinical Handbook
of
Chinese Prepared Medicines

Chun-Han Zhu

Paradigm Publications   *Brookline, Massachusetts*

1989

Copyright © 1989 Paradigm Publications
44 Linden Street, Brookline, Massachusetts 02146

ISBN 0-912111-43-7

Library of Congress Cataloging in Publication Data

Zhu, Chun-Han, 1945-
  Clinical Handbook of Chinese Prepared Medicines / Chun-Han Zhu.
        p.   cm
        Includes bibliographical references.
        ISBN 0-912111-43-7 : $25.00
        1. Materia medica, Vegetable--China--Handbooks, manuals, etc.
  I. Title
        [DNLM: 1. Drugs, Chinese Herbal. 2. Drugs, Non-Prescription.   QV
767 Z63c]
  RS164.Z48   1989
  615' .32'0951--dc20
  DNLM/DLC
  for Library of Congress   89-22942
                                CIP

Paradigm Publications
Publisher: Robert Felt
Editing, Design, and Introductory Sections: Richard Feit
Cover Art: John Bergdoll Associates
Cover Photo: Eugene Freeman

Typesetting Software
by
Textware International, Cambridge, Massachusetts

Contents

Part II
Traditional Chinese Prepared Medicines
—Source, Format and Administration, Composition and Rationale—

With gratitude to my mother, Mrs. Jun-Xiu Zhu, and to my father, Dr. Mei Zhu, who, as a practitioner and teacher of traditional Chinese medicine for more than half a century, has been my driving force, and in whose footsteps I now follow.

Chun-Han Zhu
Brookline, MA
August, 1989

Preface

The **Clinical Handbook of Chinese Prepared Medicines** is intended as an introductory text and clinical reference guide for practitioners already familiar with the basic foundations of traditional Chinese medicine. Material has been organized in two large sections:

Part I presents a basic introduction to Chinese prepared medicines, and includes:

• a summary of current approaches to the use of Chinese prepared formulae, and a brief overview of their history and manufacture, including a discussion on current efforts to control product quality and uniformity (Chapter One).

• a detailed discussion of prepared medicine formats (Chapter Two).

• guidelines for the internal administration and external application of prepared medicines (Chapter Three).

Part II is the heart of the **Handbook**. It contains individual listings of the most commonly used, and/or clinically significant, prepared medicines available in the United States, presented according to the format on page xi, following.

Each chapter in this section is preceded by a brief review of the disease patterns by which the formulae in that chapter are related, and a summary of formula differentiation.

All formulae may be accessed by pinyin transliteration, English translation, and product name(s) in the Index, beginning on page 339. It should be noted that the pinyin transliteration of the formula name and the English translation offered at the head of each formula listing will rarely correspond to the product name as it appears on the package.

Each formula described in the text has been assigned a handbook reference number, which accompanies the formula each time it occurs in the text. Note that handbook reference numbers are *not* included when the formula is discussed within its own individual section in a chapter.

The handbook reference number appears as two numerals, separated by a decimal point (**0.1** in the example on page xi). The numeral to the left of the decimal point corresponds to the chapter number in which the formula is listed; the numeral to the right of the decimal point corresponds to the formula's numerical listing within that chapter. **Bu Zhong Yi Qi Wan [13.6]**, for example, will be found as the sixth formula in Chapter 13. The pinyin name of all prepared formulae discussed in the text are highlighted in bold type for ease of reference. All product names, when different from the pinyin name, are highlighted in italic.

There are treatment categories for which Chinese prepared formulae are not commonly available, or for which only a small number of formulae are produced. The decision to preserve these categorizations has resulted in occasional chapters with only one or two entries.

Formula Name in Pinyin †

0.1

Formula Name in Chinese Characters
Translation of Chinese Name

Source: This section references the text and/or physician generally credited with having first introduced the formula. Formulae with no apparent origin in the medical literature are generally ascribed to development by common usage. In such cases, this section has been omitted.

Primary Functions and Applications: These include traditional Chinese indications, guiding symptomatology, and, where appropriate, Western medical disease categories.

Format and Administration: Includes the name of the manufacturer(s) of the medicine; the manufacturer's name for the formula; formats in which the formula is available; recommended dosages; and contraindications, where applicable.

Pinyin Name of Formulae		
Constituent Substances		
Pinyin Name	Pharmaceutical Name	Composition

It is the rare Chinese prepared medicine whose formula name, format, or composition is consistent from manufacturer to manufacturer, or from textbook to textbook. Inconsistency is the rule rather than the exception in this field. The recently published second volume of the *Zhong Guo Ji Ben Zhong Chen Yao (Fundamentals of Chinese Prepared Medicines, 1988)* has attempted to remedy this situation through the standardization of the names and constituents of some 700 common medicines. However, that work's usefulness for the current project has had two important limitations: many of the medicines commonly available in the U.S. are not included there; and the amounts of the constituent herbs in each formula have not been included. Composition has thus been gathered from product labels and from *Zhong Yao Cheng Yao Xue (Traditional Chinese Prepared Medicines)*, Tianjin Science and Technology Press, 1984. Formulae in the **Handbook** that also appear in *Zhong Guo Ji Ben Zhong Chen Yao* are indicated by a dagger (†) in the title beside the pinyin name. Where the formulae of such medicines differ from those of medicines commonly available, such differences are noted in the text.

The percent composition of some formulae are unavailable, and therefore incomplete in some tables.

The use of certain rare animal substances (such as tiger bone and rhinocerus horn), though listed as ingredients on the product labels, must be questioned. Substitutes for these constituents are often made by manufacturers without being reflected in their product literature. Practitioners sensitive to the use of animal products in general, and to the inclusion of products derived from endangered species in particular, will find effective botanical substitutes among formulae in related categories.

Composition and Rationale: Offers the functions of the constituent substances in the context of the particular formula.

Part I

An Introduction
to
Chinese
Prepared Medicines

1 History and Manufacture

1.1 Introduction

Due in part to the rapidity with which traditional Chinese medicine has been transposed to this country, many of the early, awkward, first efforts at translation, of both medical terminology and medical practice, have settled quietly and unchallenged into common usage. Such has been the case with the so-called "patent" medicines, a misnomer that has become vernacular when referring to any of the traditional ready-to-take medical formulations developed in China. Although the processes used in the preparation of Chinese herbal pills, powders, plasters, tinctures and wines have been codified and formalized, there is little of the sense of proprietary exclusivity, in either product or process, that we usually associate with the term "patent." To be sure, secret family recipes still exist, as is the case with the small, red "emergency pill" that accompanies **Yunnan Baiyao [12.10]**, for example. Yet most so-called "patent" medicines belong entirely to the public domain, and as long as they are made according to now formally established standards of quality, they may be produced and marketed by anyone, without exclusive license, permission, or rights.

Considerably more than mere proprietary advantage alone directed the development of pills, powders, plasters, wines, and liniments from raw natural substances. Assurance of uniform and controlled dosage, retention of potency, control of such variables as rate of metabolic absorption, efficient distribution and lower cost through large-scale production, have all contributed to the development of a sophisticated pharmaceutical science and industry.

We would not be far wrong in speculating, too, that the overtaxed Sung-dynasty merchant, as well as the frazzled Ming mother, appreciated the simple convenience and economy of a well-prepared herbal pill, powder, or syrup as much as does his or her modern counterpart. *Yan Bian Lian*, the phrase commonly used when referring to these *Zhong Cheng Yao* ("Chinese Ready-to-be-Taken Medicines"), may best express the fundamental reason-for-being of ready-to-take medicaments in any tradition: "Effectiveness, Convenience, Economy."

Yet this most conspicuous advantage of mass-produced traditional Chinese formulae is also its most apparent flaw: standardization makes

2

the system less interactive. An overwhelming majority of cases seen by traditional physicians in China are treated with individualized prescriptions, prepared by combining medicinal substances for each disorder on a case-by-case basis. Although most such prescriptions are based on classical formulations (as are most prepared formulae), it is in the ability to *modify* those formulae that the true potential of this modality lies, and by which the herbalist's skill is measured. The necessarily generalized therapeutic targets of pre-manufactured formulae address only the most common symptoms of specific syndromes, and in most cases precludes such customization.

Thus, while prepared formulae are indeed recommended by physicians practicing in China, they are usually intended as supplemental therapy, or for specialized or emergency cases (portal-opening formulae, for example, are almost exclusively prescribed in the prepared format). In general, they are infrequently prescribed alone, and, more often than not, are chosen by patients themselves for self or family care, as many Westerners now employ vitamin therapy and nutritional supplements.[1] The use of Chinese prepared formulae in their country of origin may be more accurately described as doctor-assisted self-prescription than as herbal medicine in its truest sense.

Clearly, such a situation is possible only when a class of primary-care professional herbalists is accessible to a patient population educated in the use of these preparations. The absence of these conditions in the West points to a phenomenon that has had a profound impact on the development of Oriental medicine here: the relative lack of penetration of traditional herbal medicine into the mainstream of Oriental medical education and practice.

Of the important modalities in traditional Chinese medicine (acupuncture, herbal medicine, massage, diet therapy, and exercise therapy), only acupuncture has been allowed, even encouraged, to develop in its entirety, to evolve new applications in its new milieu, to define its scope of education, and to set standards for entry to its professional practice. Traditional Chinese herbal medicine, on the other hand, has developed here much more hesitantly. It has produced fewer comprehensive educational programs, found its way into fewer professional licensing regulations, and has generally attracted less national attention. It has been the acupuncturist, rather than the herbalist, who has defined Oriental medicine for the West, and acupuncture, not herbalism, with which we associate the system and understand its history.

Various factors have contributed to this phenomenon. The significant level of clinical and theoretical skills and primary-source scholarship that are demanded of the practitioner of traditional Chinese herbal medicine have helped postpone its cultural penetration in the West. Certainly the fact that most of the important early teachers, notably Soulie De Morant, Tin Yau So, Nguyen Van Nghi, Van Burren, and J.R. Worsley, were trained principally as acupuncturists, must also be considered.

By whatever premise we choose to understand its evolution, the present stage in the development of the entire modality of Chinese herbal medicine in the West explains much about our understanding and application of the prepared medicines themselves. Without a public conversant in their use, responsible self-prescribing is limited, and access to the medicines therefore becomes dependent on the professionals who provide their health care. Because most providers are themselves not specifically trained as herbal physicians, their use of prepared medicines in patient care represents for many the upper level of their herbal medicine skills. These factors have in many cases combined to elevate prepared medicines, and those health-care providers who use prepared medicines as their sole form of herbal therapy, to a place in the hierarchy of traditional Oriental medicine not enjoyed by their counterparts in China.

Two related axioms should thus be emphasized to help guide the practitioner in the effective use of Chinese prepared medicines.

Prepared formulae are most effective when their prescription is grounded in a thorough understanding of traditional Chinese medical theory and herbal practice. This is not to say that their use should be avoided when such expertise is absent. Yet without comprehensive education and training of the practitioners who choose to use them, the true potential of prepared herbal medicines as effective adjuncts to primary-care therapy, and as valuable additions to the home medicine chest, may not be fully realized.

Finally, the practitioner should be aware that, except in certain acute cases, prepared formulae are best presented in the context of a comprehensive treatment plan, and are rarely intended to stand alone as independent therapeutic entities.[2] Used properly, they are extremely effective, and represent wonderful adjuncts to many therapeutic modalities, providing safe and inexpensive supplemental medicines.

1.2 History and Manufacture

The history of the manufacture of ready-prepared medicines is a long one, paralleling the history of pharmacology in China. The 1973 unearthing at Ma Huang Dui in Hunan Province of medical manuscripts dating from approximately the second century B.C.E., offers evidence that these preparations were being recommended by physicians for their patients as early as the Warring States period (403—221 B.C.E.). The *Wu Shi Er Bing Fang*, one of the works discovered at Ma Huang Dui, lists not only some 224 individual drugs, but the substances recommended for use as carriers and binders in their processing as medicaments. Though we have developed more sophisticated carriers than the cart-grease, turtle-brains and scalp oil recommended in that work, most forms that are now familiar to us, including pills, powders, syrups, plasters and tinctures, were described there.[3]

It was not until the late Han dynasty, with the publication of the *Shang Han Za Bing Lun (Treatise on Fevers and Miscellaneous Diseases)* in 219 C.E., that the foundations of contemporary Chinese pharmacology were laid. Considered the progenitor of all later works in herbal medicine, the *Shang Han Lun* contains 113 herbal formulae, more than 60 of which are described in prepared medicine format. It is a testament to the scope of that work, and to the modality itself, that such *Shang Han Lun* formulae as **Wu Ling San, Shen Qi Wan [11.2]** and **Zhi Sou Ding Chuan Wan [3.17]**, are, some seventeen centuries later, still considered by practicing physicians to be staples of the modern Chinese pharmacy.

The significant interest in medicine evidenced in the Sung Dynasty, and the revision of the materia medica instituted by T'ai-tsu (927-976), the first emperor of that era, led ultimately to the compilation of the *Tai Ping Hui Min He Ji Jiu Fang (Formularies of the People's Welfare Pharmacies)*, compiled by the physician Chen Shiwen, and published in 1155. Describing some 788 prepared medicines, and introducing the procedures to be used in their preparation, this work is considered the first medical text exclusively devoted to prepared formulae. It was also destined to become the basic manual for the first, formal pharmacological manufacturing facility to be established in Imperial China, the *Shu Yao Suo* (lit., Medicine Processing Facility).[4] Although the *Shu Yao Suo* was precedent setting by virtue of its formalization of procedure and medicinal recipes, its beneficiaries were limited to those fortunate enough to have access to the Imperial Hospital. Citizens in need of medical care depended primarily upon local doctors, who prepared medicines on a custom basis from a repertoire either inherited or collected regionally.

Large-scale production of prepared formulae did not occur until well into the Ming (1368-1644) and Qing (1644-1911) dynasties. In the burgeoning entrepreneurial climate of the times, encouraged in part by governmental decentralization of pharmaceutical production, the growing number of small, privately owned pharmacies began to develop the competitive marketing strategies that would later drive the pharmacological industry in modern China: improved and innovative production methods (through development of new medicinal formats and more efficient manufacturing processes); and product specialization (through advertisement of secret family recipes, and production of new, specialized formulae).

The most successful of these first private enterprises was the Tong Ren Tang Pharmacy, founded in 1669 in Beijing. Located since 1702 on Da Zha Lan Street, a narrow lane wide enough for but a single car in a bustling business section of Beijing, the Tong Ren Tang herbal pharmacy has been run by members of the same family for over 317 years, and is the largest, as well as the oldest Chinese herbal pharmacy still in operation today. Its virtually unrivaled reputation among pharmaceutical firms in China harkens back to Tong Ren Tang's early connections to royalty: the pharmacy's original owner was a pharmacist in the Imperial hospital in Beijing during the seventeenth century, and, during the nineteenth century, the firm was the exclusive purveyor of medicines to the Imperial Palace.

Zhao Congru, current manager of Tong Ren Tang, points to the high standards of production and raw materials to which Tong Ren Tang continues to adhere as the basis for the firm's continued high regard. Herbs are painstakingly sorted and selected by senior pharmacists from those grown in specific geographic areas: *Huang Lian (Rhizoma Coptidis)* from Szechuan Province; *Chen Pi (Pericarpium Citri Reticulatae)* from Xin Hui county in Guandong; *Dang Gui (Angelica Sinensis)* from Min county in Gan Su; *Sheng Di (Radix Rehmanniae Glutinosae)* from He Nan.

Corroborating Tong Ren Tang's assertions of high standards of manufacturing was an article that appeared in the February 14, 1985 issue of the *Jian Kang Bao* (Health News Newspaper). During a routine inventory of medicines in the warehouse on the site of the original pharmacy, *Jian Kang Bao* reported, 130-year old samples of prepared medicines, including **Da Huo Luo Dan [6.2] Su He Xiang Wan [5.4a]** and **Ren Shen Zai Zao Wan [6.3]** were discovered, still fresh and potent in their original wax packages.

Today, some 2000 employees work in four divisions of Tong Ren Tang (three factories, one each for production of medicines, liquors, and extracts, and a retail store), producing 495 varieties of prepared medicines. The most famous prepared medicines produced by Tong Ren Tang include **Niu Huang Qing Xin Wan [6.5]** (of which ten million were produced in 1986), **An Gong Niu Huang Wan [5.2]**, **Ren Shen Zai Zao Wan [6.3]**, **Shen Rong Wei Sheng Wan, Su He Xiang Wan [5.4a]**, **Zi Xue Dan [5.1]**, **Da Huo Luo Dan [6.2]**, **Ju Fang Zhi Bao Dan [5.2a]**, **Nu Jin Dan**, and **Hu Gu Jiu**.

Following Tong Ren Tang in size and notoriety is the Hangzhou Second Traditional Chinese Pharmaceutical Works in Zhejiang Province, an outgrowth of one division of Huqing Yutang Pharmacy, first established in Hangzhou in 1874. Known primarily for production of tonic prepared medicines for general health, this modern factory of more than 1000 employees produces over 90 kinds of prepared medicines. Among the best known supplements prepared here are **Ching Chun Bao**, used to maintain health and promote longevity, and **Shuang Bao Su [13.12]**, a general tonic similar to **Ren Shen Feng Wang Jiang [13.1a]**.

Other pharmaceutical companies of note include Shanghai First, Second and Third Traditional Chinese Pharmaceutical Works in Shanghai; Da Ren Tang in Tianjin; and Zhong Lian Traditional Chinese Pharmaceutical Works in Wuhan, Hubei Province.

Clinical and laboratory research over the past three decades have led to both the development of new formulae and to adaptations of traditional ones. Such formulae as **Shen Jing Suai Ruo Wan [13.9]** and **Jiang Ya Wan [7.15]**, both developed by the famous contemporary physician Shi Jinmo, and **Bi Yan Pian [1.11]** developed through clinical trial, are new members of the pharmacopoeia. **Guan Xin Su He Wan [5.4]**, an important formula for the treatment of heart disease, is a modification of the traditional Song dynasty Chinese prepared medicine **Su He Xiong Wan [5.4a]**, which is still used widely to treat unconsciousness, coma, and stroke.

1.3 Quality Control

The intense pharmaceutical development in China during the past three decades has made evident the need for standardization and quality control mechanisms in the production and distribution of traditional prepared formulae. No longer were the zealously guarded manufacturing processes and secret family recipes, passed down exclusively through paternal transmission, appropriate for the growing national and international patient populations. In response to the Chinese government's call for standardization, regional manufacturers of prepared medicines were organized early in the 1950's to establish a consensus on production methods, nomenclature, and formulation. Among the outcomes of these meetings were the publications of the first modern Drug Code (in 1953) and, in 1957, of the text *Wan San Gao Dan Ji Cheng (Collection of Prepared Medicines)*, in which 2,782 prepared medicine formulae were codified.

Although the 1953 and the later, 1977, editions of the Drug Code of the People's Republic of China *(Zhong Hua Ren Min Gong He Guo Yao Tian)* established guidelines for correct preparation and administration of prepared medications, until recently, little was done to enforce them at the level of manufacture.[5] The Drug Code Administration Law of 1985 *(Zhong Hua Ren Min Gong He Guo Yao Tian Guan Li Fa)* was structured to address this situation, and represents China's most comprehensive effort thus far in drug quality control. Manufacturers must now obtain a license, based on adherence to acceptable standards of preparation, in order to produce prepared formulae. Certain articles of that law have been highlighted here to offer some insight into the present state of the traditional pharmaceutical industry in China. A related law, the *Drug Advertisement Regulations Act* of 1985, is summarized below in section 1.3.2.

1.3.1 Drug Control Regulations Act, July 1, 1985

The Drug Control Regulations Act (formally the *Administrative Law of Medicine of the People's Republic of China)*, was issued by the Chinese National Administrative Bureau of Drugs on September 20, 1984, and became effective July 1, 1985. Qi Moujia, director of the National Administrative Bureau of Drugs, stated that the purpose of the Drug Control Regulations Act is to guarantee the quality of drugs (*China Daily*, July 3, 1985). At about the time of its enactment, there were 6,499 different prepared medicines produced in China, 1,000 of which were considered to be commonly used.

•Chapter 1, Article 3, of the law states that the People's Republic of China encourages the development of both modern medicine and traditional Chinese medicine, and that the Chinese government will protect the geographical source of the herbs and encourage the cultivating of Chinese herbal medicines.

•Chapter 2, Article 4, establishes a licensing procedure for drug manufactories, which includes license expiration dates and renewal protocol.

•Chapter 2, Article 5, states that any factory that produces medicines must have specific personnel appropriate for such production, including pharmacists, engineers, and technicians. Further, this section states that such personnel must be provided with proper space, buildings, and equipment suitable for the production of the medicines for which the manufactory is licensed, as well as the equipment and expertise to assess medicinal quality.

•Chapter 2, Article 6, states that the process of producing Chinese herbal medicines must follow the requirements of the Pharmacopoeia of the Peoples Republic of China, or the requirements issued by the local government.

•Chapter 2, Article 7, states that the materials and supplementary materials used to produce the medicine, as well as the container holding the medicine, must conform to certain regulations.

•Chapter 2, Article 8, states that the medicine must be inspected for quality before it leaves the factory. If the medicine fails the inspection, it cannot be released.

•Chapter 5, Article 33, standardizes certain specific medicines, allowing no deviation from established ingredients. It is illegal to use additional ingredients that are not medicinal ingredients, or to substitute ingredients. It is also illegal to *use* medicines that have been produced by factories that do not have the proper license.

•Chapter 5, Article 34, states that certain standards must be met in terms of herbal quality. This means, for example, that if an herbal formula requires 10% ginseng, it is illegal to make the formula with 7% ginseng. In addition, it is illegal to use herbal medicines that have exceeded their expiration date.

•Chapter 5, Article 35, states that the clinical personnel who come into contact with the herbal medicines must have annual health exams to insure protection of the herbal contents from any contamination.

•Chapter 10 includes the legal responsibilities of the manufactory.

One year after the Drug Control Regulations Act went into effect, the June 19, 1986 edition of the *China Daily* reported that in the latest round of inspections (March, 1986), 1,763 of China's 1,950 pharmaceutical factories were certified as being up to the law's standards, as were 19,095 out of 24,944 sales and distribution companies. Under the law, uncertified factories must bring all products up to standard to continue production and uncertified sales and distribution centers are denied access to products from factories. During this first year after the law became effective, the Chinese government destroyed poor quality or expired medicines (both modern medicine and Traditional Chinese Medicines) worth over 180 million R.M.B. Yuan. In September, 1986, as a result of this law, several people who were involved in the production and sales of fake medicines in Jinjiang Province were given prison sentences up to 11 years (*People's Daily,* September 12, 1986). Liu Yonggang, Deputy Director of the State Pharmaceutical Administration, stated in the June 19, 1986 *China Daily* that the law guarantees the safety and effectiveness of medicine in China. According to Liu, "control of the quality of medicine will be our top priority for the rest of the decade."

1.3.2 Drug Advertisement Regulations Act, September 17, 1985

The Drug Advertisement Regulations Act, which was issued by the Chinese National Industrial and Commercial Administration and the Health Ministry in 1985, regulates all advertisement of medicines in all media, including advertisements in medical journals, general and medical newspapers, television and radio, and even billboards along the sidewalks and streets.

The law states that if the advertiser is also the drug manufacturer, a permit must be obtained to produce the medicine. If the advertiser is only in sales and distribution, and not involved in the manufacturing, a proper license to sell the medicines, as well as any appropriate business licenses, must be on file. Anyone advertising the sale of medicines must have the approval of the local Public Health Administration. Anyone advertising the sale of a specific medicine must present to the local Provincial Public Health Administration and the local Provincial Industrial and Commercial Administration the permit number of the manufactory that is producing that particular medicine. In addition, they must show the leaflet explaining the medicine and the trademark of the medicine. If this medicine has received any awards or prizes for its effectiveness, this information must also be included. The content of the advertisement cannot be changed after the advertisement has been approved. If changes are necessary, the process must be initiated again.

Article 9 states that the Provincial Public Health Administration has the right to stop any advertisement that has been published in the media with changes that were not approved. Additional conditions that may result in withdrawal of an advertisement by the local authorities include:

- Evidence through clinical trials that this medicine has serious or unexpected side effects;
- Evidence of substandard medicinal quality;
- Discontinuation of the production of the formulae for any reason.

1.3.3 *The Fundamentals of Chinese Prepared Medicines, 1988*

Late in 1984, 108 experts in Chinese medicine and health care representing 21 provinces and 52 institutions convened in Beijing to begin work on a modern standardization of prepared medicine formulae, manufacture and application. Six thousand prepared medicines were presented for standardization in the first months of that conference, that number eventually being reduced to 838 by 1985, and to 700 by January, 1987. These 700 standard formulae were published in 1988 as Volume II of the as-yet incomplete three-volume work *Zhong Guo Ji Ben Zhong Chen Yao (Fundamentals of Chinese Prepared Medicines)*.

Many of the medicines presented in this **Handbook** are not listed in that work. Those that are are indicated here by a dagger (†) placed after the pinyin transliteration of the medicine name (*see p.xi, above*). These have been compared to the new standardizations, and differences in formulation or nomenclature have been noted.

Endnotes

[1] This is in distinct contrast to the situation in Japan, where the use of prepared formulae is a highly regarded speciality in itself.

[2] Again, we point to Japan, where the use of prepared formulae in some cases is similar to the constitutional remedy of the Western homeopath.

[3] Paul U. Unschuld, **Medicine in China: A History of Pharmaceutics.** Berkeley: University of California Press, 1986.

[4] The name *Shu Yao Suo* was later changed to *He Ji Ju*, literally, Bureau of Prescription Compounding.

[5] A valuable summary of both the 1953 and 1977 editions of the Drug Codes of the People's Republic of China may be found in Paul U. Unschuld, **Medicine in China: A History of Pharmaceutics**, op.cit.

2 Prepared Medicine Formats

Prepared medicines are available to the practitioner in both traditional formats (such as the large, waxed honey pills of **Wu Ji Bai Feng Wan [12.12]**), and as medicines whose production methods reflect contemporary packaging trends and formats (such as the bubble-packed **Yunnan Baiyao [12.10]** capsules). In many cases, the original formats of prepared medicines represented little more than herbal decoctions or powders bound in a medium, with correspondingly low levels of potency. The convenience of the prepared format was thus exchanged for the cumbersome quantities of medicine required for adequate dosages. Not until the 1950's were methods of distillation and low heat extraction developed that would enable more appropriate concentrations. Credit for much of the original pioneering development of higher concentration medicines is generally given to the Tong Ren Tang Chinese Herbal Pharmacy in Beijing. Concentrated pills and tablets, water soluble granules, potent alcohol and water extracts, and injectable solutions have brought the herbal medicine pharmacy to another level of *Yan Bian Lian* (effectiveness, convenience and economy). Though the influence of modern biomedical science is evident in these developments, the medical practice itself has not moved far from its traditional applications, and the customary appellation for prepared medicines, *Wan San Gao Dan (Pill, Powder, Ointment, Elixir)*, still appears as Chinese characters on the signposts of contemporary pharmacies.

2.1 Traditional Formats of Chinese Prepared Formulae

2.1.1 Pills

Pills are produced by combining powdered medicinal substances with either water, honey, rice paste or wax as binding media. The resultant mixture is shaped into solid spheres, and dried for easy storage and handling. In general, pills are considered to be the most potent of the traditional prepared medicine formats. Because the pill must first be dissolved in the stomach, the absorption rate of the active ingredients is relatively slow, and therapeutic effects prolonged.

•*Water Pills*

Water pills use boiled water as their primary medium. A powdered medicinal agent is sprinkled over a flat bamboo tray moistened with boiled water. When the tray is shaken, small, irregular spheres of powdered herbs and water are formed. This process is repeated until the the pills have grown to the appropriate size. The total volume of the medium in these preparations is lower than in other pill formats (approximately 5% to 7%), thus offering a relatively higher concentration of active ingredients. Water pills are usually somewhat smaller, and dissolve faster, than pills bound with other media. Formulae whose therapeutic targets include food mass dispersal, appetite improvement, heat clearage or fire dispersion are often prepared as water pills. **Liu Shen Wan [7.11]** is an example of water pill format.

•*Honey Pills*

Pills that use cooked honey as a binding medium are produced in both large (6-9 gram) and small (less than 3 gram) sizes. The honey itself, which comprises approximately 50% of the gross weight of the pill, contributes to the overall therapeutic value, and is often considered to be a medicinal constituent. Honey is credited with moistening the lungs and arresting cough, and with moistening the intestines and relieving constipation. When used in tonics, it augments supplementation (due to its slower absorption rate). No less important is the sweetness that honey imparts to otherwise less than flavorful herbal mixtures. To prevent moisture loss and subsequent hardening during extended storage, honey pills are sealed in wax shells or in waxed boxes. Examples include **Wu Ji Bai Feng Wan [12.12]**, **Ren Shen Zai Zao Wan [6.3]**, and **Da Huo Luo Dan [6.2]**.

•*Water-Honey Pills*

Among the most common pill formats are those that combine both water and honey as the binding medium. The small, black-bean sized spheres are dried in a slow oven or by open-air ventilation. They are harder and more long-lasting than pills made with honey alone. Because they have a relatively low moisture content, water-honey pills are also more easily stored.

•*Pills made from Flour-Based Paste*

A paste of rice or wheat flour may be used to bind medicinal ingredients, and is often used to mitigate toxic side effects and to buffer herbal pills for more gentle digestion. Because the paste medium produces a relatively hard, slowly dissolving pill, absorption rate is decreased, and the therapeutic effect of the herbal medicine is prolonged. **Ci Zhu Wan [14.12]** is an example of a flour-based pill.

•*Wax Pills*

Pills that use beeswax as a binding medium have the slowest absorption rate of all prepared medicine formats. Solid at room temperature, the wax softens after being swallowed. As with flour-paste pills, wax pills are often used when the constituents contain toxic substances, and are most frequently used in formulae having a clinical focus of detoxification and analgesia through dispersion of static blood. Neither wax nor flour-paste pills are commonly used today. Wax pills are produced in two sizes. The larger pills weigh 3 grams, and should be dissolved in warm water or warm wine for proper administration. The smaller pill may be swallowed directly with warm water.

2.1.2 Powders

The common use of herbal powders may be traced back at least as far as the *Wu Shi Er Bing Fang*, a medical text containing descriptions of thirteen herbal powders for internal use (two to be taken with water, eleven to be taken with wine) and eight carbonized powders for topical application.

Hua Tou, the noted Han dynasty physician, developed the herbal powder **Ma Fei San** as an anesthetic for surgery. The powder was dissolved in a small amount of wine, and the resultant compound administered to the patient, who reportedly fell into a comatose state profound enough to permit surgical removal of an abdominal tumor. Although the exact ingredients of Hua Tou's anesthetic are unknown, it is believed to have contained *Da Ma (Cannabis Sativae)*, *Wu Tou (Radix Aconti)* and/or *Yang Jin Hua (Flos Daturae)*.

Today, powders are swallowed directly, carried in gelatin capsules and then swallowed, or decocted in water. In their external application, powders may be used directly on the skin, or mixed with such media as alcohol, vinegar, sesame oil, or water to form a paste before application.

Because of the increased surface area offered by powders, their absorption rate when taken internally is higher than that of pills. Examples include **Hai Feng San, Chi Li San, Shi Dan Chuan Bei San** and **Shi Dan Chen Pi San**.

2.1.3 Pastes

Pastes are prepared by frying medicinal substances in vegetable oil or mixing them with pork fat or beeswax to form an ointment. Pastes are usually used to treat skin diseases, bruises, and sprains. Examples include **Hua Tou Gao [7.6]** and **Jing Wan Hong [7.32]**.

2.1.4 Plasters

The traditional plaster is made by spreading a medicinal paste on a piece of cloth or animal skin. The paste itself is most commonly composed of substances that relieve muscular pain on the back or limbs, reduce pain in the abdomen due to cold, relieve pain related to gynecologic disorders, and treat carbuncles on the skin. These substances are generally fried in sesame oil, which is then strained and mixed with the lead-based mineral Pb_2O_5, called *Qian Dan (Minium)*. After the paste is applied to the cloth or skin backing, the plaster is folded in half and allowed to harden. Solid at room temperature, the plaster must be warmed and softened. The cloth is then opened to expose the medicinal paste inside and applied to the skin. By helping to retain heat and prevent local cooling, plasters are effective in improving circulation of blood and qi at the site of application. **Gou Pi Gao [4.9]** is an example of a traditional plaster.

2.1.5 Elixir

The word *dan*, translated here as "elixir," originally referred to a class of Taoist longevity compounds made with cinnabar *(Zhu Sha)*, which imparted a deep red color to preparations containing it (*dan* means *red* in Chinese). Because of the reference to Taoism, many pills labeled *dan*, whether or not they contained cinnabar, were relabeled *wan* ("pill") during the Cultural Revolution. Modern usage of the word *dan* is more general, and refers either to compounds containing a significant proportion of any mineral (including, but not limited to, cinnabar), or to preparations considered to be of extraordinary value.

2.1.6 Gelatins

Gelatins are derived from animal skin, bone, hide, horn and shell. They are almost without exception considered supplements. Gelatins are simmered in wine or water until melted, and either taken alone or combined with other herbs to make pills or teas.

2.1.7 Wine or Liquors

Alcohol extracts of herbal combinations are made by combining medicinal agents with 60% to 65% clear grain alcohol (sorghum alcohol is traditional). Herbal liquors are prescribed to reinforce the effect of the herbal medicines by improving blood circulation. They are used as supplements, and to treat bi patterns (obturation: joint pain, muscle pain, or rheumatism due to wind-damp).

2.1.8 Water-Based Forms

Water-based forms of prepared medicines traditionally combine both alcohol and water to produce an herbal extract. The proportion of water to alcohol varies depending on the therapeutic target of the medicine and the medicinal constituents.

Water-based extracts are generally used to treat acute gastric disorders such as vomiting or diarrhea. *Examples include:* **Shi Di Shui [2.4b]**, **Liu Shen Shui [2.5]**, and **Yun Xiang Jing [4.13]**.

Certain water-based medicines contain toxic substances (such as fungicides). They are indicated for external use only in the treatment of skin diseases.

2.1.9 Distillates

The use of distillates is relatively uncommon, and is generally limited to formulae containing high percentages of volatile oils, or formulae requiring the removal of contaminants from original solutions.

2.1.10 Teas

One class of herbal formulae combines coarsely powdered medicines (often including regular green tea) with a binding medium to form small blocks. A small piece of the tea block is broken off, placed in boiled water, and taken as a tea. Examples include **Wu Shi Cha [1.1]** and **Shen Qu Cha [2.2]**.

2.1.11 Liniments

Liniments are liquid, oil-based medicines for external use. Examples include **Die Da Wan Hua You [12.7]** and **Chu Feng You**.

2.1.12 Ding

Ding are manufactured with finely powdered substances bound with starch paste or honey, and shaped into oblongs, spheres or spindles. They are distinguished from pills in that they require some preparation (most commonly grinding and mixing with liquid) before administration. Most *ding* are used both internally (after grinding and mixing with warm water) and externally (after grinding and mixing with vinegar and sesame oil), though some are restricted to either internal or external applications. Examples include **Zi Jin Ding [7.29]** and **Wan Ying Ding**.

2.2 Modern Formats of Chinese Prepared Formulae

2.2.1 Tablets

Tablets are made with powdered herbs and liquid herbal extracts, either in combination or individually bound with starch. Tablets are produced either uncoated as in **Niu Huang Jie Du Pian [7.10]**, or sugar coated as in **Li Fei [3.13]** and **Chuan Bei Jing Pian [3.1]**. Sugar-coated tablets are especially easy to swallow, and are more rapidly absorbed than honey pills, starch pills or concentrated pills (though their absorption rate is less than that of water pills). A dose of four tablets is equivalent to one honey pill.

Three forms of tablets are produced, distinguished by the relative proportion of the herbal medicine to the binding media:

> 1) Large tablets, produced with raw herbal powder only, such as **Yin Chiao Jie Du Pian [1.6]** and **Niu Huang Jie Du Pian [7.10]**;

2) Smaller tablets, made with starch-bound, concentrated herbal extracts, such as **Ji Xue Teng Qin Gao Pian [4.2]**;
3) Tablets made with combinations of herbal extract and herbal powder, the most common production method for tablets. **Yin Chiao Jie Du Pian [1.6]** is also available in this format.

2.2.2 Concentrated Pills

Concentrated pills represent a higher potency format of the traditional water pill. They are made from a combination of herbal powder and herbal extract, then shaped into spheres and coated with one of the substances making up the formula. Because the herbal medicine in such pills is concentrated, dosages may be correspondingly lower. These pills readily absorb moisture, and must be stored carefully and kept dry. **Jian Nao Wan [14.3]** is an example of a concentrated pill.

2.2.3 Soluble Granules

Herbal extracts are occasionally mixed with a binding medium, then dried and powdered to produce a semi-soluble product. These medicines are reconstituted in hot water and administered as tea. Though this format maintains many advantages of medicinal tea, potency is usually compromised by the long drying times under high temperatures, the use of starch binders, and the practice of including the dregs of the cooked herbs in the final powder. A small number of Japanese manufacturers of traditional Chinese prepared formulae prepare products that maintain higher potencies through the addition of ground, raw herbs, and the absence of binders. **Gan Mao Tui Re Chong Ji [1.4]** is an example of Chinese produced soluble granules.

2.2.4 Syrups

Mild and sweet, syrups are highly concentrated herbal decoctions blended with honey or sugar syrup, and, occasionally, with alcohol. Blood supplementers, yin enrichers and cough suppressants are often formulated as syrups. Examples include **Chuan Bei Bi Ba Gao [3.14]** and **Qi Xing Cha [9.2]**.

2.2.5 Plural Sera

Sera of individual botanical substances have been developed for intramuscular and intravenous injection. For example, two milliliter doses of *Chai Hu (Radix Bupleuri)* serum, injected intravenously, have been used successfully to reduce extremely high fever smoothly and without such side effects as excess sweating or agitation. A serum of *Chan Su (Secretio Bufonis)* has been used intravenously to elevate blood pressure in critical cases of shock, and in cases of respiratory failure. *Dan Shen (Radix Salviae Miltiorrhizae)* has been used both intramuscularly and intravenously in the treatment of heart disease. Factors such as the potential for anaphylaxis and the requirements for equipment sterility necessitate that injection formats be administered only by qualified physicians. Because of the highly accelerated rate of metabolic absorption, the herbal injection form is not considered appropriate for long-term use in chronic cases. Although considerable research has been conducted in China and Japan on the physiological effects of intramuscular injection of herbal preparations, little is available in English translation.

2.2.6 Adhesive Plasters

Contemporary plasters are essentially the same as their traditional counterparts: herbal formulations bound into a paste and carried on a piece of backing material for application to the skin. They differ primarily in the nature of the backing material used to carry the formulae. The herbal paste in the traditional plaster must be formed into a tar-like substance to provide adhesion to its backing, and must be heated and softened before application. The modern plaster takes advantage of adhesive backings, and does not require preparation before application. All plasters, both modern and traditional, should not be applied to open wounds or to inflamed areas of the skin, especially where exudate is present.

2.2.7 Capsules

Herbal formulae that are not readily produced in pill or tablet form, or that require faster absorption, are often powdered, or, less commonly, made into a liquid extract, and packed into clear capsules. Powder capsules include **Guan Xin Su He Wan [5.4] Ge Jie Da Bu Wan [13.4]** and **Yunnan Bai Yao [12.10]**.

3 Guidelines for the Administration of Chinese Prepared Formulae

3.1 Functions and Applications

Like other traditional sciences in China, the practice of herbal medicine was not exempt from the profound influence of Western biomedical science on Chinese culture. The results of this acculturation are no more evident than in the leaflets that accompany prepared medicines. In an attempt to present herbal medicines in a more acceptable, "scientific" light, Chinese product information and supporting literature has tended to de-emphasize traditional indications, and to favor a certain unique notion of "medical" nomenclature. Suffering from less than accurate English translation, these colorful, intercultural hodgepodges of medical pathologies are often more valuable as souvenirs than as clinical guides. Such publications certainly do not help free traditional Oriental medicine from its burden of perceived eccentricity and secondary scholarship. That they might also be used to judge the entire body of traditional herbal medicine, or to discourage wider acceptance of these valuable remedies, is truly unfortunate. A cursory glance at the number of formulae intended for use in cough, for example, and the bewildering similarity in the indications listed on the accompanying flyers, will indicate that something other than the manufacturer's product information may be necessary for effective dispensing.

Though cough may be the primary symptom in a case, the therapeutic approaches to its treatment, from a traditional Chinese medical standpoint, will depend on whether that cough is from non-diffusion of lung qi, impairment of depurative downbearing, lung qi depletion or lung yin depletion. Assuming that an accurate diagnosis has been reached, the practitioner must then examine the individual constituents of each cough formula to determine the most appropriate prescription. Incorrect prescribing may, in certain cases, cause aggravation of symptoms. A cough due to yin depletion and excess dryness, for example, if treated with a formulae intended to address cough caused by wind-cold may, because of inappropriate thermic properties, further damage yin and produce even greater dryness.

Both the *Primary Functions and Applications* section of the **Handbook** and the section *Composition and Rationale*, are intended to assist the practitioner in determining the most appropriate formula. The *Primary Functions and Applications* section presents each prepared formula from a traditional Chinese medical perspective according to specific guiding symptomology; and, where appropriate, by common Western disease categories. The *Composition and Rationale* section is intended to provide some detail about formula structure and function by reviewing the general functions of the individual constituents.

Even though prepared medicines are prescribed frequently based on symptomatology alone, the list of symptoms addressed by a given formula should be considered only the most superficial indicator for its use. Accurate discrimination between formulae of a similar nature must include consideration of the ongoing interplay between the individual guiding symptoms, and the overall picture of disharmony that they present. Sophisticated herbal prescribing, and the accurate diagnosis on which it is based, depends on a clear understanding of the differentiation of disease syndromes and patterns, the origin and progression of disease, and the interactions of the constituent herbal substances, according to the theories that bind them into a unified whole. This book can offer no substitute for such skill.

3.2 Internal Administration

Though insufficient to determine precise prescribing information, the leaflets that accompany patent medicines offer adequate dosage guidelines and administration procedures. Most prepared medicines require administration twice a day, though of course there are many exceptions to this rule. Depending on both the format and the nature of the condition being treated, prepared medicines are administered internally in the following ways:

> •Swallowed with water or water decoctions of specific herbal "guides" or "conductors" (*yao yin*) (see 3.4.2, below);

> •Swallowed without liquid, or with a minimum amount of liquid, and followed by one hour without liquids, a method recommended for medicines that warm the middle warmer and relieve stomachache, such as **Sai Mei An [11.7]**);

•Swallowed with a mixture of milk or syrup, a method often used for children;

•Dissolved slowly in the mouth, a method usually reserved for such throat-clearing medicines as **Liu Shen Wan [7.11]** or **Qing Yin Wan [7.8]**;

•Dissolved slowly with heat, a method usually preferred in the preparation of gelatin forms and pills made with wax. If *A Jiao (Gelatinum Asini)* is the only ingredient, the medicine should be melted in white wine in a double boiler, and the medicine/wine combination taken by the patient;

•Decocted in water and taken as tea, a method used with such tea-block forms as **Shen Qu Cha [2.2]**. These are heated in one cup of cold water, brought to a boil, and cooked down to two-thirds of a cup over a ten-minute period. Such decoctions can be taken cold or hot.

In all cases, patients should be advised not to increase the amount or the frequency of the dosage in an attempt to obtain faster results, especially when the patient is very young or very old.

3.3 Topical Application

3.3.1 Topical Application of Pastes or Lotions
Clean the area thoroughly before application of pastes or lotions.

3.3.2 Topical Application of Powders
Powders are generally used as astringents, to reduce inflammation, control bleeding, promote tissue regeneration and relieve pain, and may be applied without special preparation of the sight.

•*Powder Mixtures for External Use:* Powders may be mixed with liquids to form a paste, which is then applied to the affected area. Liquids commonly used in such applications include:

•Common black and red tea, used to reduce inflammation, resolve fire toxin, and relieve pain;

•Liquor (60 to 65 percent alcohol), to move static blood, promote blood circulation and relieve pain;

•Cooking oil in which Szechuan pepper (*Hua Jiao - Fructus Zanthoxyli*) has been fried, to assist in the treatment of itching skin and to dry damp;

•Dark sesame oil, to keep the skin moist and prevent dryness;

 Vinegar, to "dry" the mixture, thereby increasing its ability to reduce mucus and fluid;

•Milk, which has nourishing and tonic properties, to prevent skin dryness.

•*Powders applied to mucus membranes:* Using a straw whose end has been cut at an angle to form a scoop, certain medicinal powders may be blown directly into the ear (for boils and infections), the throat (for soreness and horseness, as with **Fu Fang Xi Gua Shuang [7.12]**), or the mouth (for gums and teeth).

•*Powders for the eyes:* Certain Chinese prepared medicines are finely powdered for application to the eyes. The top of a small glass tube is wetted with water, and touched to the powder, which is then applied to the inside of the lower eyelid.

3.3.3 Topical Application of Plasters

Traditional plasters such as **Gou Pi Gao [4.9]** require steaming or gentle dry heating to soften the medicinal ingredients prior to application. Modern plasters such as **Shang Shi Bao Zhen Gao [4.11]**, with their ingredients attached to an adhesive patch, may be applied directly to the skin without heating.

The area to be treated should be cleaned with gentle soap and warm water (a warm bath is most effective) before application. Peel open the plaster, or peel the plaster off its protective backing, and apply as many plasters as necessary for adequate coverage. The plaster will remain potent for approximately four to five days, after which new plasters should be re-applied, if required. Plasters may be worn while bathing or swimming without diminishing their effectiveness.

Discontinue use if pronounced redness, itching, or skin irritation follow application. Do not apply plasters to open wounds. Plasters contain aromatic ingredients; storage in air-tight containers is thus required.

3.4 Combining Prepared Formulae with Other Herbal Medicines

Although prepared medicines, by their nature, are less readily modified than whole herb preparations, the traditional Chinese physician does have the ability to address individual patient needs by combining prepared formulae with other herbal preparations. Combinations with herbal decoctions, with herbal medicine "conductors," and with other prepared formulae, all broaden the therapeutic scope of these medicines.

3.4.1 Combining Prepared Formulae with Herbal Decoctions

The most sophisticated adjustment made to standard prepared medicine prescriptions is the administration of prepared medicines with customized herbal decoctions, a technique that requires the skills of a trained herbalist. This combination method is commonly used with such specialized (and often expensive) formulae as **An Gong Niu Huang Wan [5.2]**, **Ju Fang Zhi Bao Dan [5.2a]**, **Ren Shen Zai Zao Wan [6.3]**, and **Da Huo Luo Dan [6.2]**. It is also employed where specific prepared medicines are needed to assist the function of the herbal tea. In such cases, the prepared medicine is traditionally taken during the day, and the herbal decoction at night. Because this method requires thorough knowledge of herbal medicine, further explanation of its application is beyond the scope of this book.

3.4.2 Using Herbal Conductors (Yao Yin)

There was a time when all prepared medicines were taken with their specifically appointed *yao yin (conductor)*, usually a commonly available kitchen ingredient with properties that helped to direct the medicine toward its therapeutic target and to aid in the medicine's absorption. Though not as widely used today as in the past, herbal conductors are important components of herbal therapy. It is commonly held that the current decrease in their use is a comment more on today's fast pace and complex life style than on their lack of efficacy.

The following herbal conductors are among the most common:

•*Ginger (Sheng Jiang):* Ginger is effective in expelling wind-cold, warming the middle warmer, and controling vomiting. It may be used in tea form to great effect as a *yao yin* in cases of wind-cold pathogens involving vomiting or nausea due to cold in the stomach, or to relieve abdominal pain and diarrhea due to cold pathogen. To prepare the tea, cook 3 to 5 slices (10 to 15 grams) of ginger in one cup of boiling water for 10 minutes. Allow the tea to cool, and swallow with the prescribed medicine.

•*Rhizoma Phragmatis (Lu Gen)* is effective in clearing heat, increasing body fluid, relieving thirst, and controlling vomiting, and becomes an effective herbal conductor when combined with medicines that treat wind-heat syndromes or skin rash (including measles in its beginning stages). It is often used in combination with the popular **Yin Chiao Jie Du Pian [1.6]**. To prepare the tea, boil 10 to 15 grams of *Lu Gen* (fresh phragmatis is preferred to dried) for 15 to 20 minutes in one cup of water, strain, cool, and take with the prepared medicine.

•*Wine:* Through wine's pungent taste and hot thermic property, channel circulation may be promoted and wind-cold pathogens expelled. Wine may thus be used as an effective herbal conductor when taken with such prepared medicines as **Da Huo Luo Dan [6.2]** and **Qi Li San [12.3]** to treat bi patterns (muscular pain or joint pain caused by wind cold damp); when prepared medicines are used to treat amenorrhea due to blood stasis caused by cold; or when prepared medicines are used to treat sports injuries (bruises). In such cases, 25 to 50 cc of 80 to 130 proof white wine, or slightly less clear grain alcohol, should be taken at either slightly heated or room temperature. Vary the dose according to the size and sex of the patient, and according to the patient's sensitivity to alcohol (inebriation is not the intended objective of this therapy).

•*Salt*, by virtue of its five-phase association, may be used to lead medicine to the kidneys. To enhance the effectiveness of such formulae as **Liu Wei Di Huang Wan [13.18]** and **Jian Bu Hu Chian Wan**, an herbal conductor of two grams of salt to ½ cup of warm water should be used.

•*Rice Gruel* should be taken simultaneously with certain bitter medicines and purgatives to minimize their deleterious effects on stomach qi. Gruel is prepared by cooking rice in an excess of water until soft and cereal-like, and then decanting. Gruel is gently nourishing, and may be taken in virtually unlimited quantities.

•*Dark Brown Sugar* expels cold and moves and nourishes the blood. When using prepared medicine to treat gynecological disorders due to blood depletion or coldness, such as dysmenorrhea, amenorrhea, or hypomenorrhea, dark brown sugar is an effective herbal conductor. Dissolve 25 to 50 grams of the sugar in a cup of warm water.

• *Fresh Lotus Rhizome Juice and Daikon Juice* have the ability to control bleeding due to repletion heat. Clean the lotus rhizoma or daikon and grate, or chop it into pieces, add a small amount of cold water, and press out the juice.

•*Cong Bai (Herba Alli Fistulosi) - Scallion Bulbs. Cong Bai*, the white part of the green scallion, supplements yang qi and eliminates exogenous cold pathogens. When using diaphoretic medicines to treat wind-cold pathogens, scallion bulbs may be used as the herbal conductor to help induce sweating. Chop the white part of two or three scallions into pieces and simmer in a cup of water for 10 minutes.

• *Honey* may be selected as an effective herbal conductor when using prepared medicines as laxatives, or as lung yin enrichers in the treatment of dry cough. In such cases, dissolve one tablespoon of honey in one cup of warm water.

• *Suan Zao Ren (Semen Zizyphi Spinosae, dried)* may be used as the herbal conductor with prepared medicines that calm the spirit and quiet the heart. Simmer 10 grams of *Suan Zao Ren* in a cup of water for 10 to 15 minutes, strain, and take with the appropriate prepared medicines.

• *Da Zao (Fructus Zizyphi Jujubae)* is commonly used as an herbal conductor when administering prepared medicines to fortify the spleen and stomach. Simmer 5 to 10 dates in a cup of water for 30 to 45 minutes, strain and drink.

•Six grams each of *Dan Zhu Ye (Herba Lophatheri Gracilis)* and *Deng Xin Cao (Medulla Junci Effusi)*, simmered for 15 minutes in a cup of water, may be used to accompany prepared medicines in the treatment of dysuria.

3.4.3 Combining Prepared Medicines

Two general approaches are commonly used when combining prepared medicines to extend therapeutic range:

1. Combining medicines of similar function to emphasize a single therapeutic objective; and

2. Combining medicines that address individual symptoms within a single disorder.

A thorough understanding of Chinese herbal medical theory, and of the specialized functions of the formulae, provide the most appropriate guidelines to direct the practitioner in prescribing combinations of prepared medicines. The common, clinically tested examples that follow illustrate methods based on such understanding.

•In the treatment of toothache or sore throat when combined with offensive breath due to stomach heat, **Niu Huang Jie Du Pian [7.10]** may be combined with other heat-clearing medicines such as **Ching Wei Huang Lian Wan.**

•When treating skin rash, eruption or itching caused by wind damp, **Fang Feng Tong Shen Wan** (to clear heat and expel wind) may be combined with **Lian Qiao Bai Du Pian [7.28]** (to treat skin disorders).

•When treating hoarseness caused by lung yin depletion, **Yang Yin Qing Fei Wan [3.12]** (to enrich lung yin and increase body fluid) may be combined with **Qing Yin Wan [7.8]** (to specifically treat hoarseness caused by dryness).

•When treating amenorrhea with hypochondriacal distention due to excessive anger, **Fu Ke Zhong Zi Wan [12.15]** (to nourish blood, regulate menses, and eliminate blood stasis) may be combined with **Shu Gan Wan [11.1]** (to move stagnant liver qi).

•When treating wind heat syndromes accompanied by cough, **Yin Chiao Jie Du Pian [1.6]** (to clears wind heat) may be combined with such cough medicines as **Chuan Bei Jing Pian [3.1]** or **Zhi Sou Ding Chuan Wan [3.17]**.

•When treating menstrual disorders accompanied by poor digestion due to qi and blood depletion, **Fu Ke Ba Zhen Wan [13.10]** (to strengthen qi and blood, and regulate menses) may be combined with **Xiang Sha Liu Jun Zi Wan [11.4]** (to strengthen middle warmer qi and improve digestion).

•When treating abdominal pain and diarrhea due to internal cold, **Fu Zi Li Zhong Wan [8.1]** (to warm the middle warmer and relieve abdominal pain) may be combined with **Huo Xiang Zheng Qi Wan [2.1]** (to regulate the stomach and intestines, and to control diarrhea, vomiting, and nausea).

•To treat headache on the side of the head due to wind heat, **Yin Chiao Jie Du Wan [1.6]** may be combined with **Shu Gan Wan [11.1]**.

•To treat leg or back pain due to kidney and liver depletion (accompanied by difficulty walking) **Jian Bu Hu Chien Wan** may be combined with **Shu Gan Wan [11.1]**.

•To treat invasion of exogenous pathogen in patients with an underlying, serious depletion of qi, combine **Yin Chiao Jie Du Wan [1.6]** with **Bu Zhong Yi Qi Wan [13.6]**.

3.5 General Contraindications and Cautions

•Strong purgatives, as well as medicines that move qi and/or blood, should not be used during pregnancy.

•Strong diaphoretics should not be used in cases of yin depletion, nor when there has been serious loss of body fluid, including loss from vomiting, diarrhea, or bleeding.

•A patient should not take supplements exclusively during invasion of exogenous pathogens (common cold, flu, or acute viral or bacterial conditions). Exclusive use of supplements at these times may cause the illness to worsen or to be prolonged. Only with careful assessment of the patient and the condition is it possible, in some instances, to combine supplements with exterior resolvants.

•A few prepared medicines have specific dietary cautions (referred to as *ji kou, forbidden mouth*), often listed on the accompanying leaflet.

•While taking **Du Zhong Hu Gu Wan [4.3]**, a medicine used to treat chronic bi (pain in the joints due to wind-cold and damp), patients are advised not to eat beans (including soybeans) or seafood.

•It is recommended that oily or spicy food be avoided while taking heat clearers.

•**Shen Ling Bai Zhu Wan [13.7]**, and other medicines used to treat poor digestion, should not be taken while eating cold, oily, or raw food.

•Certain supplements used to strengthen kidneys require that the patient refrain from sexual practices during therapy.

3.6 Treating Children with Prepared Medicines

Determining appropriate dosages is essential when using prepared medicines in the treatment of pediatric disorders. Dosages that are too small will prevent the expected therapeutic results; excessive dosages may damage the qi. The product literature accompanying many prepared medicines is unclear at best, confusing at worst, making determination of appropriate pediatric dosages difficult. Some prepared medicines designed specifically for children leave dosages for infants under one year of age unspecified.

In the absence of specific dosage information, the following guidelines may be used to determine appropriate amounts and frequency of administration.

When using a medicine that is designed specifically for children, the dose for infants up to one month old should be one-third that used for a child of one year. The dosage for infants one month to six months of age should be two-thirds that used for a child of one year. Infants between the ages of six months and one year should be given dosages equal to between two-thirds and a full dose for a child of one year.

Occasionally, only adult dosages are given on labels of medicines intended for use by both children and adults. In such cases, a general rule of thumb is to give one half the recommended adult dose to children older than seven. For children three to seven, give one-third to one-half the adult dose. Children younger than three should be given less than one-third the adult dose.

In adjusting dosages of prepared medicines for children, the practitioner should consider such factors as the overall strength of the child, the severity of the disease, the season, as well as any known history of sensitivity to medication. Dosages should be less for children who are weak, underdeveloped, or underweight. Dosages should be increased in severe illnesses. Avoid the use of too many warm medicines in the summertime, and too many cold medicines in the wintertime. In general, use no more than the dose necessary to obtain a positive clinical response.

Children present their own unique challenges to the administration of prepared medicines. They often refuse to swallow the medicine, or may be inclined to vomit after the medicine has been swallowed. In all cases, parents or care givers are advised to be calm and reasonable; never force a child to take medicine against his or her will. Whenever possible, the importance of the medicine to the child's wellbeing should be clearly communicated. Medicines to be administered to infants should be mixed with a small amount of warm water or milk to which some honey or sugar has been added. If the child vomits after taking the medicine, reduce the amount of medicine given in each dose, and increase the frequency of administration.

Large pills, especially honey pills, may be cut into several small pieces and given to the child in small portions. If too many are given, vomiting may result. If children frequently vomit after swallowing the medicine, parents should be instructed to massage the acupuncture points *nei guan* (PC-6) and *he gu* (LI-4) for the child.

| Select Pediatric Formulary ||
Disorder	Formula
Jaundice (hemolytic) in newborn caused by cold-damp	**Fu Zi Li Zhong Wan [8.1]** with an herbal conductor of *Yin Chien Hao (Herba Artemesia Capillaris)*
	Wu Ling San with an herbal conductor of *Yin Chien Hao (Herba Artemesia Capillaris)*
Stomatitis	**Fu Fang Xi Gua Shuang [7.12]**
High Fever, pneumonia, meningitis	**Hu Po Bao Long Wan [6.4]**
Wind-heat (sore throat, fever, headache, cough)	**Sang Ju Gan Mao Pian [1.3]**: 2-4 tablets, 3 times a day for children over three; less for younger children.
Eczema, boils, constipation	**Lian Qiao Bai Du Pian [7.28]**

Continued

Select Pediatric Formulary *(Continued)*	
Disorder	**Formula**
High fever and spasms due to such central nervous system infections as meningitis	**Zi Xue Dan [5.1]**: ½ to 1 gram for children over three.
	An Gong Niu Huang Wan [5.2]: half a pill twice a day for children over three; less for younger children.
Cough due to damp heat, accompanied by thick, yellow phlegm. Nausea and a full sensation in the chest may be present.	**Qing Chi Hua Tan Wan [3.7]**: half to two thirds the adult dose for children over three; less for younger children.
Chronic cough, to supplement the lungs, treat dryness of the mouth, dry throat, and hoarseness	**Qiu Li Gao [3.13]**: 10 grams dissolved in hot water, drunk twice a day.
Dysentery and diarrhea with abdominal pain	**Jia Wei Xiang Lian Pian [7.6]**: use half the adult dose for children over two; less for younger children.
Cough, with thick yellow sputum, sore throat, constipation or nasal bleeding.	**Qing Fei Yi Huo Pian [3.5]**: 2-4 tablets, twice a day for children over three; less for younger children.
Edema due to cold-damp, cold limbs, nephritis.	**Jin Gui Shen Qi Wan [11.2]**: half the adult dose for children over three; less for younger children.
Wind-cold that has turned to heat, with fever, cough, asthma, and yellow phlegm	**Zi Bao Ding**: one honey pill, twice a day for children over one year; less for younger children.

Continued

Select Pediatric Formulary *(Continued)*	
Disorder	**Formula**
Spleen depletion accompanied by chronic diarrhea and poor appetite	**Shen Ling Bai Zhu San [13.7]:** one half to two thirds the adult dose for children over three; less for younger children.
Malnourishment and underdevelopment from qi and blood depletion due to spleen qi depletion	**Fu Ke Ba Zhen Wan [13.10]:** one half to two thirds the adult dose, twice a day, for children over three; less for younger children.
Poor appetite, spontaneous sweating, poor sleeping, and general debility	**Ren Shen Gui Pi Wan [13.8a]:** one half to two thirds the adult dose, twice a day, for children over three; less for younger children.
Underdevelopment, qi and blood depletion	**He Che Da Zao Wan [13.17]:** one half to a full adult dose for children over three; less for younger children.
Qi and blood depletion syndromes, with diarrhea and feeling of coldness	**Bu Zhong Yi Qi Wan [13.6]:** one half to a full adult dose, twice a day, for children over three; less for younger children.
Stomatitis or mouth ulcer, acute tinnitis due to liver heat	**Long Dan Xie Gan Wan [7.13]:** one half to a full adult dose, twice a day, for children over three; reduced for younger children.
Viral or bacterial infections such as influenza	**Chuan Xin Lian Pian [7.26]:** one half to a full adult dose, three times a day for children over three; less for younger children.

Continued

Select Pediatric Formulary *(Continued)*	
Disorder	**Formula**
Nausea and vomiting due to summerheat	**Shi Di Xue**: a solution of one part medicine to ten parts water has been used successfully to treat heat rash.
Nighttime crying	**Liu Wei Di Huang Wan [13.18]**: one half to a full adult dose for children over three; less for younger children.

3.7 Naming Conventions for Chinese Prepared Medicines

As noted above in the Section 1.3, **Quality Control**, standardization of the names and formulae of prepared medicine, though underway, has not yet been achieved. Herbal formulations still vary based on geographic regions in which they are produced, and from manufacturer to manufacturer. Thus, the name alone will not always be an adequate determinant of consistency in prescription. A good example of such variation is **Ren Shen Zai Zao Wan [6.3]**, which is the name for some twenty different formulations. To add to the confusion, the same formula may be produced by different manufacturers under different names. **Chuan Xin Lian [7.26]**, for example, is produced under nine different titles, all with the same formula.

Care should be taken to avoid confusing formulae with similar sounding Chinese names. **Yin Qiao Jie Du Pian [1.6]**, **Ling Qiao Jie Du Pian**, and **Xi Ling Jie Du Pian [1.8]**, for example, though similar sounding, have significantly different functions and applications. **Niu Huang Qing Xin Wan [6.5]** is used to clear heat in the heart, eliminate wind phlegm and reduce spasms, while **Wan Shi Niu Huang Qing Xin Wan [5.3]** is used to clear heat, resolve fire toxin and resuscitate a patient unconscious from heat in the heart. **Ren Shen Gui Pi Wan [13.8a]** is used to supplement the blood and calm the spirit, whereas **Ren Shen Jian Pi Wan [13.8b]** removes food mass. **Liu Shen Wan [7.11]** is used to treat serious cases of throat infection, though **Liu Shen Shui [2.5]** addresses digestive disorders. **Da Huo Luo Dan [6.2]** addresses wind syndromes (paralysis due to stroke); **Xiao Huo Luo Dan [4.7]** treats cold bi patterns and sports injuries, and relieves pain.

Part II

Traditional Chinese
Prepared Medicines

1

Exogenous Pathogen Formulae:
Wind-Heat and Wind-Cold Patterns

To resolve wind-cold pathogens with warmth and pungency
1.1 Wu Shi Cha
1.2 Chuan Xiong Cha Tiao Wan
To resolve wind-heat pathogens with coldness and pungency
1.3 Sang Ju Gan Mao Pian
1.4 Gan Mao Tui Re Chun Ji
1.5 Gan Mao Dan
1.6 Yin Qiao Jie Du Pian
1.7 Ling Yang Shang Feng Ling
1.8 Xi Ling Jie Du Pian
1.9 Zhong Gan Ling
1.10 Bi Yuan Wan
1.11 Bi Yan Pian
1.12 Bi Min Gan Wan

Pattern Identification

Pathogen dispelling, the general therapeutic principle governing the use of the formulae in this chapter, relies upon a strategy of offense, whereby therapy is directed toward virtual expulsion of the pathogen. In cases where the pathogen has lodged in the more superficial aspects of the body (that is, when prominent symptoms appear in those aspects of the body most immediately in contact with the environment), the method of choice for dispelling that pathogen is exterior resolution. Diaphoresis is generally the focus of exterior resolution, and is often the term chosen to refer to that method.

Exogenous wind, the pathogen most commonly involved in cases addressed by these formulae, presents two general symptom patterns: patterns of heat and patterns of cold. Pathogens manifesting in patterns of cold are dispelled by resolving the exterior with warm, pungent substances. Pathogens manifesting in patterns of heat are dispelled by resolving the exterior with cold, pungent substances.

The nature of the patient, as well as of the pathogen, must always be considered when determining treatment. In times of exogenous pathogen penetration, when signs of repletion are often more apparent, careful attention must be paid to any signs of overall depletion, as such signs might indicate the need for inclusion of supplements into the therapeutic program. Particular attention must of course be paid to the yin depletion patient, for whom diaphoresis is contraindicated unless accompanied by yin enrichment.

Formulae Differentiation

Because of the significantly greater number of common prepared formulae for wind-heat than for wind-cold, the practitioner faced with a clear tai yang illness will be somewhat limited in his or her treatment approach. Most significantly, treatment differentiation of exterior depletion and exterior repletion patterns, so crucial to effective treatment of tai yang disorders, cannot be readily made with the use of Chinese prepared formulae alone. The classical representative formulae for the resolution of wind-cold pathogens as characterized in tai yang illnesses include *Ma Huang Tang (Ephedra Decoction)* for repletion, and *Gui Zhi Tang (Cinnamon-Twig Decoction)* for depletion, as well as their common derivatives, *Xiao/Da Ching Lung Tang (Minor/Major Cyan Dragon Decoction,)* and *Ge Gen Tang (Pueraria Decoction)*. These are not generally available as Chinese prepared formulae, and must be sought elsewhere. Where such formulae are available, such as *Ma Xing Shi Gan Tang*

(Ephedra, Apricot Seed, Gypsum and Licorice) (called **Zhi Sou Ding Chuan Wan [3.17]** in its prepared medicine form), the prominence of cough as a guiding symptom has led to their inclusion among the antitussive formulae in Chapter Three of this *Handbook*.

Cough is a symptom that often accompanies contraction of exogenous wind (both heat and cold), and therefore lung agents are often included in exterior-resolving formulae. Both **Sang Ju Gan Mao Pian [1.3]** and **Gan Mao Dan [1.5]** contain the lung diffuser *Jie Geng (Radix Platycodi)*, and should be considered when slight cough is present.

Cough may also be addressed by the formula **Ling Yang Shang Feng Ling [1.7]**, though the approach here is the moistening of lung dryness through the use of the lung clearer and moistener *Tian Hua Fen (Radix Tricosanthis)*, and the clearing of intense heat with the use of *Ling Yang Jiao (Cornu Antelopis)*.

Gan Mao Dan [1.3] is a mild formula for the treatment of exogenous wind-heat, and is often suggested for children.

Formulae such as **Yin Qiao Jie Du Pian [1.6]**, **Ling Yang Shang Feng Ling [1.7]** and **Xi Ling Jie Du Pian [1.8]** are structured to deal with more pronounced aspects of heat, and contain such heat clearers and toxin resolvants as *Jin Yin Hua (Flos Lonicerae)*, *Lian Qiao (Fructus Forsythiae Suspensae)*, and *Shan Zhi Zi (Fructus Gardeniae Jasminoidis)* to achieve that end. Though the target of these formulae is primarily exterior resolution rather than clearage (the treatment principle for qi-aspect thermic disorders), they are related to the heat-clearing, fire-draining and toxin-resolving formulae of Chapter 7. They may be considered for use in those transitional stages when defense-aspect *(wei)* patterns move into the qi aspect, and when taiyang illnesses move toward yangming.

The two formulae included for the resolution of exogenous wind-cold have special as well as general applications: **Wu Shi Cha [1.1]** when abdominal symptoms are prominent in an exogenous cold pattern (this formula is appropriately cross referenced to Chapter 9 when dispersion of digestate accumulation is foremost; and to Chapter Two for contraction of summerheat-damp); and **Chuan Xiong Cha Tiao Wan [1.2]** when headache is prominent in wind-cold contraction.

Bi Yuan Wan [1.10], **Bi Yan Pian [1.11]**, and **Bi Min Gan Wan [1.12]** address exterior patterns where the prominent symptoms include sinusitis and rhinitis.

Wu Shi Cha † 午時茶
Midday Tea

Source: *Chen Xiu-yuan Yi Shu Quan Ji (Dr. Xiu-yuan Chen's Complete Medical Book),* Qing Dynasty (1644-1911).

Primary Functions and Applications: **Wu Shi Cha** expels wind-cold, disperses digestate accumulation, and fortifies the stomach. It is used to treat wind-cold syndromes (such as those often seen in cases of common cold, intestinal flu, and acute gastroenteritis), with such symptoms as chills, fever, headache, stuffy nose, a full sensation in the chest, stomach distension due to food mass, diarrhea, and vomiting. It is commonly used to treat the poor digestion that often accompanies traveling or moving to a new location, called *shui tu bu fu* in Chinese (failure to acclimatize).

Format and Administration: **Wu Shi Cha** is produced in 9-gram blocks, and wrapped 2 blocks per package.

Recommended Dosage: Two blocks each time, once or twice a day. The blocks may either be soaked in 8 ounces of boiled water, or boiled in 8 ounces of water for 2 minutes, after which the liquid is decanted and taken while still hot. Immediately after drinking the tea, induce perspiration by covering the patient with a blanket

Contraindications: **Wu Shi Cha** is not recommended in cases of wind-heat syndromes, with symptoms such as high fever, swollen and sore throat, yellow tongue coating, and dark urine.

Wu Shi Cha		
Constituent Substances		
Pinyin Name	**Pharmaceutical Name**	**% Composition**
Huo Xiang	*Herba Agastaches seu Pogostemi*	2.13
Bai Zhi	*Radix Angelicae*	2.13
Zi Su Ye	*Folium Perillae*	2.13
Fang Feng	*Herba Ledebouriellae Sesloidis*	2.13
Qiang Huo	*Rhizoma et Radix Notopterygii*	2.13
Chai Hu	*Radix Bupleuri*	2.84
Zhi Shi	*Fructus Ponciri*	1.42
Chen Pi	*Pericarpium Citri Reticulatae*	1.42
Shan Zha	*Fructus Crataegi*	1.42
Mai Ya	*Fructus Hordei Germinantus*	2.13
Shen Qu	*Massa Medica Fermentata*	21.98
Hou Po	*Cortex Magnoliae Officinalis*	2.13
Cang Zhu	*Radix Atractylodis*	1.42
Qian Hu	*Radix Peucedani*	2.84
Jie Geng	*Radix Platycodi*	2.13
Gan Cao	*Radix Glycyrrhizae Uralensis*	1.42
Hong Cha	*Black Tea*	—

Composition and Rationale: *Huo Xiang, Bai Zhi, Zi Su Ye, Fang Feng, Qiang Huo,* and *Chai Hu* remove wind-cold, induce sweat, and relieve headache; *Zhi Shi, Chen Pi, Shan Zha, Mai Ya,* and *Shen Qu* regulate qi, remove qi stagnation, strengthen the spleen, and remove food mass; *Hou Po* and *Cang Zhu* eliminate dampness, regulate the middle burner, and fortify the spleen; *Qian Hu* and *Jie Geng* open the lung, eliminate phlegm and suppress cough; *Gan Cao* harmonizes; and *Hong Cha* buffers the diaphoretic medicines and relieves headache.

Zhong Guo Ji Ben Zhong Chen Yao (Fundamentals of Chinese Prepared Medicines, 1988) includes *Chuan Xiong (Rhizoma Ligustici Wallichii)* and *Lian Qiao (Fructus Forsythiae Suspensae)* in its standard formula for **Wu Shi Cha.**

Chuan Xiong Cha Tiao Wan † 1.2
川芎茶調散
Tea-Blended Ligusticum Pills

Source: *Tai Ping Hui Min He Ji Ju Fang (The People's Welfare Pharmacies),* Song Dynasty (960-1279).

Primary Functions and Applications: **Chuan Xiong Cha Tiao Wan** expels wind-cold, relieves headache due to the invasion of exogenous wind (as well as headaches from rhinitis and sinusitis), and is indicated when such symptoms as chills, fever, and stuffy nose are prominent. **Chuan Xiong Cha Tiao Wan** is used in the treatment of all headaches, including migraine and chronic, located in any of the following channels: shaoyang (sides of head), jueyin (top of head), taiyang (back of head, neck, upper back) and yangming (forehead).

Contraindications: Do not use **Chuan Xiong Cha Tiao Wan** in cases of headache due to depletion of qi, blood, or yin, or when the headache has been caused by the ascension of yang.

Format and Administration: **Chuan Xiong Cha Tiao Wan** is produced by the Lanchow Chinese Medicine Works and the Shanghai Chinese Medicine Works as small pills, packaged 200 per bottle.

Recommended Dosage: Eight pills, twice or 3 times a day

Chuan Xiong Cha Tiao Wan		
Constituent Substances		
Pinyin Name	**Pharmaceutical Name**	**% Composition**
Bo He	*Herba Menthae*	32
Chuan Xiong	*Rhizoma Ligustici Wallichii*	16
Jing Jie	*Herba seu Flos Schizonepetae Tenuifoliae*	16
Fang Feng	*Herba Ledebouriellae Sesloidis*	8
Qiang Huo	*Rhizoma et Radix Notopterygii*	8
Bai Zhi	*Radix Angelicae*	8
Gan Cao	*Radix Glycyrrhizae Uralensis*	8
Xi Xin	*Herba cum Radice Asari*	4

Composition and Rationale: *Bo He, Jing Jie,* and *Fang Feng* expel wind; *Chuan Xiong* moves blood, expels wind, and relieves pain, especially in shaoyang and jueyin headaches; *Qiang Huo* expels wind and relieves pain, especially in taiyang headaches; *Bai Zhi* expels wind-cold and relieves pain, especially in yangming headaches; *Xi Xin* expels wind-cold and relieves pain; and *Gan Cao* harmonizes the other herbs.

1.3   Sang Ju Gan Mao Pian †
桑菊感冒片
Mulberry and Chrysanthemum Common Cold Tablet

Source: *Wen Bing Tiao Bian (Treatise on Differentiation and Treatment of Seasonal Febrile Diseases),* by Wu Tang, 1798.

Primary Functions and Applications: **Sang Ju Gan Mao Pian** dispels wind-heat in the upper burner and opens (diffuses) lung qi, thus suppressing cough. It is indicated in acute seasonal febrile disorders due to wind-heat, and in the presence of headache, cough, slight fever, sore throat, slight thirst, and dry mouth. This formulae is useful in cases of early-stage epidemic flu, bronchitis, tonsillitis, pharyngitis, and conjunctivitis (pink eye), as well as other illnesses with fever, thirst, and cough when the condition is one of repletion.

Format and Administration: **Sang Ju Gan Mao Pian** is produced by the Tientsin Drug Manufactory as uncoated 0.6 gram tablets, packaged 8 per vial.

Recommended Dosage: Four to 8 tablets, twice or three times a day, accompanied by copious quantities of fluids (juices and water are fine).

Sang Ju Gan Mao Pian		
Constituent Substances		
Pinyin Name	**Pharmaceutical Name**	**% Composition**
Sang Ye	*Folium Mori Albae*	19.84
Ju Hua	*Flos Chrysanthemi Indicae Morifolii*	7.95
Lian Qiao	*Fructus Forsythiae Suspensae*	11.90
Xing Ren	*Semen Pruni Armeniacae*	15.87
Jie Geng	*Radix Platycodi*	15.87
Lu Gen	*Rhizoma Phragmatis*	15.80
Gan Cao	*Radix Glycyrrhizae Uralensis*	6.35
Bo He	*Herba Menthae*	6.30

Composition and Rationale: *Sang Ye* and *Ju Hua* expel wind-heat in the lungs; *Lian Qiao* clears heat; *Xing Ren* and *Jie Geng* diffuse the lung, suppress cough, and clear the throat; *Lu Gen* clears heat and relieves thirst; *Bo He* expels wind-heat; and *Gan Cao* harmonizes the other herbs.

Gan Mao Tui Re Chun Ji
感冒退熱沖劑
Common Cold, Fever-Abating Soluble Preparation

1.4

Primary Functions and Applications: **Gan Mao Tui Re Chun Ji** dispels wind-heat and reduces inflammation, and is used primarily to eliminate fever due to wind-heat. It is prescribed in cases of tonsillitis accompanied by fever, and in cases of chronic or acute traecheitis. Symptoms indicating its use include sore throat, fever, headache, and cough with phlegm. However, because of the heat-clearing and fire-toxin-resolving functions of all the herbs in this formula, the medicine is appropriate for a wide range of disorders in which heat is present, and its applicability extends to the treatment of sores, carbuncles, and parotitis.

Viral infections sometimes lead to underlying bacterial infection. In early stages of viral infection, for example, the patient will have clear phlegm and a runny nose. Later, however, if the viral stage has led to an underlying bacterial infection, the phlegm will have become yellow. This medicine is indicated in these later stages, where heat signs are present.

Gan Mao Tui Re Chun is a mild remedy, and is best used in mild cases, for children, or as a prophylactic when a patient suspects pathogenic exposure.

Format and Administration: **Gan Mao Tui Re Chun Ji** is produced by the Shanghai Chinese Medicine Works as *Ganmao Tuire Chongji*. Four herbs are contained in a plastic bag with sugar. The soluble granules are to be dissolved with warm water before consumption. Because this medicine absorbs moisture readily, it should be stored in a dry, cool area.

Recommended Dosage: One small bag, 3 times a day. If the fever rises above 38 °C (roughly 100 °F), take 2 bags, 4 times a day.

Contraindications: **Gan Mao Tui Re Chun** is not appropriate for the treatment of wind-cold syndromes.

Gan Mao Tui Re Chun Ji		
Constituent Substances		
Pinyin Name	Pharmaceutical Name	% Composition
Da Qing Ye	*Folium Daqingye*	33.33
Ban Lan Gen	*Radix Isatidis seu Baphicanthi*	33.33
Cao He Che	*Rhizoma Bistortae*	16.67
Lian Qiao	*Fructus Forsythiae Suspensae*	16.67

Composition and Rationale: This formula contains four botanical substances, each of which has the same general function as a broad-spectrum antibiotic. In classical Chinese medical terms, it clears heat and resolves fire toxin. It is interesting to note that all four herbs belong to the category of heat-clearing agents, and although none by itself has the property of expelling wind, they attain that property in combination.

Gan Mao Dan
感冒丹
Common Cold Pills

1.5

Source: **Gan Mao Dan** was developed by the 20th-century physician Shih Chinmo.

Primary Functions and Applications: **Gan Mao Dan** is used to treat invasion of wind-heat. It is indicated in the presence of such symptoms as fever (with slight chills), headache, swollen or sore throat, cough, runny nose, red eyes, skin rash or eruptions, and fatigue. If the wind-heat has affected the spleen and stomach, nausea and vomiting may also be present. In the presence of such symptoms, this formula may be used in the treatment of influenza, measles, acute conjunctivitis, tonsillitis, pharyngitis, ear pain due to flu, and nasal infection.

Format and Administration: **Gan Mao Dan** is produced by the Beijing Tung Jen Tang as *Kanmaotan* in small pills, and packaged 200 pills per bottle.

Recommended Dosage: Twenty pills, twice a day.

Gan Mao Dan		
Constituent Substances		
Pinyin Name	**Pharmaceutical Name**	**% Composition**
Jin Yin Hua	*Flos Lonicerae Japonicae*	5
Lian Qiao	*Fructus Forsythiae Suspensae*	5
Shan Zhi Zi	*Fructus Gardeniae Jasminoidis*	7
Lu Gen	*Rhizoma Phragmatis*	10
Chi Shao	*Radix Paeoniae Rubra*	16
Bai Mao Gen	*Rhizoma Imperatae Cylindricae*	10
Dan Dou Chi	*Semen Preparatum Insulsum Sojae*	14
Bo He	*Herba Menthae*	3
Sang Ye	*Folium Mori Albae*	10
Jing Jie	*Herba seu Flos Schizonepetae Tenuifoliae*	5
Zi Yuan	*Radix Asteris*	5
Jie Geng	*Radix Platycodi*	5
Chen Pi	*Pericarpium Citri Reticulatae*	5

Composition and Rationale: *Jin Yin Hua* and *Lian Qiao* clear heat and resolve fire toxin; *Zhi Zi* and *Lu Gen* clear excess heat, reduce fever, and clear heat in the qi stage; *Chi Shao* and *Bai Mao Gen* clear heat in the blood stage; *Dan Dou Chi, Bo He, Sang Ye*, and *Jing Jie* expel wind-heat, and induce mild sweating to reduce fever; *Zi Yuan* and *Jie Geng* suppress cough and eliminate phlegm; and *Chen Pi* fortifies the spleen, regulates the stomach, and relieves nausea and vomiting.

1.6   Yin Qiao Jie Du Pian †
銀翹解毒片
Lonicera and Forsythia Toxin-Vanquishing Tablets

Source: *Wen Bing Tiao Bian (More Discussions on Febrile Disease)*, Qing Dynasty (1644-1911).

Primary Functions and Applications: **Yin Qiao Jie Du Pian** is used primarily to dispel wind-heat in the spring and summer, and to treat the early (*wei*) stage of seasonal febrile diseases. Guiding symptoms include a possible slight aversion to wind, headache, thirst, cough, and throat pain. Fever may or may not be present. The tongue in such cases will be red with a white or yellowish coating. The pulse will be floating (indicating the presence of wind) and rapid (indicating the presence of heat). **Yin Qiao Jie Du Pian** may be used in cases of common cold, flu, and acute cases of pneumonia, bronchitis, pharyngitis, otitis media, parotitis, measles, and tonsillitis.

Format and Administration: **Yin Qiao Jie Du Pian** is produced by a number of manufactories, in several formats. Both Tientsin Drug Manufactory and Beijing Tung Ren Tang produce the formula as uncoated tablets (8 per vial), and as coated tablets in 20-tablet bottles. Beijing Tung Ren Tang also produces 100-tablet bottles, and the Tientsin Drug Manufactory 60- and 120-tablet vials. Practitioners should be aware that Tientsin Drug Manufactory produces a form of **Yin Qiao Jie Du Pian** called "Superior," which may contain caffeine, as well as paracetamolum and chlorpheniraminum. Since the formula varies from time to time, practitioners are advised to inspect the label carefully before using.

Recommended Dosage: Three to 5 coated pills, twice or 3 times a day with warm water. For tablets without coating, use 2 to 4, twice or 3 times a day.

Yin Qiao Jie Du Pian		
Constituent Herbs		
Pinyin Name	**Pharmaceutical Name**	**% Composition**
Jin Yin Hua	*Flos Lonicerae Japonicae*	17.76
Lian Qiao	*Fructus Forsythiae Suspensae*	17.76
Niu Bang Zi	*Fructus Arctii*	10.60
Jie Geng	*Radix Platycodi*	10.66
Bo He	*Herba Menthae*	10.66
Lu Gen	*Rhizoma Phragmatis*	8.88
Gan Cao	*Radix Glycyrrhizae Uralensis*	8.88
Dan Zhu Ye	*Herba Lophatheri*	7.10
Jing Jie	*Herba seu Flos Schizonepetae Tenuifoliae*	7.10

Zhong Guo Ji Ben Zhong Chen Yao (Fundamentals of Chinese Prepared Medicines, 1988) includes *Dan Dou Chi (Semen Preparatum insulsum Sojae)* in its standardized formula for *Yin Qiao Jie Du Pian*.

Composition and Rationale: **Yin Qiao Jie Du Pian** is extremely popular, and is widely used in China to treat the early stages of common colds and flu. *Jin Yin Hua, Lian Qiao, Niu Bang Zi, Lu Gen* and *Dan Zhu Ye* remove heat and clear fire toxin; *Jin Yin Hua, Bo He, Jing Jie* clear wind; *Jie Geng* soothes the throat and diffuses the lung; *Lu Gen* and *Dan Zhu Ye* relieve thirst and promote salivation.

There are two important modifications of **Yin Qiao Jie Du Pian**: **Xi Ling Jie Du Pian [1.8]** and **Ling Qiao Jie Du Pian [1.6a]**.

Ling Qiao Jie Du Pian [1.6a] adds *Ling Yang Jiao (Cornu Antelopis)* to the classical **Yin Qiao Jie Du Pian** formula. *Ling Yang Jiao* is a cold, liver-calming, and wind-extinguishing agent, and renders the formula particularly useful in the treatment of early stage wind-heat syndromes with cold and phlegm.

1.7   # Ling Yang Shang Feng Ling
羚羊傷風靈
Antelope Horn Wind-Damage Formula

Primary Functions and Applications: **Ling Yang Shang Feng Ling** dispels wind-heat, taking advantage of the important heat-clearing functions of antelope horn. It is used to treat common cold or flu caused by virus, to reduce fever, and to relieve such symptoms of wind-heat disorders as headache, stiff neck, throat pain, cough, phlegm, tonsillitis, and bronchitis (recall that wind-heat may be differentiated from wind-cold by the absence of chills at the beginning of the wind-heat disease). Finally, **Ling Yang Shang Feng Ling** may be used either in cases of acute bronchitis or in acute flare-ups of chronic bronchitis when accompanied by heat signs.

Format and Administration: **Ling Yang Shang Feng Ling** is produced by the Tian Jin Drug Manufactory, in coated tablet format, 24 per bottle.

Recommended Dosage: Four tablets, twice a day. In serious cases, 3 to 8 tablets, 3 times a day.

Ling Yang Shang Feng Ling		
Constituent Substances		
Pinyin Name	**Pharmaceutical Name**	**% Composition**
Ling Yang Jiao	*Cornu Antelopis*	0.50
Tian Hua Feng	*Radix Tricosanthis*	3.70
Lian Qiao	*Fructus Forsythiae Suspensae*	22.50
Dan Zhu Ye	*Herba Lophatheri*	11.30
Jing Jie	*Herba seu Flos Schizonepetae Tenuifoliae*	11.28
Ge Gen	*Radix Puerariae Lobetae*	3.70
Gan Cao	*Radix Glycyrrhizae Uralensis*	9.40
Jin Yin Hua	*Flos Lonicerae Japonicae*	22.50
Niu Bang Zi	*Fructus Arctii*	15.00
Bo He	*Herba Menthae*	0.08

Composition and Rationale: *Lian Qiao, Dan Zhu Ye, Gan Cao* and *Jin Yin Hua* clear heat; *Ling Yang Jiao* and *Tian Hua Fen* clear lung heat and help eliminate phlegm; *Ling Yang Jiao* and *Gan Cao* together suppress cough; *Tian Hua Fen* and *Niu Bang Zi* soothe the throat; *Jing Jie, Bo He* and *Niu Bang Zi* clear wind-heat; *Bo He* helps relieve headache; *Tian Hua Fen* promotes body fluid; *Ge Gen* raises body fluid and eliminates stiff neck; *Dan Zhu Ye* calms the heart and the spirit.

Zhong Guo Ji Ben Zhong Chen Yao (Fundamentals of Chinese Prepared Medicines, 1988) includes *Dan Dou Chi (Semen Preparatum insulsum Sojae)* and *Jie Geng (Radix Platycodi)* in its standardized formula for **Ling Yang Shang Feng Ling.**

Ling Yang Shang Feng Ling is a modification of the standard formula, **Yin Qiao Jie Du Pian [1.6]**, and its function is similar to yet another modification of that formula called **Ling Qiao Jie Du Pian [1.6a].** **Ling Yang Shang Feng Ling** is more effective in treating stiffness (especially neck stiffness) whereas **Ling Qiao Jie Du Pian [1.6a]** is more effective in relieving the heat that causes throat pain.

Xi Ling Jie Du Pian

1.8

犀羚解毒片
Rhinocerus and Antelope Horn Toxin-Resolving Tablets

Primary Functions and Applications: **Xi Ling Jie Du Pian** dispels wind-heat and resolves fire toxin, and is used to treat common colds caused by wind-heat. Guideing symptoms include high fever and sore throat at the onset of the illness, with slight or no chill. This medicine is used to treat common colds and flu that have become lodged in the upper half of the body. In addition, it may be used to treat measles in children, but only after a large quantity of very red rash has appeared, accompanied by fever.

Xi Ling Jie Du Pian is one of the most important modifications of the formula **Yin Qiao San.** Among the modifications, the addition to that common formula of *Xi Jiao* and *Ling Yang Jiao* are the most significant. The extremely cold properties of these agents enhance its heat-clearing function, and direct its therapeutic action toward heat in the heart and liver, with such guiding symptoms as high fever, dark red rash and agitation. **Xi Ling Jie Du Wan** is also more effective than **Yin Qiao San** in the treatment of heat in the lung.

Format and Administration: **Xi Ling Jie Du Pian** is produced by the Shantung Native Produce Branch, Tsingtao, China, as *Rhinocerus & Antelope Horn Febrifugal Tablets*. It is available in small vials, each containing twelve pills.

Recommended Dosage: Four pills every 4 hours. When treating cases of influenza, take before meals. In the presence of dark, pus-like phlegm, it may be used in higher doses (6-8 pills every 4 hours).

Xi Ling Jie Du Pian		
Constituent Substances		
Pinyin Name	**Pharmaceutical Name**	**% Composition**
Lian Qiao	*Fructus Forsythiae Suspensae*	14.6
Dan Dou Chi	*Semen Preparatum insulsum Sojae*	14.6
Niu Bang Zi	*Fructus Arctii*	11.0
Bo He	*Herba Menthae*	11.0
Bing Pian	*Borneolum*	0.7
Xi Jiao	*Cornu Rhinocerotis*	0.2
Jing Jie	*Herba seu Flos Schizonepetae Tenuifoliae*	14.6
Jin Yin Hua	*Flos Lonicerae Japonicae*	11.0
Dan Zhu Ye	*Herba Lophatheri*	11.0
Gan Cao	*Radix Glycyrrhizae Uralensis*	11.0
Ling Yang Jiao	*Cornu Antelopis*	0.3

Composition and Rationale: *Lian Qiao* and *Jin Yin Hua* clear heat and resolve fire toxin; *Dan Dou Chi* expels wind-heat; *Niu Bang Zi* expels wind-heat and promotes eruption in cases of measles; *Bo He* clears wind-heat, relieves headache, and promotes measle eruption; *Bing Pian* clears heat, relieves pain, and opens the portals; *Xi Jiao* clears blood heat, clears heat in the heart, and resolves fire toxin; *Jing Jie* expels wind;*Dan Zhu Ye* clears heat and discharges heat through urination; *Gan Cao* clears heat and suppresses cough; *Ling Yang Jiao* clears lung heat and extinguishes liver wind.

Zhong Gan Ling

1.9

重感靈
Heavy Cold Formula

Primary Functions and Applications: **Zhong Gan Ling** dispels wind-heat, clears heat, and reduces inflammation. It is used primarily to treat influenza, and is indicated in the presence of slight chills, high fever, headache, soreness, pain in the limbs, throat pain, and cough (indicators of wind-heat in the upper burner). The herbs in this formula are quite cold in nature.

Format and Administration: **Zhong Gan Ling** is produced by the Meizhou City Pharmaceutical Manufactory, Guandong, China, as coated tablets, packaged 48 per bottle.

Recommended Dosage: Four to 6 tablets for adults, 1 to 3 tablets for children, 3 times a day.

Contraindications: Do not use **Zhong Gan Ling** when the patient is very cold, and experiences serious, strong chills.

Zhong Gan Ling		
Constituent Substances		
Pinyin Name	**Pharmaceutical Name**	**% Composition**
Qing Hao	*Herba Artemesiae Apiaceae*	7
Ban Lan Gen	*Radix Isatidis seu Baphicanthi*	14
Mao Dong Qing	*Radix Ilicis Pubescentis*	27
Shi Gao	*Gypsum*	4
Qiang Huo	*Rhizoma et Radix Notopterygii*	3
Ge Gen	*Radix Puerariae Lobetae*	27
Ma Bian Cao	*Herba Verbenae*	18

Composition and Rationale: All the herbs in this formula are directed toward clearing heat and resolving fire toxin. In addition, *Ban Lan Gen* cools the blood and soothes the throat, and *Ge Gen* expels wind and raises fluid to relieve stiff neck.

1.10 Bi Yuan Wan †
鼻瀟丸
Deep Source Nasal Congestion Pills

Primary Functions and Applications: **Bi Yuan Wan** is used to dispel wind-heat and to open nasal passages. It is indicated in conditions of acute or chronic rhinitis and sinusitis. Guiding symptoms include runny nose, yellowish, thick, foul-smelling nasal mucus (indicative of bacterial infection), stuffy nose or obstruction in the nose, and in cases of nasal polyps and local blood stasis.

Format and Administration: **Bi Yuan Wan** is produced by the Min-Kang Drug Manufactory, I-Chang, China. It is available as tablets, packaged 100 per bottle.

Recommended Dosage: Twelve pills, 3 times a day, for adults only. Due to the strength of **Cang Er Zi,** do not exceed the recommended dosage.

Bi Yuan Wan		
Constituent Substances		
Pinyin Name	**Pharmaceutical Name**	**% Composition**
Cang Er Zi	*Fructus Xanthii*	72.1
Xin Yi Hua	*Flos Magnoliae Liliflorae*	13.8
Qian Cao Gen	*Radix Rubiae*	4.7
Jin Yin Hua	*Flos Lonicerae Japonicae*	4.7
Ju Hua	*Flos Chrysanthemi Indicae Morifolii*	4.7

Zhong Guo Ji Ben Zhong Chen Yao (Fundamentals of Chinese Prepared Medicines, 1988) includes some 13 additional ingredients in its standard formula for **Bi Yuan Wan,** including *Tian Hua Fen, Bai Zhi, Bo He, Jing Jie, Huang Qin, Jie Geng, Zhi Zi, Lian Qiao, Di Gu Pi, Chi Shao, Gan Cao, Mai Dong,* and *Yuan Shen.*

Composition and Rationale: *Cang Er Zi* and *Xin Yi Hua* open nasal passages and expel wind; *Qian Cao Gen* clears blood heat, controls bleeding, and moves blood; *Jin Yin Hua* clears heat in the upper burner, reduces inflammation, and resolves fire toxin; *Ju Hua* clears wind-heat, relieves headache, and brightens the eyes.

Bi Yan Pian †   1.11
鼻炎片
Rhinitis Tablets

Primary Functions and Applications: **Bi Yan Pian** dispels wind-heat and opens nasal passages. It is indicated in cases of acute or chronic rhinitis, nasal sinusitis accompanied by runny nose with large amounts of yellowish, thick, foul-smelling discharge (indicative of bacterial infection), stuffy nose, and hay fever or other allergic reactions accompanied by rhinitis. In chronic cases, there will be dizziness accompanied by headache. As it reduces inflammation (through the use of such cold agents as *Huang Bai, Lian Qiao,* and *Ye Ju Hua),* **Bi Yan Pian** is used in the treatment of cases complicated by nasal infection.

Because of its effectiveness, and because it does not produce such undesirable side effects as the drowsiness or dry mouth frequently observed with antihistamines, **Bi Yan Pian** is quite popular and widely used for clearing stuffy or runny nose associated with common cold or flu with heat signs. In 1980, it was awarded a "High Quality (Silver Medal) Seal" from the National Pharmaceutical Exhibition.

Format and Administration: **Bi Yan Pian** is produced by the Chung Lien Drug Works, Hankow, China as *Bi Jen Pian.* It is available in tablet form, packaged 100 tablets per bottle.

Recommended Dosage: Three to 4 tablets, 3 times a day, with warm water and after meals. For children ages 5-10, halve the dose. The formula contains a small amount of the slightly toxic *Cang Er Zi,* and the recommended dosage should not be exceeded.

Bi Yan Pian		
Constituent Substances		
Pinyin Name	**Pharmaceutical Name**	**% Composition**
Cang Er Zi	*Fructus Xanthii*	22.5
Xin Yi Hua	*Flos Magnoliae Liliflorae*	22.5
Gan Cao	*Radix Glycyrrhizae Uralensis*	6.5
Huang Bai	*Cortex Phellodendri*	6.5
Jie Geng	*Radix Platycodi*	4.15
Wu Wei Zi	*Fructus Schizandra Chinensis*	4.15
Lian Qiao	*Fructus Forsythiae Suspensae*	6.5
Bai Zhi	*Radix Angelicae*	6.5
Zhi Mu	*Rhizoma Anemarrhenae Ashphodeloidis*	4.15
Ye Ju Hua	*Flos Chrysanthemi Indicae Indici*	4.15
Fang Feng	*Herba Ledebouriellae Sesloidis*	4.15
Jing Jie	*Herba seu Flos Schizonepetae Tenuifoliae*	4.15

Zhong Guo Ji Ben Zhong Chen Yao (Fundamentals of Chinese Prepared Medicines, 1988) lists a significantly different formula for **Bi Yan Pian**, containing *Cang Er Zi, Xin Yi Hua, Lian Qiao, Bai Zhi, Jing Jie, Bo He, Huang Qin, Zhi Zi,* and *Di Gu Pi.*

Composition and Rationale: Cang Er Zi and *Xin Yi Hua* open nasal passages and expel wind; *Huang Bai, Lian Qiao, Zhi Mu,* and *Ye Ju Hua* clear heat and resolve fire toxin; *Radix Platycodi* expels wind, soothes the nasopharynx, and discharges pus; *Wu Wei Zi* nourishes the kidney, collects the lung qi, and suppresses cough; *Bai Zhi* expels wind, relieves headache, discharges pus, and opens nasal passages; *Fang Feng* expels wind and relieves headache; and *Jing Jie* expels wind and opens the portals and the nasal passages.

Bi Tong Pian [1.11b] has a similar function, and in most cases may be used interchangeably with **Bi Jen Pian.**

Both **Bi Yan Pian** and **Bi Yuan Wan [1.10]** are both effective in the treatment of stuffy nose, and may be used for headaches due to sinusitis. Of the two formulae, **Bi Yan Pian** is recommended for use in more severe nasal infections, and in the presence of pus-like discharge.

Bi Min Gan Wan
鼻敏感丸
Nasal Allergy Pills

1.12

Primary Functions and Applications: **Bi Min Gan Wan** expels wind, eliminates inflammation, relieves headache due to the invasion of exogenous wind, and reduces allergy-induced asthma. It is used in the treatment of rhinitis and acute or chronic sinusitis and bronchitis, and in the treatment of common colds or flu, particularly those accompanied by runny or stuffy nose. Symptoms may also include headache and dizziness.

Format and Administration: **Bi Min Kan Wan** is produced by the Fo Shan United Drug Manufactory as *Pe Min Kan Wan* in 50-tablet bottles.

Recommended Dosage: Two to 3 pills, 3 times a day. For mild cases, administer for one or two 30-day courses. In severe cases, several courses should be completed.

Bi Min Gan Wan		
Constituent Substances		
Pinyin Name	**Pharmaceutical Name**	**% Composition**
Cang Er	*Xanthium Sibiricum*	—
Huo Xiang	*Herba Agastaches seu Pogostemi*	—
Xiong Dan Zhi	*Vesica Fel Ursi*	—
Niu Huang	*Calculus Bovis*	—
Ye Ju Hua	*Flos Chrysanthemi Indicae*	—
Bai Zhi	*Radix Angelicae*	—
Xin Yi Hua	*Flos Magnoliae Liliflorae*	—

Composition and Rationale: *Xion Dan Zhi, Ye Ju Hua* and *Niu Huang* clear heat and resolve fire toxin; *Cang Er* clears stuffy nose, expels wind, and relieves pain; *Huo Xiang* expels wind and eliminates dampness; *Bai Zhi* expels exogenous wind-cold, relieves headache, and clears stuffy nose; and *Xin Yi Hua* expels wind-cold and clears stuffy nose.

2

Summerheat, Summerheat-Damp and Summertime Wind-Cold Clearing Formulae

2.1   Huo Xiang Zheng Qi Wan
2.2   Shen Qu Cha
2.3   Kang Ning Wan
2.4   Ren Dan
2.5   Liu Shen Shui

Pattern Identification

The heat and damp that occur in many geographical locations during the summer months combine to become an influential exogenous factor called *Summerheat*. The pattern of symptoms produced when penetration of summerheat gives rise to a pattern of heat (fever, thirst and agitation, for example) is called *Summerheat-Heat*. When contraction of summerheat coincides with the complications of damp, the resulting symptom pattern is called *Summerheat-Damp*.

Many formulae in this section might have been included appropriately in Chapter 9, **Digestate Accumulation Dispersing Formulae**. However, the exterior-resolving characteristics of these formulae have made them popular when abdominal symptoms of digestate accumulation or damp accompany contraction of exogenous pathogens.

The seasonal nature of summerheat is the primary factor that distinguishes it from pathogens with non-seasonal etiology. However, the basic therapeutic approaches to seasonal and non-seasonal disorders due to thermia and damp are similar: clear heat, and when necessary, drain damp.

Formulae Differentiation

Huo Xiang Zheng Qi Wan [2.1] may be understood as reflecting the functions of its namesake herb *Huo Xiang (Herba Agastaches seu Pogostemi)*, which is distinguished by its ability to simultaneously transform damp and resolve the exterior. The general emphasis of this formula is on damp abduction; its specific guiding symptom is diarrhea. Diarrhea plays a similarly important role in the symptom pattern addressed by **Shen Qu Cha [2.2]**, a formula often catalogued with agents that disperse digestate accumulation. **Kang Ning Wan [2.3]** is indicated when the combination of abdominal symptoms, headache and body ache accompany penetration of wind-cold pathogens during the summertime. A nearly identical formula produced in Hong Kong called *Po Chai Pills* will be familiar to many practitioners.

Ren Dan [2.4] and **Liu Shen Shui [2.5]** address conditions of greater heat and fire toxicity apt to occur during the summer (such as sunstroke and heat exhaustion).

Huo Xiang Zheng Qi Wan †
藿香正氣丸
Agastaches Qi-Correcting Pills

2.1

Source: Tai Ping Hui Min He Ji Ju Fang *(Formularies of People's Welfare Pharmacies)*, 1151 C.E.

Primary Functions and Applications: **Huo Xiang Zheng Qi Wan** dispels wind-cold, eliminates damp, and regulates qi in the central burner. **Huo Xiang Zheng Qi Wan** is essentially used to treat gastric disorders caused by seasonal damp where symptoms of damp predominate over symptoms of wind-cold. Diarrhea is the primary symptom in these cases, although other symptoms such as fever, vomiting, and diminished appetite may also be present. Acute gastroenteritis may also be treated effectively with this formula.

Although this formula can be used at any time of the year, it is most effective when used during the humid summer months, when disorders related to the exogenous pathogen damp occur most frequently.

Symptoms indicating its use include fever, chills, headache, distention in the central burner, abdominal pain, nausea, vomiting, and diarrhea with gurgling and copious flatulence. In such cases, the tongue coating will be white and slimy.

Format and Administration: **Huo Xiang Zheng Qi Wan** is produced by the Lanchow Chinese Medicine Works as *Lophanthus Antifebrile Pills*, packaged 100 pills per bottle, or in vials of 12 tablets. This medicine is also available in a potent, quick-acting liquid format, called **Huo Xiang Zheng Qi Shui [2.1a]**, which omits *Jie Geng* from the formula, and adds oils of *Huo Xiang* and *Su Ye*.

Recommended Dosage: For pills in the glass bottle, 10 pills 3 times a day. For pills in the glass vial, 4-8 pills, 3 times a day.

Contraindications: Do not use **Huo Xiang Zheng Qi Wan** in cases accompanied by such heat signs as dry mouth, thirst, yellow tongue coating, or fever without aversion to cold.

Huo Xiang Zheng Qi Wan		
Constituent Substances		
Pinyin Name	**Pharmaceutical Name**	**% Composition**
Huo Xiang	*Herba Agastaches seu Pogostemi*	12
Bai Zhi	*Radix Angelicae*	12
Da Fu Pi	*Pericarpium Arecae Acacia seu Catechu*	12
Zi Su Ye	*Folium Perillae*	12
Fu Ling	*Sclerotium Poriae Cocus*	12
Bai Zhu	*Rhizoma Atractylodes Macrocephalae*	8
Hou Po	*Cortex Magnoliae Officinalis*	8
Jie Geng	*Radix Platycodi*	6
Chen Pi	*Pericarpium Citri Reticulatae*	6
Gan Cao	*Radix Glycyrrhizae Uralensis*	12

Zhong Guo Ji Ben Zhong Chen Yao (Fundamentals of Chinese Prepared Medicines, 1988) includes *Ban Xia* in its standardized formula for **Huo Xiang Zheng Qi Wan**.

Composition and Rationale: *Huo Xiang* is an aromatic herb that transforms damp, expels wind-cold, and regulates the central burner; *Bai Zhi* dissipates damp and resolves the exterior by expelling wind-cold; *Da Fu Pi* moves stagnant qi and dispels damp; *Zi Su Ye* expels wind-cold and harmonizes the center; *Fu Ling* strengthens splenogastric function and eliminates damp; *Bai Zhu* fortifies the spleen, reduces damp, and warms the center; *Hou Po* directs counterflow qi downward and eliminates damp; *Jie Geng* opens lung qi; *Chen Pi* regulates central burner qi and dries damp; and *Gan Cao* harmonizes the other herbs and clears summerheat.

Ping Wei Pian [2.1a] is a formula related by function to **Huo Xiang Zheng Qi Wan**. It contains *Bai Zhu (Rhizoma Atractylodes Macrocephalae), Hou Po (Cortex Magnoliae Officinalis), Chen Pi (Pericarpium Citri Reticulatae),* and *Gan Cao (Radix Glycyrrhizae Uralensis)*. This formula is produced in prepared medicine form by the Sing-kyn Drug House as *Tabellae Ping Wei*, and is particularly effective in the treatment of damp occurring in the humidity of the summer season, and for such symptoms as abdominal distension, poor appetite, nausea or vomiting, fatigue, and heaviness in the limbs. The presence of diarrhea in such cases always points to the use of **Huo Xiang Zheng Qi Wan**.

Shen Qu Cha
神麯茶
Fermented Mass Tea

Primary Functions and Applications: **Shen Qu Cha** expels wind-cold and regulates splenogastric function. Because it contains diaphoretics, summerheat-clearing agents, spleen supplements, and damp relievers, it is indicated in the treatment of wind-cold invasion during the summertime, when humidity is at its peak. The symptoms accompanying such disorders include fever and slight chills, generalized feelings of heaviness and aching, poor appetite, abdominal distension, nausea, vomiting, and diarrhea. **Shen Qu Cha** may also be used to treat the digestive problems that often accompany traveling or moving to a new location (called *shui tu bu fu* in Chinese), with such symptoms as poor appetite, weight loss, nausea, poor digestion, and diarrhea.

Format and Administration: **Shen Qu Cha** is produced by United Pharmaceutical Manufactory as blocks of tea, 8 blocks per box.

Recommended Dosage: Simmer one block of dried herbal medicine in 8 ounces of water until the liquid has been reduced to 6 ounces, and decant. Drink when lukewarm and discard the dregs. Decrease the dose for children.

If chills are present, add 3 grams of freshly chopped ginger root before decocting.

Shen Qu Cha		
Constituent Substances		
Pinyin Name	**Pharmaceutical Name**	**% Composition**
Qing Hao	*Herba Artemesiae Apiaceae*	4.7
Huang Qin	*Radix Scutellaria*	4.7
Xiang Ru	*Herba Elsholtziae Splendentis*	4.7
Qiang Huo	*Rhizoma et Radix Notopterygii*	4.7
Du Huo	*Radix Duhuo*	4.7
Qing Pi	*Pericarpium Citri Reticulate Vinde*	4.7
Hu Po	*Succinum*	4.7
Cao Guo	*Fructus Amomi Cardamomi Tsaoko*	4.7
Mu Gua	*Fructus Chaenomelis Lagenariae*	4.7
Jie Geng	*Radix Platycodonis Grandiflori*	4.7
Shan Yao	*Radix Dioscorea*	5.0
Fu Ling	*Sclerotium Poriae Cocus*	5.0
Gan Cao	*Radix Glycyrrhizae Uralensis*	5.0
Shen Chu	*Fermented wheat flour*	38.0

Composition and Rationale: *Qing Hao* and *Huang Qin* clear heat; *Xiang Ru, Qiang Huo,* and *Du Huo* expel wind-cold; *Qing Pi, Hu Po, Cao Guo,* and *Mu Gua* remove qi stagnation, eliminate dampness, and disperse digestate accumulation; *Jie Geng* opens the lung and eliminates phlegm; *Shan Yao, Fu Ling, Gan Cao,* and *Shen Chu* fortify the spleen, stimulate the appetite, and regulate the stomach.

2.3

Kang Ning Wan
康寧丸
Healthy and Quiet Pills

Primary Functions and Applications: **Kang Ning Wan** regulates the central burner, improves digestion, and expels wind-cold during the summertime. This is a popular and commonly used medicine in China, both at home and when traveling, and is especially useful when the quality of the food and water in a new location is suspect. The name "healthy and peaceful" reflects the sense of wellbeing commonly experienced after taking the medicine. It is used to treat gastric disorders due to summertime wind-cold and damp, with symptoms that include abdominal pain, nausea, vomiting, diarrhea, regurgitation, gastric hyperacidity, abdominal distension, and poor appetite. Wind-cold symptoms such as low-grade fever, slight chills and headache, may also be present. In the presence of these symptoms, this formula may be used to treat gastroenteritis (bacterial or viral) and motion sickness. If there is a known history of motion sickness, **Kang Ning Wan** should be taken half an hour to one hour before traveling.

Format and Administration: **Kang Ning Wan** is produced by United Pharmaceutical Manufactory as *Pill Curing*. The pills are available in either a small package or a small vial. The more common vial format is packaged 10 vials per box.

Recommended Dosage: One or 2 packages or vials, 3 times a day. For children under 3 years of age, break the pills of half to one package and mix with water, 3 times a day.

Kang Ning Wan		
Constituent Substances		
Pinyin Name	**Pharmaceutical Name**	**% Composition**
Tian Ma	*Rhizoma Gastrodiae Elatae*	3.6
Bai Zhi	*Radix Angelicae*	7.2
Ju Hua	*Flos Chrysanthemi Indicae Morifolii*	3.7
Bo He	*Herba Menthae*	3.2
Ge Gen	*Radix Puerariae Lobetae*	7.2
Tian Hua Fen	*Radix Tricosanthis*	5.5
Cang Zhu	*Radix Atractylodes*	7.2
Yi Yi Ren	*Semen Coicis Lachryma-Jobi*	9.0
Fu Ling	*Sclerotium Poriae Cocus*	15.5
Mu Xiang	*Radix Saussureae seu Vladimiriae*	7.2
Hou Po	*Cortex Magnoliae Officinalis*	7.2
Ju Hong	*Pericarpium Citri Erythrocarpae*	3.6
Huo Xiang	*Herba Agastaches seu Pogostemi*	7.2
Shen Qu	*Massa Medica Fermentata*	7.2
Gu Ya	*Fructus Oryzae Sativae Germinatis*	5.5

Composition and Rationale: Tian Ma and Bai Zhi expel wind, stop headache and relieve body aches; Ju Hua, Bo He, Ge Gen, and Tian Hua Fen expel wind-heat, reduce fever and relieve headache; Can Zhu, Yi Mi, and Fu Ling supplement the spleen and eliminate damp; Mu Xiang, Hou Po, Ju Hong, and Huo Xiang regulate central burner qi, move central burner qi stagnation, relieve nausea and vomiting, and dry damp; and Shen Qu and Gu Ya strengthen the spleen, regulate digestion, and disperse food mass.

An herbal formula produced in Hong Kong called **Bao Ji Wan [2.3a]** *(Po Chai Pills)* has fifteen ingredients, and is nearly identical to **Kang Ning Wan**, except that it contains Chi Shi Zhi *(Halloysitum Rubrum)*, which warms the central burner and stops diarrhea, instead of Tian Ma *(Rhizoma Gastrodiae Elatae)*. Thus, though the clinical focus of **Bao Ji Wan [2.3a]** is similar to that of **Kang Ning Wan**, it is especially useful in the presence of diarrhea. **Kang Ning Wan**, on the other hand, through the action of *Tian Ma*, is especially useful in the treatment of exogenous pathogens and for the relief of headache and body aches.

The recommended dosage for **Bao Ji Wan [2.3a]** is 1 or 2 vials, 4 times per day.

2.4   Ren Dan
人丹
People's Elixir

Primary Functions and Applications: **Ren Dan** clears summerheat; opens the portals and awakens the spirit; resolves heat toxin and clears summerheat-damp; and regulates the function of the spleen and the stomach. A medicine commonly used during the summer season, it is often considered when any prolonged activity in the hot sunshine is anticipated (trips, picnics, beach outings, parade viewing, and working in fields). It is excellent for the treatment of problems caused by hot, humid weather, and for heat exhaustion and sunstroke (characterized by dizziness, vomiting, diarrhea, abdominal pain and, in severe cases, unconsciousness). **Ren Dan** is often used to treat motion sickness, and may be taken one half hour before embarking, or when discomfort is already apparent. Finally, it is used to treat the nausea, dizziness, poor appetite, diarrhea, and fatigue due to travel or moving to a new location, called *shui tu bu fu*. Interestingly, different locales produce **Ren Dan** made according to slightly different formulae.

Format and Administration: **Ren Dan** is produced by the United Pharmaceutical Manufactory, Guangzhou, China as small silver pills, 320 per package.

Recommended Dosage: Thirty to 60 small pills each time for adults, 10 pills per dose for children 5 and under (2-3 pills may be allowed to dissolve in the mouth until the entire dosage has been taken). **Ren Dan** is a very mild medicine, and 40-50 pills can be taken without adverse side effects.

Ren Dan		
Constituent Substances		
Pinyin Name	**Pharmaceutical Name**	**% Composition**
Gan Cao	*Radix Glycyrrhizae Uralensis*	45
Ding Xiang	*Flos Caryophylli*	2
Bo He	*Herba Menthae*	4
Bing Pian	*Borneolum*	2
Jie Geng	*Radix Platycodonis Grandiflori*	40
Er Cha	*Acacia seu Catechu*	4
Sha Ren	*Semen et Pericarpium Amomi*	1
Zhang Nao	*Camphora*	2

Composition and Rationale: *Gan Cao* harmonizes other herbs and treats halitosis; *Ding Xiang* warms the central burner and, as a cold-pain dissipator, relieves stomachache; *Bo He* expels summerheat and dispels damp; *Bing Pian* clears heat, wakes the spirit and the brain, clears the portals, and resolves heat toxin; *Jie Geng* opens lung qi and benefits the throat; *Er Cha* drains damp, clears heat, and resolves heat toxin; *Sha Ren* regulates the central burner qi, strengthens the spleen, dries damp, and controls vomiting; and *Zhang Nao* opens the portals and awakens the spirit.

Ji Zhong Shui [2.4a] is a liquid remedy closely related to **Ren Dan** and **Liu Shen Shui [2.5]**. It is used for gastric disorders due to exhaustion, or to improper eating during the summer or while traveling. **Ji Zhong Shui [2.4a]** is produced by the United Pharmaceutical Company. Use one half to one bottle as a single dose. If symptoms persist after four hours, the dose may be repeated.

Shi Di Shui [2.4b] is another formula related to **Ren Dan**. **Shi Di Shui [2.4b]** and **Ren Dan** are more commonly used in northern China; **Ji Zhong Shui [2.4a]** and **Liu Shen Shui [2.5]** are more common in the south.

2.5   Liu Shen Shui
六神水
Six Spirits Fluid

Primary Functions and Applications: **Liu Shen Shui** is used in emergency conditions to treat the symptoms of sunstroke caused by summerheat, especially during the summertime, when the humidity is high. The symptoms of sunstroke include dizziness, vomiting and/or abdominal pain. It is also used to treat other intestinal disorders that occur during the summertime, including diarrhea, abdominal pain, nausea, and vomiting.

Format and Administration: **Liu Shen Shui** is produced by the United Pharmaceutical Manufactory in small vials, 12 vials per box.

Recommended Dosage: Dilute half the contents of a vial in warm water. Repeat in 2-3 hours, if necessary. Additional medicines are often taken following **Liu Shen Shui**, such as **Huo Xiang Zheng Qi Wan [1.1]** (for slight chills or slight fever, nausea, or diarrhea); or **Xiang Sha Liu Jun Zi Wan [11.4]** (if fever and chills are absent, but fatigue and digestive problems — no appetite, stomach distension, diarrhea, nausea — are prominent).

Decrease the dose proportionally for children. **However, do not administer to infants.**

Contraindication: **Do not use Liu Shen Shui during pregnancy.**

Liu Shen Shui		
Constituent Substances		
Pinyin Name	**Pharmaceutical Name**	**% Composition**
Zhang Nao	*Camphora*	26.32
Da Huang	*Rhizoma Rhei*	21.05
Sheng Jiang	*Rhizoma Recens Zingiberis Officinalis*	26.32
Rou Gui	*Cortex Cinnamomi Cassiae*	10.53
La Jiao	*Fructus Capsici Frutescentis*	5.26
Bo He You	*Herba Menthae (Oil)*	25cc per liter

Composition and Rationale: *Zhang Nao* opens the portals and resuscitates; *Da Huang* clears heat; *Sheng Jiang* expels the exogenous pathogen, warms the central burner, and controls vomiting; *Rou Gui* builds yang qi and warms the central burner; *La Jiao* warms the central burner; and *Bo He You* clears heat, expels wind-heat, and moves stagnant qi.

Shi Di Shui [2.4b], a medicine commonly used in northern China, is similar to **Liu Shen Shui** in formulation, function, and application. **Shi Di Shui [2.4b]** and **Ren Dan [2.4]** are the most popular medicines to prevent and treat sunstroke. **Shi Di Shui [2.4b]** and **Liu Shen Shui** are more potent than **Ren Dan [2.4]** because they are liquid. **Shi Di Shui [2.4b]**, **Liu Shen Shui** or **Ren Dan [2.4]** are taken as soon as slight discomfort is felt, and are thus effective as prophylactics. Families commonly carry **Shi Di Shui [2.4b]** or **Ren Dan [2.4]** when going on outings into the countryside. **Shi Di Shui [2.4b]** or **Ren Dan [2.4]** is commonly given to factory workers to prevent the heat exhaustion that often occurs during the long summertime hours in work environments that lack air-conditioning or proper ventilation.

3

Antitussives:
Formulae to Stop Cough, Transform Phlegm, and Relieve Asthma

Pattern Identification

Cough is a compelling guiding symptom, and is often given a therapeutic category of its own. Its etiology may be found in all the major disease patterns of the lungs. Depending on the nature and cause of the illness, treatment methods and formulae structures focus on various combinations of *diaphoresis, dispersion* (through transformation of phlegm), *securing astriction* (through constraint of the lungs), and *heat clearage* to achieve their therapeutic objectives.

Penetration of exogenous pathogens and brewing phlegm-damp account for the majority of cases involving non-diffusion of lung qi and impaired depurative downbearing. Impaired depurative downbearing may assume the characteristics of dryness or dampness depending on the origin of the disease. Depletion of lung qi and lung yin generally follow chronic respiratory distress or repeated impairment of lung qi diffusion and depurative downbearing.

Formulae Differentiation

It must be emphasized that the categories established in this chapter represent only general guidelines for formula selection. In practice, most of the formulae may be used for more than one pattern of respiratory distress. Though **Li Fei [3.13]**, for example, is cataloged here with lung-moistening formulae (to emphasize its applicability in cases of lung yin depletion), it should also be considered when depurative downbearing is required. **Zhi Sou Ding Chuan Wan [3.17]** is a classic formula when counterflow downbearing is required for the dispersal of lung qi, as well as when heat gathers in the lungs during a taiyang stage of exogenous pathogen contraction. However, it is clinically significant in the relief of asthma, and is listed here under that category.

Su Zi Jiang Qi Wan [3.2] is a representative formula for the treatment of impaired lung qi depurative downbearing, particularly when phlegm-damp is pronounced.

Ba Xian Chang Shou Wan [3.15] is particularly interesting for its kidney-yin enriching characteristic. This formula is based on the representative kidney-yin enriching formula **Liu Wei Di Huang Wan [13.8]**, to which a single lung-moistening depurative downbearer and a single lung-constraining antitussive have been added.

She Dan Chen Pi Mo [3.9] deserves special consideration for its effectiveness in cases of whooping cough.

Chuan Bei Jing Pian
川貝精片
Fritillaria Essence Tablet

3.1

Primary Functions and Applications: **Chuan Bei Jing Pian** relieves cough, eliminates phlegm, and moistens the lungs. It may be used in cases of acute or chronic cough with copius expectoration, acute or chronic bronchitis, and asthma.

In cases where cough and phlegm are due to exogenous pathogens, diaphoretic formulae such as **Sang Ju Gan Mao Pian [1.3]** (for wind-heat) or **Chuan Xiong Cha Tiao Wan [1.2]** (for wind-cold) must be included in the therapy.

Format and Administration: **Chuan Bei Jing Pian** is produced by the Handan Pharmaceutical Works as *Fritillaria Extract Sugar-Coated Tablets,* and packaged 60 per bottle.

Recommended Dosage: Adults: 3 to 6 tablets, 3 times a day with warm water. Children, half that dose.

Chuan Bei Jing Pian		
Constituent Substances		
Pinyin Name	**Pharmaceutical Name**	**% Composition**
Chuan Bei	*Bulbus Fritillariae Cirrhosae*	21
Yuan Zhi	*Radix Polygalae Tenuifoliae*	20
Wu Wei Zi	*Fructus Schizandrae Chinensis*	17
Jie Geng	*Radix Platycodi*	15
Chen Pi	*Pericarpium Citri Reticulatae*	15
Gan Cao	*Radix Glycyrrhizae Uralensis*	12

Composition and Rationale: *Chuan Bei* moistens the lung, clears heat, suppresses cough, and eliminates phlegm; *Yuan Zhi* eliminates phlegm; *Wu Wei Zi* suppresses cough and relieves asthma; *Jie Geng* and *Chen Pi* eliminate phlegm; and *Gan Cao* harmonizes the other herbs, moistens the lungs, and suppresses cough.

3.2   Su Zi Jiang Qi Wan †
蘇子降氣丸
Perilla Seed Qi-Downbearing Pills

Source: *He Ji Ju Feng (Formulae from The People's Welfare Pharmacies),* Song Dynasty (960-1279).

Primary Functions and Applications: **Su Zi Jiang Qi Wan** eliminates phlegm and lowers counterflow qi. It is used to treat cold phlegm accumulation in the lung that has resulted in asthma, shortness of breath, and cough. The phlegm in such cases will be white and foamy. **Su Zi Jiang Qi Wan** is also indicated in cases where depletion of kidney yang has resulted in failure to support the qi of the lungs, causing asthma, shortness of breath, and cough.

In the presence of the above symptoms, **Su Zi Jiang Qi Wan** is indicated in the treatment of chronic bronchitis and emphysema.

Format and Administration: **Su Zi Jiang Qi Wan** is available in small, 18 gram bags, 10 bags per box.

Recommended Dosage: Three grams, 3 times per day, on an empty stomach.

Contraindications: **Su Zi Jiang Qi Wan** contains many ingredients that have dry, warm properties, and cannot be used for patients who have lung heat (indicated by the presence of yellow phlegm and fever).

Su Zi Jiang Qi Wan		
Constituent Substances		
Pinyin Name	**Pharmaceutical Name**	**% Composition**
Su Zi	*Fructus Perillae Frutescentis*	10.6
Ban Xia	*Rhizoma Pinelliae Ternatae*	10.6
Hou Po	*Cortex Magnoliae Officinalis*	10.6
Qian Hu	*Radix Peucedani*	10.6
Chen Pi	*Pericarpium Citri Reticulatae*	10.6
Chen Xiang	*Lignum Aquilariae*	7.6
Dang Gui	*Radix Angelicae Sinensis*	7.6
Sheng Jiang	*Rhizoma Recens Zingiberis Officinalis*	10.6
Da Zao	*Fructus Zizyphi Jujubae*	10.6
Gan Cao	*Radix Glycyrrhizae Uralensis*	10.6

Composition and Rationale: Su Zi, Ban Xia, Hou Po, Qian Hu, and *Chen Pi* lower counterflow qi, eliminate phlegm, and relieve asthma; *Chen Xiang* warms kidney yang and relieves asthma; *Dang Gui* nourishes the blood and reduces dryness; *Sheng Jiang* warms the middle burner and regulates stomach qi; and *Da Zao* and *Gan Cao* moisten the lung, suppress cough, eliminate phlegm, and harmonize the other herbs.

Ma Xing Zhi Ke Pian †
麻杏止咳片
Ephedra and Apricot Kernal Cough Tablets

3.3

Source: This herb formula is a modification of *Ma Xing Shi Gan Tang,* a popular formula for cough and asthma that first appeared in the Han dynasty medical classic, *Shang Han Lun.*

Primary Functions and Applications: **Ma Xing Zhi Ke Pian** suppresses cough, relieves asthma, clears lung heat, and eliminates phlegm. It is used to treat cough caused by lung heat due to wind-heat; to treat asthma associated with lung heat; and to treat cases of acute bronchitis and acute flare-ups of chronic bronchitis in the presence of heat signs. Since this formula clears heat and reduces high fever, it is used in cases of pneumonia, influenza, and bronchitis.

Format and Administration: **Ma Xing Zhi Ke Pian** is produced by the Siping Pharmaceutical Works as *Ma Hsing Chih Ke Pien, Hsiang Yang Brand,* in coated tablet format, 80 tablets per bottle.

Recommended Dosage: Four tablets, twice or 3 times a day.

Ma Xing Zhi Ke Pian		
Constituent Substances		
Pinyin Name	Pharmaceutical Name	% Composition
Ma Huang	*Herba Ephedrae*	5
Gan Cao	*Radix Glycyrrhizae Uralensis*	12
Xing Ren	*Semen Pruni Armeniacae*	15
Jie Geng	*Radix Platycodi*	22
Chen Pi	*Pericarpium Citri Reticulatae*	12
Shi Gao	*Gypsum*	12
Hua Shi	*Talcum*	11
Feng Mi	*Mel*	11

Composition and Rationale: *Ma Huang* relieves asthma and opens the lung; *Gan Cao* suppresses cough, clears heat, and eliminates phlegm; *Xing Ren* suppresses cough and relieves asthma; *Jie Geng* clears heat and eliminates phlegm; *Chen Pi* lowers counterflow qi and eliminates phlegm; *Shi Gao* clears heat and disperses fire; *Hua Shi* clears heat and discharges dampness; and *Feng Mi* moistens the lung and suppresses cough.

3.4   Chuan Bei Pi Pa Lu
川貝枇杷露
Fritillaria and Loquat Dew

Primary Functions and Applications: **Chuan Bei Pi Pa Lu** clears lung heat, suppresses cough, and eliminates phlegm. It is used to treat cough due to wind-heat or exogenous heat accumulation in the lung. Symptoms in such cases include cough with thick white or yellow phlegm, and feelings of dryness in the throat with thirst. Sore throat may or may not be present in these cases.

Format and Administration: **Chuan Bei Pi Pa Lu** is produced by the Peking Chinese Drug Manufactory, Beijing, China, as *Fritillary and Loquat Leaf mixture,* in 150 ml. bottles. This formula is also known as *Chuan Bei Pi Pa Tang Jiang* (Frittilary Loquat Sugar Elixir).

Recommended Dosage: Ten to 15 ml each time, 3 or 4 times a day. For children under 12 years of age, use half the recommended dose. For children under 5 years, use one third the dose.

Chuan Bei Pi Pa Lu		
Constituent Substances		
Pinyin Name	**Pharmaceutical Name**	**% Composition**
Chuan Bei Mu	*Bulbus Fritillariae Cirrhosae*	1.00
Pi Pa Ye	*Folium Eriobotryae Japonicae*	26.20
Bai Bu	*Radix Stemonae*	4.70
Bo He Nao	*Herba Menthae (Crystal)*	0.04
—	*Flavoring (apricot seeds) and sugar*	to 100%

Composition and Rationale: *Chuan Bei Mu* clears lung heat, moistens dryness and suppresses cough; *Pi Pa Ye* clears lung heat, eliminates phlegm and lowers counterflow qi; *Bai Bu* clears lung heat and suppresses cough; and *Bo He Nao* expels wind heat.

Qing Fei Yi Huo Pian †   3.5
清肺抑火片
Lung-Clearing Fire-Eliminating Tablets

Source: Shou Shi Bao Yuan (Longevity and Health), Ming Dynasty (1368-1644).

Primary Functions and Applications: **Qing Fei Yi Huo Pian** clears lung heat and reduces ascending fire, suppresses cough, and stimulates an increase in body fluid. It is used to clear heat, and is especially useful in clearing lung heat and in the treatment of cough with abundant thick, yellow phlegm. In addition, it is indicated in cases of tonsillitis, pharyngitis (swollen, painful throat), for sores in the mouth or nose, for toothaches or boils, for constipation due to heat in the large intestine (reddish urine may also be present here) and to stop bleeding (i.e., nose, gums) due to repletion heat.

Qing Fei Yi Huo Pian may be used in acute flare-ups of chronic bronchitis when repletion heat is present. Other medicines, such as **Chuan Bei Pi Pa Gao[3.14]** and **Li Fei [3.13]**, are more appropriate during the more stable periods of chronic bronchitis.

Format and Administration: **Qing Fei Yi Huo Pian** is produced by the Tientsin Drug Manufactory as uncoated tablets, 8 per vial, 12 vials per box.

Recommended Dosage: Four tablets, twice a day with warm water. For serious cases with high fever, double the dose. The herbs in this formula are quite gentle, and can be taken as long as necessary.

Contraindications: **Do not use Qing Fei Yi Huo Pian during pregnancy.** This herb formula is only for cases with lung heat. Do not use for patients with cough due to wind-cold, or in cases of lung yin depletion. **Qing Fei Yi Huo Pian** may cause diarrhea.

Qing Fei Yi Huo Pian		
Constituent Substances		
Pinyin Name	**Pharmaceutical Name**	**% Composition**
Huang Qin	*Radix Scutellariae Baicalensis*	21
Shan Zhi Zi	*Fructus Gardeniae Jasminoidis*	12
Da Huang	*Rhizoma Rhei*	18
Qian Hu	*Radix Peucedani*	7
Ku Shen	*Radix et Semen Sophora Flavescentis*	9
Tian Hua Feng	*Radix Trichosanthis*	12
Jie Geng	*Radix Platycodi*	12
Zhi Mu	*Rhizoma Anemarrhenae Ashphodeloidis*	9

Zhong Guo Ji Ben Zhong Chen Yao (Fundamentals of Chinese Prepared Medicines, 1988) includes *Huang Bai* and *Bei Mu* in its standardized formula for **Qing Fei Yi Huo Pian.**

Composition and Rationale: Huang Qin clears lung heat; *Zhi Zi* clears heat; *Da Huang* clears heat through the bowels; *Qian Hu* suppresses cough; *Ku Shen* clears damp-heat; *Tian Hua Fen* clears heat, increases body fluids, and relieves thirst; *Jie Geng* clears heat as it affects sore throat; and *Zhi Mu* moistens the lung.

Jie Geng Wan
桔梗丸
Platycodon Pills

3.6

Source: Jing Kui Yao Lue Fang Lun (Synopsis of the Golden Chamber), by Zhang Zhong Jing, 219 C.E..

Primary Functions and Applications: **Jie Geng Wan** opens the lung, reduces phlegm, and discharges pus from pulmonary abscesses. It assists the expectoration of phlegm and suppresses cough, and can be used to treat the effects of either wind-heat or wind-cold pathogens. It is used to discharge pus in the treatment of pulmonary abscess with foul-smelling phlegm, and for chronic bronchitis with yellow phlegm. *Jie Geng*, the primary herb, eliminates phlegm and helps discharge pus from the lung, and is used to treat sore throat and tonsillitis.

Format and Administration: **Jie Geng Wan** is produced by the Lanchow Chinese Medicine Works as pills, packaged 100 per bottle.

Recommended Dosage: Five to 10 pills, 3 times a day with warm water.

Jie Geng Wan		
Constituent Substances		
Pinyin Name	**Pharmaceutical Name**	**% Composition**
Jie Geng	*Radix Platycodi*	90
Gan Cao	*Radix Glycyrrhizae Uralensis*	10

Composition and Rationale: Jie Geng opens the lung, reduces phlegm, and discharges pus from pulmonary abscess; *Gan Cao* suppresses cough.

3.7   **Qing Chi Hua Tan Wan †**
清氣化痰丸
Qi-Clearing Phlegm-Transforming Pills

Source: Jing Yue Chuan Shu (Jing Yue's Complete Works), Zhang Jing-yue, 1624 C.E..

Primary Functions and Applications: **Qing Chi Hua Tan Wan** clears lung heat, suppresses cough, eliminates phlegm, and relieves asthma. It is commonly used in the treatment of phlegm heat, and in cases of pneumonia or chronic bronchitis due to heat in the lungs. Symptoms indicating its use include strong, loud coughing which might induce vomiting; sticky, thick phlegm; fullness in the chest; a reddish tongue with yellow fur; and a slippery, rapid pulse.

Format and Administration: **Qing Chi Hua Tan Wan** is produced by the Lanzhou Fo Ci Pharmaceutical Factory as *Pinellia Expectorant Pills*, in bottles of 200.

Recommended Dosage: Six pills, 3 times a day with warm water.

Contraindications: **Qing Chi Hua Tan Wan** is not recommended for cases of wind-cold invasion in their early stages, especially when accompanied by aversion to cold. It is also contraindicated in cases of dry cough without phlegm.

Qing Chi Hua Tan Wan		
Constituent Substances		
Pinyin Name	**Pharmaceutical Name**	**% Composition**
Ban Xia	*Rhizoma Pinelliae Ternatae*	16.7
Tian Nan Xing	*Rhizoma Arisaematis (processed with bile)*	16.7
Zhi Shi	*Fructus Citri Immaturus*	11.1
Huang Qin	*Radix Scutellariae*	11.1
Ju Hong	*Exocarpium Citri Rubrum*	11.1
Gua Lou	*Semen Trichosanthis*	11.1
Xing Ren	*Semen Armeniacae*	11.1
Fu Ling	*Sclerotium Poriae Cocus*	11.1

Zhong Guo Ji Ben Zhong Chen Yao (Fundamentals of Chinese Prepared Medicines, 1988) includes *Chen Pi* in its standardized formula for **Qing Chi Hua Tan Wan.**

Composition and Rationale: *Ban Xia* eliminates phlegm; *Tian Nan Xing* and *Gua Lou* clear lung heat and reduce phlegm; *Zhi Shi* lowers counterflow qi (promotes depurative downbearing); *Huang Qin* clears lung heat; *Ju Hong* eliminates phlegm and promotes depurative down-bearing; *Xing Ren* suppresses cough and calms asthma; *Fu Ling* drains damp and eliminates phlegm.

Chuan Ke Ling
喘咳靈
Cough and Dyspnea

3.8

Primary Functions and Applications: **Chuan Ke Ling** clears lung heat and regulates lung qi. It is used to treat coughs due to common cold or flu, and to treat pulmonary abscess.

Format and Administration: **Chuan Ke Ling** is produced by the Fu Sung Pharmaceutical Works, Kirin, China, in tablet format, in bottles of 100 tablets.

Recommended Dosage: Four tablets, 3 times a day, with warm water

Contraindications: Do not use **Chuan Ke Ling** for yin depletion cough.

Chuan Ke Ling		
Constituent Substances		
Pinyin Name	Pharmaceutical Name	% Composition
Jie Geng	*Radix Platycodi*	35
Xing Ren	*Semen Pruni Armeniacae*	25
Gan Cao	*Radix Glycyrrhizae Uralensis*	30
Niu Dan	*Fellis Bovis*	10

Composition and Rationale: *Jie Geng* opens the lung, eliminates phlegm and discharges pus; *Xing Ren* suppresses cough and relieves asthma; *Gan Cao* suppresses cough and clears lung heat; and *Niu Dan* clears heat.

3.9   She Dan Chen Pi Mo †
蛇膽陳皮散
Snake Gallbladder and Tangerine Peel Powder

Primary Functions and Applications: **She Dan Chen Pi Mo** has two primary functions: the treatment of wind-heat as it affects the lung; and the treatment of the sequelae of disharmonies of the heart.

Symptoms accompanying wind-heat affecting the lung will include high fever, cough, thoracic oppression, expectoration of phlegm, and difficult breathing. For very serious cases with especially high fever, unconsciousness or spasms may be present. Such cases occur most commonly in children.

In general, disharmonies of the heart in repletion conditions will lead to symptoms of mania, uneasiness, hysteria, or epilepsy (grand mal or petit mal seizures). In the latter case, physicians in China often combine **She Dan Chen Pi Mo** with other anti-epileptic medications.

She Dan Chen Pi Mo is also used in cases of whooping cough, and in acute cases of pneumonia and bronchitis.

Format and Administration: **She Dan Chen Pi Mo** is produced by the United Pharmaceutical Manufactory, and is available in small vials, each containing 0.6 grams of powder. **She Dan Chuan Bei Ye [3.9a]** is a liquid format of the same medicine.

The name **She Dan Chen Pi Mo** is used for more than one herb formula, though the six-ingredient formula listed here is considered to be the standard. The formula **San She Tan Chen Pi Mo,** produced by the United Pharmaceutical Manufactory, Guangdong, contains only two ingredients (*She Dan* and *Chen Pi*), which together eliminate phlegm (to relieve asthma), expel wind, and strengthen the stomach (to relieve nausea). It is used to treat chronic cough with phlegm, possibly accompanied by nausea and regurgitation.

A similar two-ingredient formula, **She Dan Chuan Bei San [3.9a]**, contains *She Dan* and *Chuan Bei Mu.* it clears heat, suppresses cough, and reduces phlegm, and is used to treat the cough and phlegm caused by phlegm-heat as seen in cases of influenza, acute bronchitis, or acute tracheitis.

Recommended Dosage: One vial (0.6 grams), twice or 3 times a day for adults.

A clinical report published in *Jiang Su Zhong Yi (Journal of Traditional Chinese Medicine)* 12:39 (1965), describes the following dosages in fifty-nine children with whooping cough treated with **She Dan Chen Pi San.** All amounts were divided into 3 doses per day: children under 1 year used a total of 1 vial per day; children age 1 to 5 years used 1 1/2 vials per day; children age 6 to 10 years used 2 vials per day; children age 11 to 15 years used 3 vials per day. The most common treatment period lasted 7 to 10 days. The shortest treatment period lasted 4 days; the longest treatment period lasted 16 days. In 42 of 59 cases there was complete recovery; in 14 cases there was obvious improvement and in 3 cases there was no change.

Contraindications: **She Dan Chen Pi San** is not recommended for use with patients who show signs of depletion.

She Dan Chen Pi Mo		
Constituent Substances		
Pinyin Name	**Pharmaceutical Name**	**% Composition**
She Dan	*Agkistrodon*	0.13
Chen Pi	*Pericarpium Citri Reticulatae*	61.65
Di Long Tan	*Lumbricus (carbonized)*	12.33
Jiang Can	*Bombyx Batryticatus*	12.33
Zhu Sha	*Cinnabaris*	12.33
Hu Po	*Succinum*	1.23

Composition and Rationale: She Dan clears heat; *Chen Pi* eliminates phlegm; *Di Long* and *Jiang Can* relieve spasm and asthma; *Zhu Sha* and *Hu Po* tranquilize and calm the spirit.

Most **She Dan Chen Pi San** available in the U.S. is from Guangzhou United Pharmaceutical Co., and contains 16.67% *She Dan* and 83.33% *Chen Pi.* Its effect is similar to the original formula, although its primary use is for the treatment of cough with white or yellowish phlegm. It is also used to lower counterflow qi and thereby treat nausea and vomiting.

3.10

Hai Zao Wan †
海藻丸
Sargassium Pills

Primary Functions and Applications: **Hai Zao Wan** reduces and helps to remove nodes. It is used to treat simple goiter (due to inadequate dietary intake of iodine); to treat chronic lymphadenitis in the neck, including scrofula (tuberculosis in the neck); to prevent and treat hypertension and atherosclerosis; and as an anticoagulant to help prevent and treat blood clots.

Format and Administration: **Hai Zao Wan** is produced in 50-pill bottles, by the Lanzhow Fo Ci Pharmaceutical Factory as *Haiodin.*

Recommended Dosage: Two pills, 3 times a day.

Hai Zao Wan		
Constituent Substances		
Pinyin Name	**Pharmaceutical Name**	**% Composition**
Hai Zao	*Herba Sargassi*	60
Kun Bu	*Thallus Algae*	40

Zhong Guo Ji Ben Zhong Chen Yao (Fundamentals of Chinese Prepared Medicines, 1988) includes *Wu Mei (Fructus Mume)* in its standardized formula for **Hai Zao Wan.**

Composition and Rationale: *Hai Zao* and *Kun Bu* remove nodular phlegm accumulation. Both contain large amounts of iodine.

Er Chen Wan † 3.11
二陳丸
Double Vintage Pills

Source: *He Ji Jiu Fang (Formularies of the People's Welfare Pharmacies)*, 1151 C.E..

Primary Functions and Applications: **Er Chen Wan** dries damp, reduces phlegm caused by dampness, and regulates the qi of the middle burner. Guiding symptoms include cough with abundant expectoration, excess thin, white phlegm, a thick, white, greasy tongue coating, and a slippery pulse. **Er Chen Wan** is the primary formula for treating cough with excess phlegm accompanied by sensations of fullness in the chest, with nausea and possibly vomiting.

Er Chen Wan is also used in cases of abdominal distension with digestive disorders and possible vomiting (which may be due to exogenous pathogens associated with autumn dampness), and in cases involving dizziness or palpitations caused by the retention of damp. It is indicated in cases of chronic bronchitis with excess phlegm, for the relief of emphysematic symptoms, to reduce swelling of the thyroid in cases where that gland is enlarged; for gastric symptoms (poor appetite or excess stomach acid); and gastroenteritis with cough or phlegm.

Format and Administration: **Er Chen Wan** is produced by the Lanchow Chinese Medicine Works as *Er Chen Wan (Pinellia-Pachyma Compound Pills)* in bottles of 200 pills. Honey pills of this formula are produced in China, though they are rarely available in the U.S.

Recommended Dosage: Seven or 8 small pills, 3 times a day, or 2 honey pills, twice a day, with warm water.

Er Chen Wan		
Constituent Substances		
Pinyin Name	**Pharmaceutical Name**	**% Composition**
Ban Xia	*Rhizoma Pinelliae Ternatae*	44.45
Chen Pi	*Pericarpium Citri Reticulatae*	11.11
Fu Ling	*Sclerotium Poriae Cocus*	22.22
Gan Cao	*Radix Glycyrrhizae Uralensis*	22.22

Composition and Rationale: The name "Double Vintage" refers to the increased potency of aged *Ban Xia* and *Chen Pi*: the older these two medicines are, the more effective the formula. *Ban Xia* dries dampness, reduces phlegm, relieves vomiting, and lowers the stomach qi; *Chen Pi* regulates the middle burner qi and dries damp; *Fu Ling* strengthens the spleen and rids damp through urination; and *Gan Cao* harmonizes the other herbs.

3.12 Yang Yin Qing Fei Tang Jiang †
養陰清肺糖漿
Yin-Nourishing Lung-Clearing Syrup

Source: *Chong Lou Yu Yao (Key to get into the Magic Building)*, Cheng Neijin, 1836.

Primary Functions and Applications: **Yang Yin Qing Fei Tang Jiang** is a very nourishing formula for the supplementation of lung yin, and is effective in clearing the yin depletion type of lung heat in chronic *(not acute)* conditions. It eliminates phlegm, suppresses chronic cough or cough in the final stages of exogenous pathogen invasion (especially dry cough or cough with little phlegm and some blood), and soothes the throat.

Symptoms indicating its use include dryness and pain in the throat, with thirst and hoarseness due to a depletion of lung yin, or as the sequelae of external pathogen invasion. Common diseases also addressed include tonsillitis, pharyngitis, chronic dry cough (similar to that seen with tuberculosis or lung cancer patients), and diptheria.

Format and Administration: **Yang Yin Qing Fei Tang Jian** is produced by the Tientsin Drug Manufactory in 120 ml bottles.

Recommended Dosage: Twenty ml or 4 teaspoons, twice a day. Reduce by half for children.

Yang Yin Qing Fei Tang Jian		
Constituent Substances		
Pinyin Name	Pharmaceutical Name	% Composition
Mu Dan Pi	*Cortex Radicis Mouton*	10.52
Zhi Bei Mu	*Bulbus Fritillariae Cirrhosae*	10.52
Bai Shao	*Radix Paeoniae Lactiflora*	10.52
Yuan Shen	*Radix Scrophulariae Ningpoensis*	21.04
Sheng Di Huang	*Radix Crudae Rehmanniae Glutinosae*	26.31
Mai Men Dong	*Radix Ophiopogonis Japonici*	15.78
Gan Cao	*Radix Glycyrrhizae Uralensis*	5.27
Bo He	*Herba Menthae*	0.04

Composition and Rationale: *Mo Dan Pi* clears blood heat and reduces infection; *Zhe Bei Mu* clears heat, moistens the lungs, suppresses cough, and eliminates phlegm; *Bai Shao* nourishes yin and moistens body fluid; *Yuan Shen* nourishes yin, moistens body fluid, and reduces inflammation; *Sheng Di Huang* nourishes yin, clears heat, and reduces inflammation; *Mai Men Dong* nourishes yin, clears lung heat, and moistens the lungs; *Gan Cao* harmonizes the other herbs, clears heat, and moistens the lung; and *Bo He* diffuses the lung and soothes the throat.

3.13 Li Fei †
利肺
Lung Benefiting Formula

Primary Functions and Applications: **Li Fei**, as its name indicates, benefits the lungs, relieves asthma, and suppresses chronic cough due to lung yin depletion. It is thus used to treat lung yin depletion, with such symptoms as chronic cough without mucus (internal heat has dried out the mucus); asthma due to lung qi depletion (*not hot damp asthma exhibiting symptoms of lung-heat and dyspnea);* and coughing with blood in cases of lung yin depletion (night sweats may also be present here.)

Li Fei is used in cases of chronic pulmonary tuberculosis or lung cancer, where chronic dry cough is accompanied by expectoration of blood.

Format and Administration: **Li Fei** is produced by the Handan Pharmaceutical works as *Sugar-Coated Pulmonary Tonic Tablets,* available in 60-tablet bottles.

Recommended Dosage: Four to 6 tablets, 3 times a day with warm water, shortly (a half-hour) after meals.

Li Fei		
Constituent Substances		
Pinyin Name	**Pharmaceutical Name**	**% Composition**
Dong Chong Xia Cao	*Sclerotium Cordycipitis Chinensis*	5
Ge Jie	*Gecko*	5
Bai He	*Bulbus Lilii*	8
Wu Wei Zi	*Fructus Schizandrae Chinensis*	13
Bai Ji	*Rhizoma Bletillae Striatae*	27
Bai Bu	*Radix Stemonae*	15
Mu Li	*Concha Ostreae*	11
Pi Pa Ye	*Folium Eriobotryae Japonicae*	10
Gan Cao	*Radix Glycyrrhizae Uralensis*	6

Composition and Rationale: Dong Chong Xia Cao strengthens lung qi and suppresses cough; *Ge Jie* strengthens the lungs; *Bai He* supplements lung yin, clears lung heat, moistens the lungs, and suppresses cough; *Wu Wei Zi* suppresses cough and moistens the lungs; *Bai Ji* controls bleeding; *Bai Bu* suppresses cough and clears lung heat; *Mu Li* supplements the yin, reduces replete yang, and controls sweat; *Pi Ba Ye* clears lung heat, suppresses cough, and eliminates phlegm; and *Gan Cao* suppresses cough and clears heat.

In classical Chinese medicine, lung disorders are generally treated with lung heat clearers or lung supplements. Formulae such as **Qing Fei Yi Huo Pian [3.5]**, for example, are used to clear lung heat and treat cough, phlegm, or asthma in cases of acute or chronic bronchitis or tracheitis. **Li Fei** is used in cases of lung yin depletion to supplement the lung, and does not address the lung heat caused by exogenous pathogens.

Chuan Bei Pi Ba Gao   3.14
川貝枇杷膏
Fritillaria and Loquat Syrup

Source: Wen Re Lun (Treatise on Seasonal Febrile Diseases), Ye Gui, 1746 C.E..

Primary Functions and Applications: **Chuan Bei Pi Ba Gao** clears lung heat, suppresses cough, moistens the lung, and relieves asthma (by promoting counterflow-downbearing of lung qi). It is used in cases of cough caused by lung heat, with such symptoms as difficult expectoration of phlegm and throat pain, and is effective in both acute and chronic cases. Smoker's cough may also be relieved with its use.

Chuan Bei Pi Ba Gao may be used to nourish lung yin, and to treat pulmonary tuberculosis accompanied by expectoration of blood. Symptoms in such cases include dry cough with little or no phlegm. Such cases are usually indicative of yin depletion, which gives rise to internal heat, low grade fever, and dryness of the mouth and throat.

Format and Administration: **Chuan Bei Pi Ba Gao** is produced by the Nin Jiom Manufactory, Hong Kong, as *Natural Herb Loquat Flavored Syrup* in 10 fluid-ounce bottles.

Recommended Dosage: Ten ml each time (1 tablespoon), 3 times a day. For children, 5 ml, 3 times a day. Take directly from the bottle, or dilute with warm water. Daily use over a long period of time is acceptable, and is especially beneficial for smokers who have compromised the defensive function of their lung.

Chuan Bei Pi Pa Gao		
Constituent Substances		
Pinyin Name	**Pharmaceutical Name**	**% Composition**
Pi Pa Ye	*Folium Eriobotryae Japonicae*	--
Bei Mu	*Bulbus Fritillariae Cirrhosae*	--
Sha Shen	*Radix Adenophorae*	--
Wu Wei Zi	*Fructus Schizandrae Chinensis*	--
Chen Pi	*Pericarpium Citri Reticulatae*	--
Jie Geng	*Radix Platycodi*	--
Ban Xia	*Rhizoma Pinelliae Ternatae*	--
Bo He	*Herba Menthae*	--
Kuan Dong Hua	*Flos Tussilaginis Farfare*	--
Xing Ren	*Semen Pruni Armeniacae*	--
Feng Mi	*Mel*	--

Composition and Rationale: *Pi Ba Ye* suppresses cough and eliminates phlegm; *Bei Mu* clears lung heat, moistens the lung, suppresses cough, and eliminates phlegm; *Sha Shen* strengthens yin, clears lung heat, moistens the lung, and suppresses cough; *Chen Pi* lowers counterflow lung qi and eliminates phlegm; *Jie Geng* opens lung qi and eliminates phlegm; *Ban Xia* eliminates phlegm; *Bo He* expels wind-heat and clears lung heat; *Kuan Dong Hua* suppresses cough and is a counterflow-downbearing agent; *Wu Wei Zi, Xing Ren* and *Feng Mi* moisten the lung and suppress cough.

Ba Xian Chang Shou Wan †

3.15

八仙長壽丸

Eight Immortals Longevity Pills

Primary Functions and Applications: **Ba Xian Chang Shou Wan** is used to treat lung or kidney yin depletion, and to strengthen kidney qi and collect lung yin through the use of astringents. It is indicated in cases of chronic cough, with symptoms caused by a depletion of yin in the kidney (dry cough, lumbago, dizziness, vertigo, tinnitis, deafness, night sweats, thirst, heat in the five centers, seminal emission). In such cases, the tongue may be expected to be reddish, with little or no moss, and the pulse to be thin and rapid. **Ba Xian Chang Shou Wan** should be considered in cases of tuberculosis, asthma, or diabetes.

Format and Administration: **Ba Xian Chang Shou Wan** is produced by the Lanchow Chinese Medicine Works in pill format, 200 pills per bottle. This formula is also known as **Mai Wei Di Huang Wan [3.15a]**, and is based upon **Liu Wei Di Huang Wan [13.18]** to which *Mai Dong* and *Wu Wei Zi* have been added.

Recommended Dosage: Eight pills, 3 times a day.

Ba Xian Chang Shou Wan		
Constituent Substances		
Pinyin Name	**Pharmaceutical Name**	**% Composition**
Shou Di	*Radix Rehmanniae (processed)*	26.66
Shan Zhu Yu	*Fructus Corni*	13.33
Shan Yao	*Rhizoma Batatatis*	13.33
Dan Pi	*Cortex Moutan*	10.00
Ze Xie	*Buthus Martensi*	10.00
Fu Ling	*Sclerotium Poriae Cocus*	10.00
Mai Dong	*Radix Ophiopogonis Japonici*	10.00
Wu Wei Zi	*Fructus Schizandrae*	6.68

Composition and Rationale: *Shou Di* nourishes yin, strengthens the kidney, and supplements the blood; *Shan Zhu Yu* nourishes the liver and the kidney, controls spermatorrhea, suppresses cough, clears heat, and eliminates phlegm; *Shan Yao* strengthens the spleen and kidney and controls spermatorrhea; *Dan Pi* clears heat in the blood and reduces liver fire; *Ze Xie* clears heat in the kidney and promotes urination; *Fu Ling* strengthens the spleen, promotes urination, and discharges dampness; *Mai Dong* clears lung heat, moistens the lung, strengthens the body fluid, and supplements the yin; and *Wu Wei Zi* strengthens the kidney and lung qi and astringes the lung.

3.16

Qiu Li Gao †
秋梨膏
Autumn Pear Syrup

Source: *Yi Xue Cong Zhong Lu (Medicine for the Large General Population),* Qing Dynasty (1644-1911).

Primary Functions and Applications: **Qiu Li Gao** suppresses cough, eliminates phlegm, nourishes lung yin, and promotes the production of body fluid. It is used to treat cough, reduce phlegm, relieve asthma, especially for the patient who has phlegm with blood due to damaged body fluid and lung dryness due to yin depletion, and to treat throat dryness, with frequent thirst and hoarseness. It is used in cases of dry cough, including the dry cough which is a major symptom following tuberculosis, chronic bronchitis, or other lung diseases.

Format and Administration: Many manufactories in China currently use the name **Qiu Li Gao,** and produce a similar form of this medicine with similar ingredients. All have the same basic function and applications. It is commonly available in 12-ounce bottles.

The Tong San Yi Factory, situated on Qian Men Da Jie in Beijing, is becoming famous as the leading producer of **Qiu Li Gao,** the only prepared medicine produced there. This establishment produces **Qiu Li Gao** in two varieties: **Ling Bei Qiu Li Gao,** with primary ingredients of *Fu Ling, Chuan Bei Mu* and *Qiu Li,* plus honey; and **Yen Wo Qiu Li**

Gao, with primary ingredients of bird's nest and *Qiu Li,* plus honey. **Ling Bei Qiu Li Gao** is used to treat chronic cough due to lung dryness. **Yen Wo Qiu Li Gao** is used as a supplement to strengthen the lungs and to improve the general health of older people. Both can be used over a long period of time as a tonic to promote general wellbeing.

Recommended Dosage: Fifteen grams, twice a day.

Qiu Li Gao		
Constituent Substances		
Pinyin Name	**Pharmaceutical Name**	**% Composition**
Qiu Li	*Fructus Pyri*	95.230
Mai Men Dong	*Radix Ophiopogonis Japonici*	.095
Zhe Bei Mu	*Bulbus Fritillariae Cirrhosae*	.095
Ou Jie	*Fresh Lotus Rhizome*	.190
Qing Luo Bo	*Green Turnip*	.095

Composition and Rationale: *Qiu Li* clears lung heat, suppresses cough, moistens and nourishes the lung, and relieves thirst; *Mai Men Dong* nourishes the lung yin, reduces lung dryness, eliminates phlegm, and suppresses cough; *Zhe Bei Mu* clears lung heat, suppresses cough, and eliminates phlegm; *Ou Jie* increases body fluid, relieves thirst, and controls bleeding; and *Qing Luo Bo* regulates lung qi, suppresses cough, and eliminates phlegm.

Only pears harvested in the autumn may be used in **Qiu Li Gao.** This assures both adequate ripeness (having remained on the tree for as long as possible), and absorption of autumn's energetic factor, associated with the lung in five-phase theory.

3.17   Zhi Sou Ding Chuan Wan †
止嗽定喘丸
Cough-Suppressing Dyspnea-Stabilizing Pills

Source: *Shang Han Lun,* 219 C.E..

Primary Functions and Applications: **Zhi Sou Ding Chuan Wan** opens the lung qi, disperses lung heat, and relieves cough and asthma. It is the prepared format of the important formula *Ma Xing Shi Gan Tang (Ephedra, Apricot Seed, Gypsum, and Licorice Decoction),* the representative formulae for the treatment of the cough and asthma resulting from lung heat. Thick yellow expectoration, shortness of breath, and fever will be primary. Sweating may or may not be present.

Zhi Sou Ding Chuan Wan is also effective in cases of acute or chronic bronchitis, acute pneumonia, acute or chronic tracheitis, and pneumonia with measles in children. When treating measles, use this formula only after the rash has completely emerged; do not use at the beginning of the illness.

Format and Administration: **Zhi Sou Ding Chuan Wan** is produced by the Tientsin Drug Manufactory in pill format, in bottles of 150 pills.

Recommended Dosage: Ten pills, twice a day with warm water.

Contraindications: Due to the presence of *Ma Huang* in this formula, use **Zhi Sou Ding Chuan Wan** with caution when large doses are administered to hypertensive patients.

Zhi Sou Ding Chuan Wan		
Constituent Substances		
Pinyin Name	**Pharmaceutical Name**	**% Composition**
Ma Huang	*Herba Ephedrae*	1
Xing Ren	*Semen Pruni Armeniacae*	19
Shi Gao	*Gypsum*	15
Gan Cao	*Radix Glycyrrhizae Uralensis*	25
—	*unspecified substance*	to 100%

Composition and Rationale: Ma Huang expels wind-cold, opens the lung, and relieves asthma; *Xing Ren* brings down counterflow qi and suppresses cough and asthma; *Shi Gao* clears lung heat and stomach heat; *Gan Cao* harmonizes the other herbs, clears heat, and suppresses cough.

Qi Guan Yan Ke Sou Tan Chuan Wan   3.18
氣管炎咳嗽痰喘丸
Bronchial Cough, Phlegm and Dyspnea Pills

Primary Functions and Applications: **Qi Guan Yan Ke Sou Tan Chuan Wan** eliminates phlegm, relieves asthma, and reduces cough. It is used in cases of chronic bronchitis and bronchiectasis in the presence of abundant expectoration of thin white phlegm. This herb formula is often the medicine of choice for elderly patients exhibiting these symptoms.

Format and Administration: **Qi Guan Yan Ke Sou Tan Chuan Wan** is produced by the Beijing Tung Jen Tang as *Chu Kuan Yen Wan* in pill format, 200 pills per bottle.

Recommended Dosage: Twenty pills, twice a day with warm water.

Qi Guan Yan Ke Sou Tan Chuan Wan		
Constituent Substances		
Pinyin Name	**Pharmaceutical Name**	**% Composition**
Qian Hu	*Radix Peucedani*	4
Xing Ren	*Semen Pruni Armeniacae*	6
Yuan Zhi	*Radix Polygalae Tenuifoliae*	4
Sang Ye	*Folium Mori Albae*	8
Chuan Bei Mu	*Bulbus Fritillariae Cirrhosae*	6
Ju Hong	*Pericarpium Citri Erythrocarpae*	2
Pi Pa Ye	*Folium Eriobotryae Japonicae*	28
Kuan Dong Hua	*Flos Tussilaginis Farfare*	2
Dang Shen	*Radix Codonopsis Pilosulae*	16
Ma Dou Ling	*Fructus Aristolochiae*	2
Wu Wei Zi	*Fructus Schizandrae Chinensis*	2
Sheng Jiang	*Rhizoma Recens Zingiberis Officinalis*	8
Da Zao	*Fructus Zizyphi Jujubae*	12

Composition and Rationale: *Qian Hu* lowers counterflow lung qi and eliminates phlegm; *Xing Ren* reduces cough and relieves asthma; *Yuan Zhi* eliminates phlegm; *Sang Ye* expels wind, opens the lung, and clears lung heat; *Chuan Bei Mu* moistens the lungs, suppresses cough and eliminates phlegm; *Ju Hong* reduces thin white phlegm; *Pi Ba Ye* suppresses cough and eliminates phlegm; *Kuan Dong Hua* lowers counterflow lung qi, suppresses cough, and transforms phlegm; *Dang Shen* strengthens lung qi and spleen qi; *Ma Dou Ling* suppresses cough, relieves asthma, and clears lung heat; *Wu Wei Zi* suppresses cough and relieves asthma; and *Sheng Jiang* and *Da Zao* regulate the constructive (*ying*) and defensive (*wei*) energies.

3.19

Xiao Ke Chuan †
消咳喘
Cough-Relieving Formula

Primary Functions and Applications: **Xiao Ke Chuan** suppresses cough, assists expectoration of phlegm, and relieves asthma. It is used in cases of chronic tracheitis or bronchitis with abundant phlegm, for cough due to the common cold; and to increase the body's resistance to disease.

Format and Administration: **Xiao Ke Chuan** is produced by the Harbin Medicine Manufactory as *Hsiao Keh Chuan,* in both liquid (200 ml per bottle) and capsule (18 per bottle) format.

Recommended Dosage: Liquid, 10 ml 3 times a day; or pills, 2 pills 3 times a day with warm water. Decrease dosage to half for children.

Xiao Ke Chuan		
Constituent Substances		
Pinyin Name	**Pharmaceutical Name**	**% Composition**
Man Shan Hong	*Radix et Ramus Rhododendri Daurici*	100

Luo Han Guo Chong Ji
羅漢果沖劑
Mormordica Soluble Preparation

3.20

Primary Functions and Applications: **Luo Han Guo Chong Ji** clears lung heat, nourishes and moistens the lungs, and suppresses cough. It is used to treat cough due to lung heat, which is often associated with lung yin depletion and weak lungs. In such cases, heat produces cough with sticky phlegm or phlegm with blood. As a summer beverage, taken hot or cold, it is effective in eliminating summerheat and quenching thirst.

Luo Han Guo Chong Ji is indicated in the treatment of bronchitis, pharyngitis, and tonsillitis, with symptoms such as cough, dry and itchy throat, sticky phlegm or phlegm with blood; and for treatment of stubborn, chronic cough, such as whooping cough, or chronic cough associated with tuberculosis.

Format and Administration: **Luo Han Guo Chong Ji** is produced by the Lo Han Kuo Products Manufactory, Kwangsi, China. It is available in blocks of 12 per package.

Recommended Dosage: For each dose, dissolve 1 block in 1 cup of boiling water. Take 2 to 3 times a day.

Luo Han Guo Chong Ji		
Constituent Substances		
Pinyin Name	Pharmaceutical Name	% Composition
Luo Han Guo	*Fructus Mormordicae*	95
—	*Cane Sugar*	5

Composition and Rationale: *Luo Han Guo* expels summer heat, nourishes the lungs, suppresses cough, and relieves thirst. **Luo Han Guo** has a sweet taste and cooling property. The *luo han* fruit has a laxative effect.

Luo Han Guo Zhi Ke Lu [3.20a], a medicine related to **Luo Han Guo Chong Ji**, contains, in addition to *Fructus Mormordicae, Bei Mu (Bulbus Fritillariae Cirrhosae), He Shou Wu (Radix Polygoni Multiflori), Bei Sha Shen (Radix Glehniae)*, and *Xing Ren (Semen Pruni Armeniacae)*. It is somewhat stronger in clearing lung heat and opening lung qi. **Luo Han Guo Zhi Ke Lu** is produced by the Yulin Drug Manufactory in 100 milliliter bottles.

3.21

Ping Chuan Wan
平喘丸
Dyspnea-Calming Pills

Primary Functions and Applications: **Ping Chuan Wan** suppresses cough, relieves shortness of breath, and nourishes lung yin. It is used to treat chronic shortness of breath that has depleted lung qi and lung yin. A guiding symptom in such cases is shortness of breath that is worse in the evening, after exertion, or when in the presence of exogenous pathogens. Cough with white, thin phlegm may be present as well. In the presence of these symptoms, this formula is recommended in the treatment of chronic bronchitis and emphysema.

Format and Administration: **Ping Chuan Wan** is produced by the Sing-Kyn Drug House, Kwangchow, China in pill format, 120 pills per bottle.

Recommended Dosage: Ten pills, 3 times a day.

The manufacturer indicates on the accompanying flyer that based on their clinical experience, a single bottle can produce noticeable effects for a "general case," and that three bottles can relieve cough and shortness of breath in cases of chronic bronchitis. For such cases, and in cases of chronic asthma and emphysema, three to four 40-day courses of treatment in succession will suppress the cough, reduce phlegm, and relieve shortness of breath.

Ping Chuan Wan		
Constituent Substances		
Pinyin Name	**Pharmaceutical Name**	**% Composition**
Dang Shen	*Radix Codonopsis Pilosulae*	15
Ge Jie	*Gecko*	5
Dong Chong Xia Cao	*Sclerotium Cordycipitis Chinensis*	5
Xing Ren	*Semen Pruni Armeniacae*	15
Chen Pi	*Pericarpium Citri Reticulatae*	8
Gan Cao	*Radix Glycyrrhizae Uralensis*	10
Sang Bai Pi	*Cortex Radicis Mori Alba*	10
Bai Qian	*Radix Cynanchi Stauntonii*	8
Meng Shi	*Lapis Chloriti*	4
Wu Zhi Mao Tao	*Radix Fici Simplicissimae*	10
Man Hu Tui Zi	*Elaeagnus Glabra Thunb*	10

Composition and Rationale: Dang Shen, Ge Jie, and Dong Chong Xia Cao supplement lung qi and yin; *Xing Ren, Chen Pi,* and *Gan Cao* suppress cough and eliminate phlegm; *Sang Bai Pi, Bai Qian, Meng Shi, Wu Zhi Mao Tao,* and *Man Hu Tui Zi* relieve asthma and downbear.

4

Formulae for the Treatment of Bi Patterns

4.1   Yao Tong Pian

4.2   Ji Xue Teng Qin Gao Pian

4.3   Du Zhong Hu Gu Wan

4.4   Feng Shi Ling Pian

4.5   Feng Shi Xiao Tong Wan

4.6   Feng Shi Pian

4.7   Xiao Huo Luo Dan

4.8   Du Huo Ji Sheng Wan

4.9   Gou Pi Gao

4.10 Shang Shi Zhi Tong Gao

4.11 Bao Zhen Gao

4.12 Zhui Feng Huo Xue Pian

4.13 Yun Xiang Jing

4.14 Hu Gu Jiu

4.15 Feng Liao Xing Yao Jiu

Pattern Identification

The pathogenic factors wind, cold, and damp often combine to obstruct the characteristic flow within the channels. The joint and muscular pain, stiffness and impeded movement of the sinews that result from such obturation (stopping-up) form a recognizable pattern of symptoms termed, in Chinese, *bi*.

Therapeutic objectives in bi patterns focus primarily on restoration of flow in the channels, and are accomplished by both freeing the channels and by dispelling the predominant pathogen(s). Thus, when wind predominates, wind-dispellants and connecting-channel freeing agents are added. When damp is foremost, wind-damp dispellants are used. When cold bi is observed, the channels must be warmed and the cold dissipated with potent hot, pungent agents. In stubborn cases of bi from wind-damp-cold, static blood transformers are often included.

In all bi cases, acumoxatherapy is considered an essential concomitant of the treatment strategy.

Formulae Differentiation

Feng Shi Xiao Tong Wan [4.5] and **Feng Shi Pian [4.6]** are structured for treatment of the classical patterns of bi from wind, cold, and damp, combining warm-natured wind dissipators, wind-damp dispellants, and connecting-channel freeing agents. **Feng Shi Pian [4.6]** contains a number of exterior resolvants, and thus has more of a sense of exterior resolution in cases of wind penetration. **Zhui Feng Hu Xue Pian [4.12]** includes exterior resolution, wind dissipation, and blood nourishment, as well as connecting-channel freeing, in its strategy to treat bi.

Chronic or long-standing cases of bi often take their toll on the function of the kidneys, or on the general state of the qi and the blood (causing depletion). In such cases, supplementation should accompany channel-freeing efforts. **Du Zhong Hu Gu Wan [4.3], Du Huo Ji Seng Wan [4.8],** and **Hu Gu Jiu[4.14]** are noteworthy in this dual capacity. **Yao Tong Pian [4.1]** may also be considered as a channel-freeing, supplementing formulae. However, its emphasis is decidedly on kidney supplementation, and its inclusion here, rather than with the supplements of Chapter 13, might well be debated.

The emphasis of **Ji Xue Teng Qin Gao Pian [4.2]** is on transforming blood as well as on freeing bi, and might appropriately have been included among the blood regulating formulae of Chapter 12.

Xiao Huo Luo Dan [4.7] emphasizes analgesic stasis transformers.

For topical relief of the muscular ache and joint pain of bi patterns, the plasters **Gou Pi Gao [4.9], Shang Shi Zhi Tong Gao [4.10]** and **Bao Zhen Gao [4.11]** provide warmth as well as channel invigoration. The lotion/elixir **Yun Xiang Jing [4.13]** may be used both externally and internally (for emergency cases), and has the additional distinction of being effective in cases of frostbite.

4.1

Yao Tong Pian †
腰痛片
Lumbago Tablets

Primary Functions and Applications: **Yao Tong Pian** strengthens the kidneys and moves the blood. It is used to treat lumbago caused either by kidney yang depletion or by chronic muscular over-straining.

Format and Administration: **Yao Tong Pian** is produced by the Hu Qing Yu Tang Medicine Factory, Hangzhou, China, in both tablet format (100 per bottle, called *Anti-Lumbago Tablets*), and in honey-pill format, called *Yao Tong Wan*.

Recommended Dosage: One honey pill, or six pills, 3 times a day.

Yao Tong Pian		
Constituent Substances		
Pinyin Name	**Pharmaceutical Name**	**% Composition**
Dang Gui	*Radix Angelicae Sinensis*	17.4
Du Zhong	*Cortex Eucommiae Ulmoidis*	17.4
Xu Duan	*Radix Dipsaci*	13.04
Gou Qi Zi	*Fructus Lycii Chinensis*	13.04
Bai Zhu	*Rhizoma Atractylodis Macrocephalae*	13.04
Bu Gu Zhi	*Semen Psoralae Corytoliae*	13.04
Niu Xi	*Radix Achyranthes Bidentatae*	13.04

Zhong Guo Ji Ben Zhong Chen Yao (Fundamentals of Chinese Patent Medicines, 1988) includes *Chi Shou, Zi Xie, Tu Bie Chong, Rou Gui,* and *Ru Xiang* in its standardized formula for **Yao Tong Wan**, indicating a formula that is somewhat less tonic, and more directed toward warming and clearing the channels and relieving pain.

Composition and Rationale: *Dang Gui* supplements and moves the blood; *Du Zhong* strengthens the kidney, liver, sinews, and bones; *Xu Duan* in this context may be considered a blood nourisher and connecting-channel freer, and as such strengthens the kidney, liver, sinews, and bones, and relieves lumbago; *Gou Ji* strengthens the kidney, liver, and lumbar area; *Bai Zhu* strengthens the spleen and supplements the qi; *Bu Gu Zhi* warms kidney yang; *Niu Xi* moves the blood and strengthens the liver and kidney.

Ji Xue Teng Qin Gao Pian † 4.2
鳩血藤浸膏片
Milletia Liquid Extract Tablets

Primary Functions and Applications: *Ji Xue Teng (Millettia Reticulata Benth.),* the single constituent of **Ji Xue Teng Qin Gao Pian,** nourishes the blood, moves the blood, and clears the channels. It is used to treat amenorrhea or dysmenorrhea due to blood depletion and/or blood stasis. The primary symptom indicating such disharmony is dizziness. **Ji Xue Teng Qin Gao Pian** is commonly combined with formulae specifically designed to treat gynecologic disorders, and with supplements, if necessary. Although not as strong, this herb has the same effect as *Dang Gui (Radix Angelicae Sinensis)* in nourishing blood.

Ji Xue Teng Qin Gao Pian is also used to treat bi patterns. Symptoms in such cases include numbness of the limbs, stiff and painful joints, backache, and weakness in the knees. Because this medicine both nourishes and moves the blood, it is especially good for older or weaker patients with blood depletion causing failure to nourish the channels, resulting in channel dysfunction. It may also be used to treat aplastic anemia.

This is a mild, gentle medicine, and may be used safely for up to three months, even by patients with a depletion of yin and signs of depletion heat, without any exacerbation of symptoms.

Ji Xue Teng Qin Gao Pian has been observed to increase the white blood cell count in cancer patients whose white cell counts were reduced as a result of chemotherapy or radiation. Research in Shanghai with cancer patients undergoing chemotherapy showed an increase in white blood cell count following 3 or 4 days of treatment with this herbal medicine. Thus, the chemotherapy or radiation treatments were able to continue without prolonged interruption. (*Shanghai Traditional Chinese Medicine Journal,* No. 9, pp. 16-17, 1965).

Format and Administration: **Ji Xue Teng Qin Gao Pian** is produced by the Shanghai Native Medicine Works, Shanghai, China, as *Caulis Milletiae Tablet.* It is available in coated tablet format, 100 per bottle.

Recommended Dosage: Four tablets, 3 times a day.

Ji Xue Teng Qin Gao Pian		
Constituent Substances		
Pinyin Name	Pharmaceutical Name	% Composition
Ji Xue Teng	*Millettia Reticulata Benth.*	100

Composition and Rationale: *Ji Xue Teng* nourishes the blood and promotes blood circulation.

4.3   Du Zhong Hu Gu Wan
杜仲虎骨丸
Eucommiae and Tiger Bone Pills

Primary Functions and Applications: **Du Zhong Hu Gu Wan** strengthens the liver and kidney, nourishes and moves the blood, supplements the qi, and relieves pain. It is designed to treat both the symptoms of bi, and the underlying liver and kidney damage that results from chronic bi. It is thus used for joint pain, lumbago, joint stiffness, fatigue, feelings of cold in the limbs, weakness in the lower back and the knees, as well as for impotence and spermatorrhea.

Du Zhong Hu Gu Wan is also indicated in the treatment of elderly patients with liver and kidney insufficiency that has produced a gradual onset of slowness in walking, a feeling of numbness or near paralysis of the limbs, feelings of coldness, and dizziness.

Format and Administration: **Du Zhong Hu Gu Wan** is produced by the Guiyang Chinese Medicine Factory, Guiyang, China, as *Pilulae Corticis Eucommiae et Ossis Tigris*. It is available in pill format, 100 per box. This medicine is produced by several different manufactories under the same name; the ingredients may vary somewhat, but the general function is the same.

Recommended Dosage: Adults, 8-12 pills, 3 times a day. Children 8-11 years old, 4-6 pills, 3 times a day; 12-16 years old, 6-8 pills, 3 times a day.

Contraindication: **Do not use Du Zhong Hu Gu Wan during pregnancy.** Do not eat beans or seafood while taking this medicine.

Du Zhong Hu Gu Wan		
Constituent Substances		
Pinyin Name	**Pharmaceutical Name**	**% Composition**
Ren Shen	*Radix Ginseng*	6.2
Bai Zhu	*Rhizoma Atractylodis Macrocephalae*	3.8
Dang Gui	*Radix Angelicae Sinensis*	6.2
Chuan Xiong	*Rhizoma Ligustici Wallichii*	6.2
Ji Xue Teng	*Millettia Reticulata Benth.*	3.8
San Qi	*Radix Pseudoginseng*	6.2
Du Zhong	*Cortex Eucommiae Ulmoidis*	17.8
Hu Gu	*Os Tigris*	6.8
Mu Gua	*Fructus Chaenomelis Lagenariae*	5.5
Yin Yang Huo	*Herba Epimedii*	3.8
Wu Shao She	*Zaocys*	6.8
Lu Lu Tong	*Fructus Liquidambaris*	5.5
Cang Zhu	*Radix Atractylodis*	5.5
Xun Gu Feng	*Rhizoma seu Herba Aristolochiae*	4.0
Wei Ling Xian	*Radix Clematidis Chinensis*	4.0
Shi Nan Teng	*Ramus Photiniae*	4.0
Sang Zhi	*Ramulus Mori Albae*	3.8

Composition and Rationale: *Ren Shen* and *Bai Zhu* fortify the spleen and nourish qi; *Dang Gui, Chuan Xiong, Ji Xue Teng,* and *San Qi* nourish and move blood; *Du Zhong Hu Gu, Mu Gua,* and *Yin Yang Huo* strengthen liver and kidney and increase mobility; *Wu Shao She, Lu Lu Tong, Cang Zhu, Xun Gu Feng, Wei Ling Xian, Shi Nan Teng,* and *Sang Zhi* expel wind-cold and damp, relieve pain, and clear the channels.

Feng Shi Ling Pian
風濕靈片
Wind-Damp Tablets

Primary Functions and Applications: **Feng Shi Ling Pian** expels wind-cold, eliminates damp and relieves pain, and nourishes and moves the blood. It is used to treat bi patterns, with such symptoms as joint pain and stiffness, limb numbness, and chronic swollen joints. It is used in the treatment of rheumatoid arthritis (though it should not be used in the acute stage or during flare-ups, with fever and redness around the joints, as the formula contains warming herbs). It may also be employed in the treatment of osteoarthritis and sports injuries, including sprains or strains.

Format and Administration: **Feng Shi Ling Pian** is produced by the Gorjiu Pharmaceutical Factory, Yunnan, China as *Yunnan Rheumatilin,* in capsule format, 20 capsules per box.

Recommended Dosage: One capsule in the evening before going to bed, with or without food. Observe the recommended dosages carefully.

Feng Shi Ling Pian		
Constituent Substances		
Pinyin Name	**Pharmaceutical Name**	**% Composition**
Chuan Wu	*Radix Aconiti*	—
Tian Qi	*Radix Pseudoginseng*	—
Bai Yun Shen	*Radix Ginseng*	—
Duan Jie Shen	*Radix Cynanchi Wallichii*	—

Composition and Rationale: *Chuan Wu* expels wind-cold damp; *Tian Qi* moves the blood, reduces swelling, and relieves pain; *Bai Yun Shen* supplements the qi, reduces swelling, and relieves pain; and *Duan Jie Shen* clears the channels, regulates blood circulation, and strengthens the kidneys.

Feng Shi Xiao Tong Wan
風濕消痛丸
Wind-Damp Pain-Relieving Pills

4.5

Primary Functions and Applications: **Feng Shi Xiao Tong Wan** expels wind-cold and eliminates damp, moves the blood and relieves pain, and strengthens the sinews and bones. It is used to treat bi patterns, with such symptoms as feelings of coldness in the limbs, stiffness, pain, and swelling of the joints. It is highly recommended for the treatment of patients with chronic rheumatoid arthritis or osteoarthritis, and for elderly patients suffering from debility of the legs and problems walking due to pain and stiffness in the joints.

Format and Administration: **Feng Shi Xiao Tong Wan** is produced by the Tientsin Drug Manufactory, Tientsin, China, as *Feng Shih Hsiao Tung Wan* in pill format, 10 pills per bottle.

Recommended Dosage: Ten pills, twice a day after meals, with water or wine. It is not necessary to take with food.

Contraindications: While taking this medicine, do not eat pig's liver, mutton or sheep blood, or sweet potatoes.

Feng Shi Xiao Tong Wan		
Constituent Substances		
Pinyin Name	**Pharmaceutical Name**	**% Composition**
Xi Xian Cao	*Herba Siegesbeckiae Orientalis*	15
Chou Wu Tong	*Succus Clerodendri Exsiccatus*	15
Hu Gu	*Os Tigris*	15
Lu Jin	*Ligamentum Cervi*	10
Hong Hua	*Flos Carthami Tinctorii*	10
Mu Gua	*Fructus Chaenomelis Lagenariae*	10
Qiang Huo	*Rhizoma et Radix Notopterygii*	15
—	*Binding Substances*	to 100%

Composition and Rationale: *Xi Xian Cao* and *Chou Wu Tong* treat bi; *Hu Gu* strengthens the sinews and bones and relieves pain; *Lu Jin* strengthens the sinews; *Hong Hua* moves the blood and removes blood stagnation; *Mu Gua* strengthens the sinews, clears the channels and relieves pain; and *Qiang Hu* expels wind-cold and relieves pain.

This formula is a modification of another very effective formula, **Xi Tong Wan [4.5a]**, which contains only *Xi Xian Cao* and *Chou Wu Tong*. **Xi Tong Wan [4.5a]** has been shown to reduce arthritic inflammation in animals (see "The Treatment Effect of Guan Jie Ling on Artificially-Induced Arthritis in Laboratory Rats." Proceedings of the Annual Meeting of the Chinese Pharmacological Association, 1963, pp. 328-329.)

Xi Xian Cao and *Chou Wu Tong* are simultaneously effective in the treatment of bi and hypertension.

4.6 Feng Shi Pian †
風濕片
Wind-Damp Tablets

Primary Functions and Applications: **Feng Shi Pian** expels cold and wind damp, moves the blood, soothes muscles and sinews, and relieves pain. It may be used to treat bi patterns, rheumatism, arthritis, and rheumatoid arthritis with such symptoms as limb numbness, joint pain and difficulty walking, as well as associated neuralgia in the arms and legs.

Format and Administration: **Feng Shi Pian** is produced by the Zhong Lian Drug Manufactory, Wuhan, China, in bottles of 24 pills.

Recommended Dosage: Two tablets, once a day, with warm water or warm wine. If the pain is worse in the morning, take the medicine at that time. Avoid overdose by carefully following recommended dosage.

Contraindication: **Do not use Feng Shi Pian during pregnancy, or with hypersensitive patients.**

Feng Shi Pian		
Constituent Substances		
Pinyin Name	Pharmaceutical Name	% Composition
Ma Huang	*Herba Ephedrae*	18.5
Gui Zhi	*Ramulus Cinnamomi Cassiae*	18.5
Fang Feng	*Herba Ledebouriellae Sesloidis*	10.4
Du Huo	*Radix Duhuo*	10.4
Quan Xie	*Buthus Martensi*	15
Ma Qian Zi	*Semen Strychnotis*	18.5
Du Zhong	*Cortex Eucommiae Ulmoidis*	18.5
Niu Xi	*Radix Achyranthes Bidentatae*	2.6
Gan Cao	*Radix Glycyrrhizae Uralensis*	2.6

Composition and Rationale: *Ma Huang, Gui Zhi, Fang Feng,* and *Du Huo* expel wind-cold, warm and clear the channels, reduce numbness and tremor, and relieve pain; *Quan Xie* and *Ma Qian Zi* reduce swelling and relieve pain; *Du Zhong* and *Niu Xi* supplement the liver and kidney; *Gan Cao* harmonizes and modifies the other herbs.

Ma Huang stimulates the cerebral cortex and can increase blood pressure. *Ma Qian Zi* stimulates the central nervous system, increases blood circulation, and strengthens breathing. Since it also increases blood pressure, this medicine should not be used in cases of hypertension. Overdose may cause serious poisoning, with symptoms such as dizziness, nausea, numbness and seizures. Toxicity of *Ma Qian Zi* may be antidoted with barbiturates.

Xiao Huo Luo Dan
4.7
小活絡丹
Minor Connecting-Vessel-Quickening Pill

Source: *He Ji Ju Fang (Formularies of the People's Welfare Pharmacies),* Song Dynasty (960-1279).

Primary Functions and Applications: **Xiao Huo Luo Dan** clears the channels, moves the blood, removes wind-cold accumulation, and relieves pain. It is used to free channels stuck due to wind-cold accumulation, with such symptoms as sharp joint pain and joint stiffness, limb numbness, aching in the joints or muscles, and rheumatism. It is also used to treat sports or other traumatic injuries, including those due to overexertion. Since **Xiao Huo Luo Dan** moves blood, pain is reduced and healing accelerated.

Format and Administration: **Xiao Huo Luo Dan** is produced by the Lanchow Chinese Medicine Works in pill format, 100 pills per bottle.

Recommended Dosage: Six pills, twice or 3 times a day with warm water or wine. Because *Chuan Wu, Cao Wu,* and *Dan Nan Xing* are slightly toxic, do not increase the dosage.

Contraindication: **Do not use Xiao Huo Luo Dan during pregnancy.** Because of the presence of herbs with a hot thermic nature, do not use in cases where the joints are red and swollen or in the presence of fever.

Xiao Huo Luo Dan		
Constituent Substances		
Pinyin Name	**Pharmaceutical/Botanical Name**	**% Composition**
Chuan Wu	*Aconiti Carmichaeli*	21.25
Cao Wu	*Aconiti Kusnezoffii*	21.25
Dan Nan Xing	*Pulvis Arisaematis cum Felle Bovis*	21.25
Di Long	*Lumbricus*	21.25
Ru Xiang	*Gummi Olibanum*	7.50
Mo Yao	*Myrrha*	7.50

Composition and Rationale: *Chuan Wu* and *Cao Wu* warm the channels and relieve pain; *Dan Nan Xing* eliminates wind-phlegm and relieves limb numbness; *Di Long* calms wind and clears the channels; *Ru Xiang* moves the blood, relieves pain, reduces swelling, and promotes tissue regeneration; and *Mo Yao* moves the blood, relieves pain, reduces swelling, and promotes tissue regeneration.

Though similar in name, the function and application of **Xiao Huo Luo Dan** is quite different from **Da Huo Luo Dan**. Though both medicines can be used for joint or muscle pain due to wind-cold accumulation in the channels, **Xiao Huo Luo Dan** is used for stronger patients with these symptoms, while **Da Huo Luo Dan** is used for patients whose symptoms are accompanied by dual depletions of qi and blood.

Du Huo Ji Sheng Wan
獨活寄生丸
Duhuo and Loranthis Pills

4.8

Source: Bei Ji Qien Jin Yao Fang *(A Thousand Golden Remedies for Emergencies)*, Tang Dynasty (618-907).

Primary Functions and Applications: **Du Huo Ji Sheng Wan** eliminates wind-damp, relieves pain, nourishes blood and qi, and strengthens the liver and kidneys. It is used to treat bi patterns in weaker patients with depletions of qi and blood. Guiding symptoms include pain and coldness in the lumbar area (lumbago) or legs or joints (especially knee joints), tremor (which may be present due to insufficient blood), joint stiffness, numbness, fatigue and cold sensations with a desire for warmth. The tongue may be pale, with a thin, white tongue coating. The pulse may be thin, weak, or empty.

When such symptoms associated with bi patterns due to qi and blood depletion are present, this formula may be used in cases of chronic arthritis (rheumatoid or osteoarthritis) and sciatica.

Du Huo Ji Sheng Wan is a commonly used medicine in China for the treatment of bi, especially in cases with both qi and blood depletion. It addresses both the symptoms and root cause. In classical Chinese medical theory, bi is a combination of wind, cold, and damp. When these three factors affect the sinews and bones over a long period of time, the liver (sinews) and kidney (bones) will also be affected, ultimately leading to the depletion of blood and qi.

Format and Administration: **Du Huo Ji Sheng Wan** is produced by the Min Kang Pharmaceutical Manufactory, Szechuan, in bottles of 100 pills.

Recommended Dosage: Six pills, twice or 3 times a day.

Du Huo Ji Sheng Wan		
Constituent Substances		
Pinyin Name	**Pharmaceutical Name**	**% Composition**
Du Huo	*Radix Duhuo*	7.31
Qin Jiao	*Herba Gentiana Macrophyllae*	7.31
Fang Feng	*Radix Ledebouriellae Sesloidis*	7.31
Xi Xin	*Herba cum Radice Asari*	7.31
Du Zhong	*Cortex Eucommiae Ulmoidis*	7.31
Niu Xi	*Radix Achyranthes Bidentatae*	7.31
Sang Ji Sheng	*Ramus Visci Loranthi seu Visci*	7.31
Dang Gui	*Radix Angelicae Sinensis*	4.88
Chuan Xiong	*Rhizoma Ligustici Wallichii*	7.31
Shou Di Huang	*Radix Rehmannia Glutinosae*	4.88
Bai Shao	*Radix Paeoniae Lactiflora*	4.88
Dang Shen	*Radix Codonopsis Pilosulae*	7.31
Fu Ling	*Sclerotium Poriae Cocus*	7.31
Rou Gui	*Cortex Cinnamomi Cassiae*	7.31
Gan Cao	*Radix Glycyrrhizae Uralensis*	4.88

Composition and Rationale: *Du Huo Qin Jiao* and *Fang Feng* expel wind-damp, treat bi patterns, and relieve pain; *Xi Xin* expels wind-cold, eliminates damp, and relieves pain; *Du Zhong, Niu Xi*, and *Sang Ji Sheng* strengthen the liver and kidney, reinforce the sinews and bones, and eliminate wind-damp; *Dang Gui* strengthens the blood; *Chuan Xiong, Shou Di Huang*, and *Bai Shao* promote blood circulation; *Dang Shen, Fu Ling*, and *Gan Cao* supplement the qi and strengthen the spleen; and *Rou Gui* dispels cold and relieves pain.

Te Xiao Yao Tong Pian [4.8a] is similar in function and application to **Du Huo Ji Sheng Wan.** It contains a number of supplementing substances that benefit kidney yang that are not included in **Du Huo Ji Sheng Wan.** Thus, **Te Xiao Tao Tong Pian** is more specifically effective for the treatment of lumbago (hence its product name, *Specific Lumbagalin*), whereas **Du Huo Ji Sheng Wan** is a more general analgesic.

Yao Tong Pian [4.1] is designed for the treatment of lumbago resulting from kidney yang depletion; **Te Xiao Yao Tong Pian [4.8a]** is more appropriate for the patient with lumbago due to both kidney yang depletion and bi patterns.

Gou Pi Gao †
狗皮膏
Dog Skin Plaster

Primary Functions and Applications: **Gou Pi Gao** expels wind-cold, moves the blood, relieves pain, and relaxes the sinews. It is used to treat such symptoms of bi patterns as lumbago, leg pain, and numbness, and to treat neuralgia or rheumatism, sports or other traumatic injury, and sprains, or strains with swelling and pain.

Format and Administration: **Gou Pi Gao** is produced by the Tientsin Drug Manufactory as *Kou Pi Kao,* with one traditional plaster per envelope. The plaster comes folded in half, with the herbal medicines inside the folded area. The plaster is quite hard, and must first be heated and softened. Use the steam from a boiling kettle of water to warm and moisten the plaster on both sides while it is still folded. After the plaster is softened, gently unfold it. While it is still warm, but not too hot, place it on the affected area, with the herbs against the skin.

The original formula required the use of dog skin in the preparation of the plaster. Due to the shortage and expense of dog skin, however, some factories substitute either cloth, paper, or sheep skin. *Zhong Guo Ji Ben Zhong Chen Yao (Fundamentals of Chinese Patent Medicines, 1988)* reported that studies were completed in 1981 that indicated that dog skin is essential to the efficacy of the medicine.

A new, somewhat more convenient form of **Gou Pi Gao** is now available in which the herbs are contained within a cloth tape.

Itching, redness, or rash that develop after application may indicate an allergy to the medicine, requiring removal of the plaster. When no such adverse reaction is present, the plaster may be kept on the skin for from one to two weeks. Keep the plaster dry. When ready to remove, gently peel it off the skin. If any of the plaster remains on the skin, it may be removed with paint thinner. The plaster may be re-used a few times.

Contraindication: **Do not use on the abdomen during pregnancy. Do not apply to broken skin or open wound.**

Gou Pi Gao		
Constituent Substances		
Pinyin Name	**Pharmaceutical Name**	**% Composition**
Tian Ma	*Rhizoma Gastrodiae Elatae*	10.53
Xi Xin	*Herba cum Radice Asari*	10.53
Ru Xiang	*Gummi Olibanum*	5.26
Mo Yao	*Myrrha*	5.26
Xue Jie	*Sanguis Draconis*	5.26
Er Cha	*Acacia seu Catechu*	5.26
Chuan Shan Jia	*Squama Manitisg*	10.53
Ding Xiang	*Flos Caryophylli*	5.25
Du Zhong	*Cortex Eucommiae Ulmoidis*	10.53
Niu Xi	*Radix Achyranthes Bidentatae*	10.53
Dang Gui	*Radix Angelicae Sinensis*	10.53

Zhong Guo Ji Ben Zhong Chen Yao (Fundamentals of Chinese Patent Medicines, 1988) lists a 43-ingredient standardized formula significantly different from that shown here and on the manufacturer's label.

Composition and Rationale: *Tian Ma* and *Xi Xin* eliminate wind-cold damp and relieve pain; *Ru Xiang, Mo Yao, Xue Jie, Er Cha*, and *Chuan Shan Jia* promote blood circulation, remove blood stasis, and stop pain; *Ding Xiang* removes stagnant qi and relieves pain; *Du Zhong* and *Niu Xi* strengthen the liver and kidney, and reinforce the sinews and bones; and *Dang Gui* supplements and moves the blood.

She Xiang Zhui Feng Gao [4.9a], produced by the Guilin Fourth Pharmaceutical Factory, is similar in application to **Gou Pi Gao.**

4.10   Shang Shi Zhi Tong Gao †
傷濕止痛膏
Damp Damage Pain-Relieving Plaster

Primary Functions and Applications: Due to its convenience and rapid pain-relieving action, **Shang Shi Zhi Tong Gao** is a popular and commonly used herbal plaster in China. It is used to expel wind-damp, move the blood, and relieve pain, and is indicated in the treatment of bi patterns, with such symptoms as muscle and joint pain, arthritis (osteoarthritis or rheumatoid arthritis), and sports or other soft tissue injury, including sprains and strains.

Format and Administration: **Shang Shi Zhi Tong Gao** is produced by the Shanghai Chinese Medicine Works, Shanghai, China. The herbal medicine itself is on 2″ x 3″ adhesive-backed cloth tape, attached two to a piece of cellophane.

The affected area should be cleaned with gentle soap and warm water (a warm bath is ideal) before application. Peel the plaster off its backing and place it on the affected area, using as many plasters as necessary for adequate coverage. Since the medicine loses its effectiveness after 8 to 12 hours, fresh plasters must be applied regularly during treatment. Plasters may be worn while bathing or swimming, as water does not affect the actions of the herbal medicine. Store plasters in an air-tight container to avoid dilution of the aromatic ingredients.

Contraindication: **Do not apply during pregnancy.** Do not apply to an open wound. Discontinue use if pronounced redness, itching, or skin irritation follow application.

Shang Shi Zhi Tong Gao		
Constituent Substances		
Pinyin Name	Pharmaceutical Name	% Composition
Yun Xiang Qin Gao	*Resina Fructus Liquidambaris*	10.64
Bo He Nao	*Herba Menthae (Crystal)*	8.51
Bing Pian	*Borneolum*	8.51
Zhang Nao	*Camphora*	17.02
Dong Qing Yu	*Wintergreen Oil*	12.77
Fu Fang Din Xiang Liu Qin Gao	*Extractum Flos Caryophylli Liquidum Compositus*	42.55

Zhong Guo Ji Ben Zhong Chen Yao (Fundamentals of Chinese Patent Medicines, 1988) lists a formula for **Shang Shi Zhi Tong Gao** entirely different from that available in the U.S.

Composition and Rationale: *Yun Xiang Qin Gao* eliminates cold-damp; *Bo He Nao, Bing Pian, Zhang Nao* and *Dong Qing Yu* expel wind-heat, reduce swelling, and relieve pain. *Fu Fang Ding Xiang Liu Qin Gao* is a liquid extract of 16 herbal substances that promote blood circulation, relieve pain, expel wind-cold, and strengthen sinews and bones.

4.11

Bao Zhen Gao
寶珍膏
Jewel and Gem Plaster

Primary Functions and Applications: **Bao Zhen Gao** eliminates wind-damp and warms the channels, removing stagnation. It is used to treat bi patterns (obturation: joint pain due to the combination of wind-cold and damp) with symptoms that include shoulder pain, back pain, and aching muscles; to treat sports injury or other traumatic injuries to muscles and sinews; and in the treatment of neuralgia, rheumatism, and arthritis (acute or chronic osteoarthritis or rheumatoid arthritis).

Format and Administration: **Bao Zhen Gao** is produced by the Shanghai Medicine Works, Shanghai, China, as *Shang Shi Bao Zhen Gao* in boxes of 10 traditional plasters. The herbal medicine itself is inside a 2″ x 3″ cloth tape with an adhesive backing. Plasters are attached two to a piece of cellophane.

The affected area should be cleaned with gentle soap and warm water before application (a warm bath is most effective). Peel the plaster off and apply as many plasters as necessary for adequate coverage. The herbal medicine in the plaster is effective for 4 to 5 days, after which time new plasters may be re-applied as required. Water does not affect the herbal medicine, and the plasters may be worn while bathing or swimming.

Contraindication: **Do not use during pregnancy.** Discontinue use if pronounced redness, itching, or skin irritation follow application. Do not apply to an open wound. Since plasters contain many aromatic ingredients, it is important to store in an air-tight container.

Bao Zhen Gao		
Constituent Substances		
Pinyin Name	Pharmaceutical Name	% Composition
She Xiang	*Secretio Moschi Moschiferi*	0.62
Yun Xiang Qin Gao	*Resina Fructus Liquidambaris*	17.74
Bo He Nao	*Herba Menthae (Crystal)*	7.1
Zhang Nao	*Camphora*	7.1
Dong Qing Yu	*Wintergreen Oil*	14.2
Fu Fang Xi Xin Liu Qin Gao	*Extractum Herba Asari Liquidum Compositus*	53.25

Composition and Rationale: She Xiang warms the channels, promotes blood circulation, reduces swelling, and relieves pain; *Yun Xiang Qin Gao* eliminates cold damp; *Bo He Nao, Dong Qing Yu,* and *Zhang Nao* expel wind-heat, reduce swelling, and relieve pain; *Fu Fang Xi Xin Liu Qin Gao,* a liquid extract consisting of several different herbal medicines, promotes blood circulation, relieves pain, and expels wind-cold.

The major difference between this formula and **Shang Shi Zhi Tong Gao [4.10]** is the presence here of *She Xiang (Secretio Moschi Moschiferi)*, a powerful qi and blood mover. *She Xiang* is also able to penetrate rapidly and to lead the accompanying herbs into the deeper tissues. This medicine is particularly good for neuralgia, arthritis, and muscle pain.

Zhui Feng Huo Xue Pian
追風活血片
Wind-Chasing, Blood-Quickening Tablets

4.12

Primary Functions and Applications: **Zhui Feng Huo Xue Pian** moves the blood, relaxes the sinews, and eliminates wind-cold in the channels. It is used to treat bi patterns (obturation: joint pain due to the combination of wind-cold and damp), where the wind-cold element is stronger than the damp. Symptoms include feelings of cold and numbness in the limbs, weakness in the legs and in the lumbar area, rheumatism, chronic arthritis, and joint or muscle pain. The pain may be sharp or traveling, with more sharp pain than dull pain (the presence of dull pain indicates damp). **Zhui Feng Hu Xue Pian** is also used in the treatment of long-term sequelae of sports or traumatic injuries where there is aching in the sinews, muscles, or joints.

Format and Administration: **Zhui Feng Hu Xue Pian** is produced by the Siping Pharmaceutical Works, Kirin, China, as *Chui Feng Huohsueh* in coated tablet format, 80 per bottle.

Recommended Dosage: Four tablets, twice a day.

Contraindications: **Do not use during pregnancy.**

Zhui Feng Hu Xue Pian		
Constituent Substances		
Pinyin Name	Pharmaceutical Name	% Composition
Gui Zhi	*Ramulus Cinnamomi Cassiae*	6
Du Huo	*Radix Duhuo*	6
Ma Huang	*Herba Ephedrae*	5
Fang Feng	*Herba Ledebouriellae Sesloidis*	8
Di Feng	*Cortex Illici Difengpi*	6
Qiang Huo	*Rhizoma et Radix Notopterygii*	6
Ru Xiang	*Gummi Olibanum*	8
Zi Ran Tong	*Pyritum*	5
Mo Yao	*Myrrha*	8
Du Zhong	*Cortex Eucommiae Ulmoidis*	12
Qian Nian Jian	*Rhizoma Homalomenae Occultae*	6
Mu Gua	*Fructus Chaenomelis Lagenariae*	6
Niu Xi	*Radix Achyranthes Bidentatae*	6
Gan Cao	*Radix Glycyrrhizae Uralensis*	5
Feng Mi	*Mel*	5

Composition and Rationale: *Gui Zhi, Du Huo, Ma Huang, Fang Feng, Di Feng* and *Qiang Huo* eliminate wind-cold, warm the channels, promote channel circulation, and relieve pain; *Ru Xiang, Zi Ran Tong* and *Ma Yao* promote blood circulation, relieve pain, reduce inflammation, and promote healing of injured tissues; *Du Zhong, Qian Nian Jian, Mu Gua,* and *Niu Xi* strengthen the liver and kidneys and reinforce the sinews and bones; *Gan Cao* harmonizes the other herbs; and *Feng Mi* is used as a binding medium.

Yun Xiang Jing
雲香精
Cloud Fragrance Extract

Primary Functions and Applications: **Yun Xiang Jing** relieves pain, reduces swelling, and regulates stomach qi. It is effective in the treatment of bi patterns (obturation: joint pain due to the combination of wind-cold and damp), and is thus indicated in cases of rheumatism, arthritis (including rheumatoid arthritis), neuralgia due to wind-cold damp, and headache pain due to flu and common cold (wind-cold syndrome). It is also used to treat stomachache or abdominal pain due to improper diet (especially the consumption of too much cold food), or during a common cold or flu (indicative of a wind-cold syndrome), and can be effective in the treatment of motion sickness.

Yun Xiang Jing is indicated in the treatment of poor circulation in the extremities, and in cases of frostbite located anywhere on the body. Finally, it may be used to treat early stages of carbuncles or skin sores, and helps reduce inflammation and swelling.

Format and Administration: **Yun Xiang Jing** is produced by the Yulin Drug Manufactory, Kwangsi, China, in 30 ml bottles.

Recommended Dosage: The medicine can be used both externally and internally.

External Use: Used as a lotion, apply with a cotton ball to the affected area two or three times a day. It is not necessary to cover the area following application.

Internal Use: Use internally for headache or stomachache and abdominal pain in acute or emergency cases. Do not give internally to children younger than 3 years of age. From ages 3 to 7 years, use 1 ml; from 8 to 15 years of age, use 1.5 ml; over age 16, use 2 ml. Dilute one part medicine in nine parts water. Only one dose is taken, which may be repeated if necessary in four hours. For serious cases, the dose may be increased, but never more than twice the dose should be administered. In case of accidental internal overdose, a tea of *Huang Lian (Rhizoma Coptidis*, a cold herb), may be administered to alleviate side effects.

Contraindication: **Do not use Yun Xiang Jing internally during pregnancy.**

Yun Xiang Jing		
Constituent Substances		
Pinyin Name	Pharmaceutical Name	% Composition
Guo Jiang Long	*Semen Bauhiniae Championi*	—
Chuan Bi Feng	*Diploclisia Glaucescens*	—
Gui Zhi	*Ramulus Cinnamomi Cassiae*	—
Xi Xin	*Herba cum Radice Asari*	—
Bo He Nao	*Herba Menthae (Crystal)*	—

Composition and Rationale: *Guo Jiang Long* and *Chuan Bi Feng* move blood, relieve rheumatism, reduce swelling, and relieve pain; *Gui Zhi* and *Xi Xin* expel wind-cold, move blood, and relieve pain; *Bo He Nao* relieves pain, reduces inflammation, regulates stomach qi, and, when applied topically, relieves itching.

Similar in effect to **Yun Xiang Jing** is the liniment **Bai Hua You [4.13a]**, produced as *White Flower Analgesic Balm* by the Hoe Hin Fah Yeow Manufactory, Hong Kong.

4.14

Hu Gu Jiu †
虎骨酒
Tiger Bone Wine

Primary Functions and Applications: **Hu Gu Jiu** nourishes the hepatorenal system, supplements central qi, clears the channel, moves blood, and relieves pain. It is appropriate for the treatment of chronic *bi* syndrome, with such symptoms as numbness and stiffness of the limbs and joints, and weakness of the legs and lumbar. Patients for whom this medicine is recommended will show signs of cold, with a pale tongue with thin, white fur, and a deep and slow pulse.

Hu Gu Jiu is often prescribed for rheumatism and arthritis in the elderly.

Format and Administration: **Hu Gu Jiu** is produced by the Beijing Tong Ren Tang in 250 ml and 500 ml bottles.

Recommended Dose: Fifteen to 20 ml twice to 3 times a day.

Contraindications: **Do not use Hu Gu Jiu during pregnancy. Do not use with hypertensive patients, nor with patients who show signs of heat.**

Hu Gu Jiu		
Constituent Substances		
Pinyin Name	**Pharmaceutical Name**	**% Composition**
Hu Gu	*Os Tigris*	—
Lu Rong	*Cornu Parvum Cervi*	—
Yin Yang Huo	*Herba Epimedii*	—
Niu Xi	*Radix Achyranthes Bidentatae*	—
Gou Qi Zi	*Fructus Lycii Chinensis*	—
Yi Yi Ren	*Semen Coicis Lachryma-Jobi*	—
Mu Gua	*Fructus Chaenomelis Lagenariae*	—
Wu Jia Pi	*Cortex Radicis Acanthopanacis*	—
Cang Zhu	*Radix Atractylodis*	—
Hong Qu	*Semes Oryzae cum Monasco*	—
Chuan Wu	*Radix Aconiti*	—
Cao Wu	*Aconiti Kusnezoffii*	—
Qiang Huo	*Rhizoma et Radix Notopterygii*	—
Du Huo	*Radix Duhuo*	—
Chi Shi Zhi	*Halloysitum Rubrum*	—
Fang Feng	*Herba Ledebouriellae Sesloidis*	—

Continued

Hu Gu Jiu		
(Continued)		
Constituent Substances		
Pinyin Name	**Pharmaceutical Name**	**% Composition**
Bai Zhu	*Rhizoma Atractylodis Macrocephalae*	—
Rou Gui	*Cortex Cinnamomi Cassiae*	—
Ding Xiang	*Flos Caryophylli*	—
Tan Xiang	*Lignum Santali Albi*	—
Mu Xiang	*Radix Saussureae seu Vladimirae*	—
Sha Ren	*Fructus Seu Semen Amomi*	—
Fo Shou	*Herba cum Radice Adonis Amurensis*	—
Chen Pi	*Exocarpium Citri Sinensis*	—
Ching Pi	*Pericarpium Citri Reticulatae*	—
Wu Yao	*Radix Linderae Strychnifoliae*	—
Dang Gui	*Radix Angelicae Sinensis*	—
Bai Shao	*Radix Paeoniae Lactiflora*	—
Shou Di Huang	*Radix Rehmannia Glutinosae*	—
Chuan Xiong	*Rhizoma Ligustici Wallichii*	—
Ren Shen	*Radix Ginseng*	—
Ru Xiang	*Gummi Olibanum*	—
Mo Yao	*Myrrha*	—
Song Jie You	*Lignum Nodi Pini*	—
She Xiang	*Secretio Moschi Moschiferi*	—
Hong Hua	*Flos Carthami Tinctorii*	—
Zi Cao	*Radix Lithospermi seu Arnebiae*	—
Mu Dan Pi	*Cortex Radicis Moutan*	—
Yu Jiu	*Herba Monochoriae Korsakowii*	—
Bai Jiu	*White Wine*	—

Composition and Rationale: Hu Gu, Lu Rong, Yin Yang Huo, Niu Xi, and *Gou Qi Zi* nourish the liver and kidney and strengthen the bones and joints; *Yi Yi Ren, Mu Gua, Wu Jia Pi, Cang Zhu,* and *Hong Chu* expel wind and damp; *Chuan Wu, Cao Wu, Qiang Huo, Du Huo, Chi Shi Fang Feng,* and *Bai Zhu* warm to eliminate cold accumulation in the channels; *Rou Gui, Ding Xiang, Tan Xiang, Mu Xiang, Sha Ren, Fo Shou, Chen Pi, Qiang Pi,* and *Wu Yao* warm the interior and regulate qi to move stagnation; *Dang Gui, Bai Shao, Shou Di Huang, Chuan Xiong,* and *Ren Shen* move and nourish the blood, yin, and qi; *Ru Xiang, Mo Yao, Song Jie You She Xiang,* and *Hong Hua* move blood and clear channels; *Zi Cao* and *Mu Dan Pi* clear depletion heat; and *Yu Ju* and *Bai Jiu* nourish stomach yin.

Feng Liao Xing Yao Jiu †
馮了性藥酒
Feng Liao Xing's Medicinal Wine

4.15

Primary Functions and Applications: **Feng Liao Xing Yao Jiu** expels wind, clears the channels, eliminates cold, and relieves pain. It is indicated for wind-cold-damp bi patterns, with such symptoms as joint pain that may be described as moving, sharp, and/or heavy. This medicine is also recommended for the treatment of sports injuries, sprains, bruises, and paralysis following windstrike, but only when the patient presents with cold signs.

Format and Administration: **Feng Liao Xing Yao Jiu** is produced in 250cc and 500cc bottles.

Recommended Dosage: Ten to 15 cc twice a day.

Contraindications: Do not use **Feng Liao Xing Yao Jiu** in yin depletion cases, or in the presence of exogenous heat.

Feng Liao Xing Yao Jiu		
Constituent Substances		
Pinyin Name	**Pharmaceutical Name**	**% Composition**
Ma Huang	*Herba Ephedrae*	—
Ding Gong Tan	*Radix et Caulis Erycibes Obtusifoliae*	—
Qiang Huo	*Rhizoma et Radix Notopterygii*	—
Du Huo	*Radix Duhuo*	—
Fang Ji	*Radix Fangji*	—
Bai Zhu	*Rhizoma Atractylodis Macrocephalae*	—
Wu Jia Pi	*Cortex Radicis Acanthopanacis*	—
Dang Gui	*Radix Angelicae Sinensis*	—
Chuan Xiong	*Rhizoma Ligustici Wallichii*	—
Qing Hao Zi	*Herba Artemisiae Apiaciae*	—
Shan Zhi Zi	*Fructus Gardeniae Jasminoidis*	—
Wei Ling Xian	*Radix Clematidis Chinensis*	—
Xiao Hui Xiang	*Fructus Foeniculi Vulgaris*	—

Composition and Rationale: Ma Huang and Ding Gong Tan expel wind-cold; *Qiang Huo, Wei Ling Xian, Xiao Hui Xiang, Du Huo, Fang Ji, Bai Zhu,* and *Wu Jia Pi* expel wind-cold-damp in the upper and lower body, and move qi to eliminate stasis; *Dang Gui, Chuan Xiong, Qing Hao Zi,* and *Shan Zhi Zi* move blood, clear the channels, relieve pain, and clear heat to prevent incubation when the heat is chronic.

5

Portal-Opening Formulae

To open the portals with coldness
5.1 Zi Xue 5.2 An Gong Niu Huang Wan 5.3 Wan Shi Niu Huang Qing Xin Wan
To open the portals with warmth, and to clear *the pericardium when clouded by phlegm turbidity*
5.4 Guan Xin Su He Wan

Pattern Identification

Portal-opening is a treatment method usually reserved for emergency resuscitation. It is used in the treatment of the sudden, severe interruption of the qi dynamic (syncope) in cases such as epilepsy or windstrike; for disorientation of the spirit from inner-body heat-block during exogenous heat diseases (primarily in patterns involving heat penetration of the pericardium); and from obstruction due to phlegm-turbidity. When the treatment target is the sequelae of strike, rather than resuscitation, treatment is accomplished by wind-dispersing and channel-clearing, as discussed in Chapter 6. Portal-opening is a method of some intensity, and is applied in the presence of strong pathogens only. It is therefore important to note any signs of flaccidity and depletion (such as slackness of the jaw, for example), that would contraindicate such a treatment approach.

Formulae Differentiation

The formulae **Zi Xue Dan [5.1]**, **An Gong Niu Huang Wan [5.2]**, and **Ju Fang Zhi Bao Dan [5.2a]** are considered the "Three Treasures" of Chinese medicine for clearing severe heat. Although all three formulae are similar in heat-clearing, fire-toxin resolving, portal-opening, and spasm-reducing effects, and may be used more or less interchangeably to treat seasonal febrile disease with high-grade fever, unconsciousness, and phlegm-heat retention, each "treasure" has its specialty.

An Gong Niu Huang Huang [5.2] is the coldest of the three formulae, and is most effective in clearing heat and resolving fire toxin. It is used to treat high grade fever with unconsciousness.

Ju Fang Zhi Bao Dan [5.2a] is the least cold of the Three Treasures, and is used primarily to open the portals and to eliminate turbid phlegm retention. It is used to treat patients with spasm, seizures and/or coma.

Zi Xue Dan falls between the other formulations in thermic property, and is used primarily to treat the spasm caused by high-grade fever.

Zi Xue Dan [5.1], **An Gong Niu Huang Wan [5.2]**, and **Wan Shi Niu Huang Qing Xin Wan [5.3]** (from which **An Gong Niu Huang Wan [5.2]** is derived), are thus considered representative portal-opening formulae.

Zi Xue †   5.1
紫雪
Purple Snow

Source: He Ji Ju Fang *(Formularies of the People's Welfare Pharmacies),* 1151 C.E..

Primary Functions and Applications: **Zi Xue** is very effective when used to clear severe heat, especially in the pericardium, and is particularly useful in the treatment of children. It relieves fire toxin, and may be used to open the portals (relieve coma) and reduce spasms when due to severe heat. The heat itself may be the result of such infections as pneumonia, tonsillitis, dysentery (used with *Bai Tou Weng Tang (White Haired Gaffer Decoction)* as a *yao yin*), influenza, epidemic encephalitis (a serious brain infection due to heat pathogen in the summer), cerebrospinal meningitis in winter or spring, measles, serious cases of hepatitis and hepatic coma, cirrhosis of the liver, and epilepsy (see *Research Journal of Traditional Chinese Prepared Medicines*, No. 7, 1981, for a study on the use of **Zi Xue** in the treatment of epilepsy). Patients will have shown signs of heat from the onset of the illness, as evidenced by such signs as high-grade fever, thirst, constipation, uneasiness or unconsciousness, dark and/or scanty urine, and lack of any sensation of cold, symptoms that in these cases are due to heat in the pericardium.

Zi Xue has also been effective in the treatment of severe burns (in which cases it is used with a *yao yin* of *Qing Ying Tang [Construction-Clearing Decoction]),* for infections contracted or manifest during menstruation *(heat entering the blood mansion),* and for severe skin infections.

Format and Administration: **Zi Xue** derives its name from its purple color, its frost- or snow-like shape, and its extremely cold properties. **Zi Xue** may also be found as *Zi Xue San* (Zi Xue Powder) or *Zi Xue Dan (Dan* referring to formulations containing metallic elements). **Zi Xue** is produced by the Guangzhou United Drug Manufactory as *Tzuh-sueh Tan* in small vials containing approximately 0.8 grams of medicine. Since the cinnabar sinks to the bottom, care must be taken to insure consumption of the entire contents. It should be used until the patient's fever has been reduced and the temperature returned to normal. If the fever has not been greatly reduced within 3 days, re-confirm the diagnosis, or switch to another heat-clearing formulation.

Recommended Dosage: Adults, 2 vials, twice a day, with warm water. Children younger than 1 year, ½ vial, twice a day. For children over 1 year, use 1 vial, twice a day.

Contraindications: **Do not use Zi Xue during pregnancy.**

Zi Xue		
Constituent Substances		
Pinyin Name	**Pharmaceutical Name**	**% Composition**
Hua Shi	*Talcum*	7.1
Ding Xiang	*Flos Caryophylli*	0.7
Shi Gao	*Gypsum*	7.1
Sheng Ma	*Rhizoma Cimicifugae*	7.1
Han Shui Shi	*Calcitum*	7.1
Xuan Shen	*Radix Scrophulariae Ningpoensis*	7.1
Ci Shi	*Magnetitum*	14.3
Gan Cao	*Radix Glycyrrhizae Uralensis*	5.7
Ling Yang Jiao	*Cornu Antelopis*	3.6
Mang Xiao	*Mirabilitum Depurantum*	14.3
Mu Xiang	*Radix Saussureae*	3.6
Xiao Xi	*Nitrum*	14.3
Xue Niu Jiao	*Cornu Rhinocerotis*	3.6
She Xiang	*Secretio Moschi Moschiferig*	0.8
Chen Xiang	*Lignum Aquilariae*	3.6
Zhu Sha	*Cinnabaris*	—

Composition and Rationale:
Of the 16 substances in this formula, most are directed toward clearing heat and resolving fire toxin, including *Hua Shi, Shi Gao, Sheng Ma, Han Shui Shi, Xuan Shen, Ling Yang Jiao, Xiao Xi, Xue Niu Jiao* and *Zhu Sha. Ding Xiang, Xi Jiao,* and *She Xiang* open the portals, while *Ding Xiang, Mu Xiang* and *Chen Xiang* move qi. *Ci Shi* and *Zhu Sha* calm the spirit. In addition, *Hua Shi* promotes urination, *Mang Xiao* clears heat in the intestines and moves the stool, and *Ling Yang Jiao* and *Ci Shi* reduce spasm.

An Gong Niu Huang Wan †
安宮牛黃丸
Peaceful Palace Bovine Bezoar Pills

5.2

Source: Wen Bing Tiao Bian *(More Discussion of Febrile Diseases)*, Qing Dynasty (1644-1911).

Primary Functions and Applications: Along with **Zi Xue [5.1]** and **Jiu Fang Zhi Ban Dan**, **An Gong Niu Huang Wan** is one of the "Three Treasures" in the Chinese pharmacopoeia used to treat serious seasonal febrile disease. It is therefore used to treat high grade fever, unconsciousness, delirium, and agitation due to blockage of heart portals, with phlegm-heat accumulation. The classical Chinese medical diagnosis in such cases is pathogenic heat attacking the pericardium, causing a syndrome similar to that involving heat in the heart. Additional symptoms include red tongue with yellow or white slimy coating (in the earlier stage, the tongue coating will be white; in later stages, when the body fluid has been damaged, it will be yellow), and a rapid, full pulse.

If constipation is the primary symptom, dissolve the honey pill in warm water, mix it with 10 grams of *Da Huang (Rhizoma Rhei)* powder, and have the patient drink the resulting liquid.

An Gong Niu Huang Wan is also used in the treatment of spasms in children caused by high fever, as well as when signs of phlegm-heat accumulation are present, including stroke (apoplexy), seizures, coma due to high grade fever in acute epidemic diseases (such as epidemic encephalitis B), bacillary dysentery, and coma due to such other serious infections as septicemia.

Format and Administration: **An Gong Niu Huang Wan** is produced by the Beijing Tung Ren Tang in large honey-pill format, 10 pills per box, each pill coated in gold powder. As well as indicating the extreme value of this medicine, the gold powder is used to calm the spirit and to tranquilize.

This medicine is usually reserved for serious or emergency cases. In China, **An Gong Niu Huang Wan** serum is available for intravenous use.

Recommended Dosage: One honey pill, once or twice a day. In extremely serious cases, increase the dosage to 3 times per day. The entire honey pill, including the gold powder with which the pill is coated must be taken.

If the primary symptom is excess phlegm, simmer either 6 grams of *Tian Zhu Huang (Concretio Silicea Bambusae)* or *Zhu Li* (Succus Bambusae) for 20 minutes in 2 cups of water, and administer as a *yao yin.*

If high-grade fever is prominent, simmer 10 grams of *Jin Yin Hua (Flos Lonicerae Japonicae)* and 6 grams of *Bo He (Herba Menthae)* in 2 cups of water for 10 minutes, and administer as a *yao yin.*

Contraindication: **Do not use An Gong Niu Huang Wan during pregnancy.**

An Gong Niu Huang Wan		
Constituent Substances		
Pinyin Name	**Pharmaceutical Name**	**% Composition**
Niu Huang	*Calculus Bovis*	11.11
Xi Jiao	*Cornu Rhinocerotis*	11.11
She Xiang	*Secretio Moschi Moschiferig*	2.78
Huang Lian	*Rhizoma Coptidis*	11.11
Huang Qin	*Radix Scutellaria*	11.11
Shan Zhi Zi	*Fructus Gardeniae Jasminoidis*	11.11
Xiong Huang	*Realgar*	11.11
Bing Pian	*Borneolum*	2.78
Zhu Sha	*Cinnabaris*	11.11
Zhen Zhu	*Margarita*	5.56

Zhong Guo Ji Ben Zhong Chen Yao (Fundamentals of Chinese Prepared Medicines, 1988) includes *Yu Jin (Tuber Curcumae)* in its standardized formula for **An Gong Niu Huang Wan.**

Composition and Rationale: *Niu Huang, Xi Jiao*, and *She Xiang*
are the primary herbs in the formulae, working to clear heat, resolve fire toxin, and open the portals; *Huang Lian, Huang Qin,* and *Shan Zhi Zi,* the secondary herbs, clear heat and resolve fire toxin; *Xiong Huang* resolves fire toxin and expels accumulated phlegm; *Bing Pian* is a fragrant, portal-opening, heart turbidity unblocking agent; *Zhu Sha* and *Zhen Zhu* calm the spirit, and reduce spasm and tremor.

An Gong Niu Huang Wan is a modification of **Wan Shi Niu Huang Qing Xin Wan [5.3]**. Although they have similar functions, **An Gong Niu Huang Wan** is generally more effective.

It is from the heart portal-opening and pericardium cooling functions of *Niu Huang (Calculus Bovis)*, the principal ingredient in this formula, that the name "Peaceful Palace Bovine Bezoar Pills" is derived. In classical Chinese medical theory, the heart controls the spirit (consciousness). Seasonal febrile diseases are commonly accompanied by high-grade fever, which can cause unconsciousness and delirium. In such cases, a medicine that both clears heat and opens the heart portal is always the medicine of choice.

During the cultural revolution, the word *gong* ("palace," referring to the pericardium as the palace of the heart) was considered by the Red Guard to be a reference to feudalism, and was forbidden. Thus, the name of the medicine was changed from **An Gong Niu Huang Wan** to *Kang Re* (lit. "anti heat") *Niu Huang Wan*.

In his book *Clinical Experience with Chinese Herbal Medicines*, Dr. Mei Zhu reported the combined use of **An Gong Niu Huang Wan** powder with the following specially developed herbal conductor *(yao yin)* in the successful treatment of infantile thrush (an infection of the oral mucus membrane by *candida albicans*, characterized by superficial, confluent white patches on a red, moist, inflamed surface).

Decoction for the Treatment of Thrush		
Constituent Substances		
Pinyin Name	**Pharmaceutical Name**	**Composition**
Sheng Di	*Radix Rehmannia*	6 gr.
Lu Gen	*Rhizoma Phragmatitis*	20 gr.
Zhu Ye	*Herba Lophatheri*	6 gr.
Jin Yin Hua	*Flos Lonicerae Japonicae*	10 gr.
Gou Teng	*Ramulus et Uncus Uncariae*	6 gr.
Bo He	*Herba Menthae*	3 gr.
Shan Zha	*Fructus Crataegi*	3 gr.
Shen Qu	*Massa Fermentata*	3 gr.
Sheng Shi Gao	*Gypsum*	15 gr.

The *Sheng Di* was cooked for ten minutes in 3 cups of water, after which the remaining herbs were added, and cooked until one cup remained. This yielded two doses for the infant.

Three tenths of a gram of **An Gong Niu Huang** powder was used each day for three days (in place of the powder, a third of a honey pill each time may be used), at which time the above herbal tea was administered.

5.3 Wan Shi Niu Huang Qing Xin Wan †
萬氏牛黃清心丸
Wan's Bovine Bezoar Heart-Clearing Pills

Source: Jing Yue Quan Shu (Complete Works of Jing Yue), Ming Dynasty (1368-1644).

Primary Functions and Applications: **Wan Shi Niu Huang Qing Xin Wan** clears heat and unblocks obstructed heart portals, calms restlessness due to heat, and restores consciousness where high fever has led to coma. It is used when exogenous heat toxin has attacked the pericardium, with such symptoms as unconsciousness, delirious speech, uneasiness with high fever, stroke in its acute stage, encephalitis and cerebrospinal meningitis (both of which may be viral), infantile convulsions, or serious pneumonia. It's use is also indicated in cases of high fever caused by infection, kidney failure leading to unconsciousness with fever, liver failure leading to unconsciousness with fever; and essential hypertension.

Format and Administration: **Wan Shi Niu Huang Qing Xin Wan** is produced by the Beijing Tung Ren Tang in honey pill format, 10 pills per box.

Recommended Dosage: Adults, one honey pill twice a day. Children less than 1 year, half a pill twice a day.

Contraindications: **Do not use Wan Shi Niu Huang Qing Xin Wan during pregnancy. Do not use in yin depletion cases.**

Wan Shi Niu Huang Qing Xin Wan		
Constituent Substances		
Pinyin Name	**Pharmaceutical Name**	**% Composition**
Niu Huang	*Calculus Bovis*	1.69
Shan Zhi Zi	*Fructus Gardeniae Jasminoidis*	20.34
Huang Lian	*Rhizoma Coptidis*	33.90
Huang Qin	*Radix Scutellaria*	20.34
Yu Jin	*Tuber Curcumae*	13.56
Zhu Sha	*Cinnabaris*	10.17

Composition and Rationale: *Niu Huang* clears heat and opens the heart portals; *Zhi Zi* clears heat in the heart; *Huang Lian* and *Huang Chin* clear heat; *Yu Jin* eliminates phlegm and opens the portals; *Zhu Sha* tranquilizes the spirit.

Because this formula is relatively gentle, it is not recommended for the treatment of serious or critical cases. In such cases, one of the *Three Treasures* (**An Gong Niu Huang Wan [5.2]**, **Zi Xue [5.1]**, or **Jiu Fang Zhi Bao Dan [5.2a]**) should be considered the medicines of choice.

Guan Xin Su He Wan †

5.4

冠心蘇合丸
Coronary Liquid Styrax Pills

Primary Functions and Applications: Due to its aromatic properties, **Guan Xin Su He Wan** opens the heart portals, moves stasis in the chest, regulates qi, and relieves pain. It is used to treat symptoms related to coronary artery disease due to qi stagnation and exogenous cold, with fullness in the chest, chest pain or pressure, and angina. It may also be used to improve blood circulation in patients with cold in the extremities, and will distend the coronary arteries, improving blood supply to the coronary muscle.

Format and Administration: **Guan Xin Su He Wan** is produced in capsule format by the Tianjin Drug Manufactory, 40 capsules per box.

Recommended Dosage: Two capsules, twice a day. In China, many people take this medicine to prevent, as well as to treat, angina. It has been shown not to interfere with Western medicines used to treat heart disease.

Contraindications: Do not use this formula if the coronary artery disease is caused by blood stasis, which will be indicated by such symptoms as fixed, stabbing, strong, sharp pain that is possibly worse at night, or heart palpitations, accompanied by a dark purple tongue and a deep and choppy pulse. In such cases, **Dan Shen Pian [12.1a]** is the formula of choice.

Guan Xin Su He Wan		
Constituent Substances		
Pinyin Name	**Pharmaceutical Name**	**% Composition**
Su He Xiang	*Styrax Liquidus*	8
Bing Pian	*Borneolum*	15
Tan Xiang	*Lignum Santali Albi*	31
Ru Xiang	*Gummi Olibanum*	15
Mu Hu Die	*Semen Oroxyli Indici*	31

Zhong Guo Ji Ben Zhong Chen Yao (Fundamentals of Chinese Prepared Medicines, 1988) includes *Zhu Sha (Cinnabaris)* and *Qing Mu Xiang (Radix Saussureae)* in its standardized formula for **Guan Xin Su He Wan**.

Composition and Rationale: *Su He Xiang* opens the portals; *Bing Pian* aromatically opens the portals; *Tan Xiang* moves qi and relieves pain; *Ru Xiang* promotes blood circulation, relieves pain, and removes blood stasis; and *Mu Hu Die* moves qi.

Guan Xin Su He Wan is a modification of **Su He Xiang Wan [5.4a]**, developed in the Song Dynasty (960-1279), and used to open the heart portals and to resuscitate the patient from unconsciousness associated with windstrike *(zhong feng)*.

6

Wind-Dispelling, Wind-Extinguishing and Windstrike-Resolving Formulae

To dispel exogenous wind
6.1   Hua She Jie Yang Wan
To dispel wind and free the connecting channels
6.2 Da Huo Luo Dan 6.3 Ren Shen Zai Zao Wan 6.4 Hu Po Bao Long Wan 6.5 Niu Huang Qing Xin Wan 6.6 Niu Huang Jiang Ya Wan 6.7 Bao Ying Dan

Pattern Identification

Wind has already been presented as a pathogen requiring resolution of the exterior during contraction of exogenous wind-cold and wind-heat (Chapter 1); and as a primary component of bi patterns, one of three identifiable outcomes of wind invasion of the channels (Chapter 4).

The formulae in this chapter address three additional wind-related pathologies: itching and skin diseases caused by wind striking the channels; localized paralysis, or tetany, associated with wind invasion of the channels and sinews; and the additional spasms and convulsions of endogenous wind.

Though "stroke" makes a convenient mnemonic couple with "windstrike" *(zhong feng)*, the practitioner should be careful not to limit his or her understanding of the terms by equating them too precisely. The term "stroke" is generally understood by Western English-speakers to mean cerebrovascular accident. The Chinese medical term *zhong*, "to strike" (as in "to strike the mark"), is a somewhat more generalized term which includes, but is not limited to, our common understanding of the term "stroke." Indeed, when wind strikes, a number of related disorders may be seen.

Formulae Differentiation

Treatment in cases of skin diseases in wind-heat or wind-cold patterns usually calls for dispelling wind, either with cold- or warm-natured wind dissipators. Wind may also combine with, or be engendered by, pathogenic factors of damp and blood depletion. **Hua Shi Jie Yang Wan** combines agents that address these factors.

Da Huo Luo Dan [6.2], **Ren Shen Zai Zao Wan [6.3]**, **Hu Po Bao Long Wan [6.4]**, and **Niu Huang Qing Xin Wan [6.5]** free wind in the connecting channels. They are related to the formulae in Chapter 4 (for the treatment of bi patterns) by virtue of their association with the pathogen pattern "strike" *(zhong)*, with the important distinction that the formulae in this chapter emphasize treatment of the sequelae, while the formulae of Chapter 4 emphasize resuscitation.

Niu Huang Jiang Ya Wan [6.6] addresses the ascendant hyperactivity of liver yang, and the ensuing pattern of endogenous wind, especially as it affects the head.

Bao Ying Dan [6.7], a pediatric formula containing agents that clear heat, settle tetany, resuscitate, and calm the spirit, might well have been included among formulae that cool fire and resolve toxin. However, its use in cases of high heat and ascendant liver yang, with the wind-like symptoms of coma, spasms, and trismus, has led to its inclusion here.

6.1

Hua She Jie Yang Wan
花蛇解癢丸
Agkistrodon Itch-Relieving Pills

Primary Functions and Applications: **Hua She Jie Yang Wan** supplements the qi, nourishes the blood, eliminates wind, and relieves itching. It is used to treat itching on the skin due to wind, and is especially effective in treating the chronic itching seen in cases of depletion. In classical Chinese medical theory, itching on the skin is due to the accumulation of wind on the skin's surface. In general, two types of herbal medicines are used to eliminate the wind and to stop the itching: wind expellants and blood-supplementing wind extinguishers. **Hua She Jie Yang Wan** contains herbs that eliminate wind both by wind-dispelling and through blood supplementation. It is therefore effective in the treatment of erythematous eczema, and in cases of itching caused by drug allergies.

Format and Administration: **Hua She Jie Yang Wan** is produced by the Hanyang Pharmaceutical Works, Hong Kong as *Kai Yeung Pills*, in bottles of 50 pills.

Recommended Dosage: Five pills, 3 times a day (half that for children).

Contraindications: Do not eat seafood, bamboo shoots, or goose while taking this medicine.

Hua She Jie Yang Wan

Constituent Substances

Pinyin Name	Pharmaceutical Name	% Composition
Huang Qi	*Radix Astragali*	10
Ren Shen	*Radix Ginseng*	10
Dang Gui	*Radix Angelicae Sinensis*	10
Chuan Xiong	*Rhizoma Ligustici Wallichii*	10
Sheng Di Huang	*Radix Crudae Rehmanniae Glutinosae*	5
Bai Zhi	*Radix Angelicae*	10
Fang Feng	*Herba Ledebouriellae Sesloidis*	5
Cang Er Zi	*Fructus Xanthii*	5
Bai Hua She	*Agkistrodon seu Bungarus*	10
Wu Shao She	*Zaocys Dhumnades*	5
She Chuang Zi	*Semen Cnidii Monnieri*	10
Cang Zhu	*Rhizoma Atractylodis*	10

Composition and Rationale: *Huang Qi* and *Ren Shen* strengthen the qi and the yang energy on the surface of the body; *Dang Gui, Chuan Xiong* and *Sheng Di* nourish the blood and extinguish endogenous wind; and *Bai Zhi, Fang Feng, Cang Er Zi, Bai Hua She, Wu Shao She, She Chuang Zi,* and *Cang Zhu* expel wind, dry damp, and relieve itching.

Da Huo Luo Dan †   6.2
大活絡丹
Major Connecting-Vessel-Quickening Pill

Source: *Lan Tai Gui Fan (Regulations from Lan Tai)*, Qing Dynasty (1644-1911).

Primary Functions and Applications: **Da Huo Luo Dan** promotes the smooth circulation of blood and qi to relax muscles and sinews, expels wind and cold, stops spasms, and reduces pain. It is used to treat the numbness of the limbs caused by windstrike *(zhong feng)*, rheumatism, or poor circulation. When exogenous wind affects the patient with a constitutional depletion of qi, the resultant back pain, leg pain, or stiff limbs will present as rheumatism. **Da Huo Luo Dan** is recommended in such cases. **Da Huo Luo Dan** is useful in the treatment of the sequelae of stroke, and should be used as soon as possible after the patient's medical and neurological condition has stabilized (though it is important not to use this formula too early in cerebral hemorrhage cases). It can also be used for the treatment of the sequelae of head injuries after medical and neurological conditions are stable.

Symptoms indicating the use of **Da Huo Luo Dan** include facial paralysis, limb paralysis (paralysis may be spastic or flaccid), impaired speech output, and impaired articulation. In cases of facial paralysis due to Bell's Palsy, this is most effective when used as soon as possible following onset. **Da Huo Luo Dan** is also used to treat chest pain when caused by coronary artery disease.

Format and Administration: **Da Huo Luo Dan** is produced by the Tientsin Drug Manufactory as coated pills, 40 per tube, and by the Beijing Tung Ren Tang in honey-pill format, 10 per box.

Recommended Dosage: One honey pill, twice a day, with warm water, 60 proof yellow Chinese wine, or clear spirits such as vodka (the alcohol will help to stimulate blood circulation). In cases of paralysis or rheumatism, it is common to use this formula for several months.

Contraindication: **Do not use Da Huo Luo Dan during pregnancy.**

Da Huo Luo Dan		
Constituent Substances		
Pinyin Name	**Pharmaceutical Name**	**% Composition**
An Xi Xiang	*Benzonium*	—
Bing Pian	*Borneolum*	—
Cao Wu Tou	*Radix Aconiti Kussnezoffii*	—
Chen Xiang	*Lignum Aquilariae*	—
Chi Shao	*Radix Paeoniae Rubrae*	—
Chuan Xi	*Radix Cyathulae*	—
Chuan Xiong	*Radix Ligustici Wallichii*	—
Da Huang	*Rhizoma Rhei*	—
Dang Gui	*Radix Angelicae Sinensis*	—
Di Long	*Lumbricus*	—
Ding Xiang	*Flos Caryophylli*	—
Cao Dou Kou	*Semen Alpinae Katsumadae*	—
Fang Feng	*Herba Ledebouriellae Sesloidis*	—
Fu Ling	*Sclerotium Poriae Cocus*	—
Gan Cao	*Radix Glycyrhizae Uralensis*	—
Ge Gen	*Radix Puerariae*	—
Gu Sui Bu	*Rhizoma Gusuibu*	—
Guan Zhong	*Radix sue Herba cum Radice Potentillae*	—
Gui Ban	*Plastrum Testudinis*	—
He Shou Wu	*Rhizoma Polygoni Multiflori*	—
Hu Gu	*Os Tigris*	—
Huang Lian	*Rhizoma Coptidis*	—
Huang Qin	*Radix Scutellariae Baicalensis*	—
Huo Xiang	*Folium Agastaches sseu Pogostemi*	—
Jiang Can	*Bombyx Batryticatus*	—
Ma Huang	*Herba Ephedrae*	—
Mo Yao	*Myrrha*	—
Mu Xiang	*Radix Saussureae*	—
Niu Huang	*Calculus Bovis*	—

Continued

Da Huo Luo Dan		
(Continued)		
Constituent Substances		
Pinyin Name	**Pharmaceutical Name**	**% Composition**
Qi She	*Agkistrodon Acutus*	—
Qiang Huo	*Rhizoma et Radix Notopterygii*	—
Qing Pi	*Pericarpium Citri Reticulate Viride*	—
Ren Shen	*Radix Ginseng*	—
Rou Gui	*Cortex Cinnamomi Cassiae*	—
Ru Xiang	*Gummi Olibanum*	—
She Xiang	*Secretio Moschi Moschiferi*	—
Shou Di Huang	*Radix Rehmannia Glutinosae*	—
Song Xiang	*Resina Praeparata Pini*	—
Tian Ma	*Rhizoma Gastrodiae Elatae*	—
Tian Nan Xing	*Rhizoma Arisaematis*	—
Wei Ling Xian	*Radix Clematidis Chinensis*	—
Wu Shao She	*Zaocys Dhumnades*	—
Wu Yao	*Radix Linderae Strychnifoliae*	—
Xi Jiao	*Cornu Rhinocerotis*	—
Xi Xin	*Herba cum Radice Asari*	—
Xiang Fu	*Rhizoma Cyperi Rotundi*	—
Xuan Shen	*Radix Scrophulariae Ningpoensis*	—
Xue Jie	*Sanguis Draconis*	—

Ren Shen Zai Zao Wan † 6.3
人參再造丸
Ginseng Renewal Pill

Primary Functions and Applications: **Ren Shen Zai Zao Wan** calms internal wind, expels external wind, eliminates phlegm, and clears qi stagnation and blood stasis caused by wind and phlegm. This herbal medicine is used especially with strokes (windstrike - *zhong feng*), with such symptoms as facial paralysis, limb paralysis, hemiplegia, numbness of limbs, pain, limb contractures, poor articulation, and speech output problems. It is recommended that the medicine be administered as soon as possible after the onset of the stroke, when the patient is medically and neurologically stable. Herbal therapy in such cases will be most effective when administered in conjunction with physical and speech therapy. In addition to treating stroke, **Ren Shen Zai Zao Wan** is used to prevent strokes in patients who have already suffered transient ischemic attacks or other neurological problems associated with prestroke conditions, such as episodes of motor, sensory, or visual abnormalities.

Format and Administration: **Ren Shen Zai Zao Wan** is produced by the Shanghai Chinese Medicine Works in honey-pill format, 10 per box; and by the Tientsin Drug Manufactory, as *Tsaitsuowan*, in pill format, 50 pills per bottle.

Recommended Dosage: One honey pill twice a day, or 3 to 5 smaller pills, twice or 3 times a day, with warm water. For stroke patients with paralysis, administer for at least 6 months.

Contraindications: **Do not use Ren Shen Zai Zao Wan during pregnancy.**

Ren Shen Zai Zao Wan		
Constituent Substances		
Pinyin Name	Pharmaceutical Name	Composition (grams)
Ren Shen	*Radix Ginseng*	20
Huang Qi	*Radix Astragali*	20
Shou Di Huang	*Radix Rehmannia Glutinosae*	20
He Shou Wu	*Rhizoma Polygoni Multiflori*	20
Gui Ban	*Plastrum Testudinis*	10
Hu Gu	*Os Tigris*	10
Gu Sui Bu	*Rhizoma Drynariae*	10
Quan Xie	*Buthus Martensi*	15
Di Long	*Lumbricus*	5
Tian Ma	*Rhizoma Gastrodiae Elatae*	20
Jiang Can	*Bombyx Batryticatus*	10
Qi She Rou	*Agkistrodon*	20
Sang Ji Sheng	*Ramus Visci Loranthi*	20
Bi Xie	*Rhizoma Dioscoreae*	20
Song Jie	*Lignum Pini Nodi*	10
Wei Ling Xian	*Radix Clematidis Chinensis*	15
Ma Huang	*Herba Ephedrae*	20

(Continued)

Ren Shen Zai Zao Wan *(Continued)*

Constituent Substances

Pinyin Name	Pharmaceutical Name	Composition
Xi Xin	*Herba cum Radice Asari*	10
Fang Feng	*Herba Ledebouriellae Sesloidis*	20
Qiang Huo	*Rhizoma et Radix Notopterygii*	20
Bai Zhi	*Radix Angelicae*	20
Ge Gen	*Radix Puerariae Lobetae*	15
Qing Pi	*Pericarpium Citri Reticulate Viride*	10
Ding Xiang	*Flos Caryophylli*	10
Xuan Shen	*Radix Scrophulariae Ningpoensis*	20
Da Huang	*Rhizoma Rhei*	10
Hong Qu	*Semen Oryzae cum Monasco*	5
Huang Lian	*Rhizoma Coptidis*	20
Zhu Sha	*Cinnabaris*	10
Tan Xiang	*Lignum Santali Albi*	5
Jiang Huang	*Rhizoma Curcumae Longae*	2.5
Huo Xiang	*Folium Agastaches sseu Pogostemi*	20
Chi Shao	*Radix Paeoniae Rubrae*	10
Fu Zi	*Radix Aconiti*	10
Rou Gui	*Cortex Cinnamomi Cassiae*	20
Chuan Xiong	*Rhizoma Ligustici Wallichii*	20
Chen Xiang	*Lignum Aquilariae*	10
Wu Yao	*Radix Linderae Strychnifoliae*	10
Xiang Fu	*Rhizoma Cyperi Rotundi*	10
Xue Jie	*Sanguis Draconis*	7.5
Ru Xiang	*Gummi Olibanum*	10
Mo Yao	*Myrrha*	10
San Qi	*Radix Pseudoginseng*	5
Dang Gui	*Radix Angelicae Sinensis*	10
Ju Hong	*Pericarpium Citri Erythrocarpae*	40
Bai Zhu	*Rhizoma Atractylodis Macrocephalae*	18
Fu Ling	*Sclerotium Poriae Cocus*	10
Gan Cao	*Radix Glycyrrhizae Uralensis*	20
Dou Kou	*Semen Alpinae Katsumadai*	10
Shen Qu	*Massa Medica Fermentata*	40
Niu Huang	*Calculus Bovis*	2.5
Shui Niu Jiao	*Cornu Bubali*	15
Tian Zhu Huang	*Concretio Siliceae Bambusae*	10
Bing Pian	*Borneolum*	2.5
She Xiang	*Secretio Moschi Moschiferi*	5

Composition and Rationale: Ren Shen, Huang Qi, Shou Di Huang, He Shou Wu, Gui Ban, Hu Gu, and Gu Sui Bu supplement yin, and fortify qi, blood, kidney, and bone; Quan Xie, Di Long, Tian Ma, and Jiang Can calm internal wind, release contracture, and reduce spasm; Qi She Rou, Sang Ji Sheng, Bi Xie, Song Jie, Wei Ling Xian, Ma Huang, Xi Xin, Fang Feng, Qiang Huo, Bai Zhi, Ge Gen, and Chuan Xiong expel wind and clear the channels; Chen Xiang, Wu Yao, Xiang Fu, Xue Jie, Ru Xiang, Mo Yao, San Qi, and Dang Gui promote blood circulation and free qi stagnation and blood stasis; Ju Hong, Bai Zhu, Fu Ling, Gan Cao, Dou Kou, and Shen Qu regulate qi, fortify spleen and supplement jing; Niu Huang, Shui Niu Jiao, and Tian Zhu Huang clear heat in the heart and eliminate phlegm; Bing Pian and She Xiang open the heart portals.

6.4

Hu Po Bao Long Wan †
琥珀抱龍丸
Succinum Dragon-Embracing Pills

Source: This formula is a modification of **Bao Long Wan [6.4a]** which originally appeared in the Ming Dynasty text *Shou Shi Bao Yuan (Protection of Vital Energy for Longevity).*

Primary Functions and Applications: **Hu Po Bao Long Wan** clears heat in the heart, transforms phlegm, stops convulsions, and calms the spirit. It is used to treat syndromes caused by phlegm-heat in the lungs in children. Guiding symptoms include fever, cough, and phlegm congestion with dyspnea. Wheezing may also be present. In serious cases with extreme elevations in temperature, there may be agitation, convulsions, or loss of consciousness.

In the presence of fever, **Hu Po Bao Long Wan** may be used to treat acute bronchitis, pneumonia, epidemic encephalitis B, epidemic cerebrospinal meningitis, tetanus, spasms caused by high fever (including opisthotonos and lockjaw), high fever associated with measles, and unconsciousness.

Format and Administration: **Hu Po Bao Long Wan** is produced as *Po Lung Yuen Medical Pills* in Hong Kong, in honey-pill format, 10 honey pills per box.

Recommended Dosage: For children less than 1 month of age, use one third of a pill, twice a day; for serious cases, use 3 times a day. For children between 1 month and 3 months of age, use one half a pill, twice a day; for serious cases, use 3 times a day. For children 1 year or older, use 1 pill, twice or 3 times a day.

Hu Po Bao Long Wan		
Constituent Substances		
Pinyin Name	Pharmaceutical Name	% Composition
Niu Huang	*Calculus Bovis*	7.8
Tian Zhu Huang	*Concretio Siliceae Bambusae*	7.8
Dan Nan Xing	*Pulvis Arisaematis cum Felle Bovis*	3.1
She Xiang	*Secretio Moschus*	0.6
Quan Xie	*Buthus Martensi*	4.7
Jiang Can	*Bombyx Batryticatus*	15.5
Zhu Sha	*Cinnabaris*	4.7
Hu Po	*Succinum*	7.8
Xiong Huang	*Realgar*	1.6
Chi Fu Ling	*Sclerotium Poriae Cocus*	15.5

Composition and Rationale: *Niu Huang* clears heat in the heart, resolves fire toxin, and calms the spirit; *Tian Zhu Huang* and *Dan Nan Xing* clear heat and eliminate phlegm; *She Xiang* opens the heart portals and resuscitates; *Quan Xie* calms excessive liver wind; *Jiang Can* stops convulsions; *Zhu Sha* calms the spirit; *Hu Po* tranquilizes and helps *Niu Huang* clear heat in the heart; *Xiong Huang* resolves fire toxin; and *Chi Fu Ling* clears damp-heat and promotes urination.

Zhong Guo Ji Ben Zhong Chen Yao (Fundamentals of Chinese Prepared Medicines, 1988) presents significantly different constituents as its standardized formula for **Hu Po Bao Long Wan.** They are *Tan Xiang, Zhi Shi, Chi Shao, Ren Shen, Fu Ling, Shan Yao, Gan Cao, Tian Zhu Huan, Dan Nan Xing, Zhu Sha,* and *Hu Po.*

6.5   Niu Huang Qing Xin Wan †
牛黃清心丸
Bovine Bezoar Heart-Clearing Pills

Primary Functions and Applications: There are a number of formulae similar to **Niu Huang Qing Xin Wan**, differing from manufacturer to manufacturer.

Wan Shi Niu Huang Qing Xin Wan [5.3], for example, is a formula directed mainly at clearing heat and unblocking obstructed portals. **Niu Huang Qing Xin Wan** can clear repletion heat, but is more directed at treating such sequelae of stroke as paralyis (arm, leg, or facial), impeded speech, and dizziness.

Format and Administration: **Niu Huang Qing Xin Wan** is produced by the Beijing Tung Ren Tang as large honey pills, 10 per box.

Recommended Dosage: Adults, one honey pill, twice a day. Children younger than 1 year, half a pill, twice a day.

Niu Huang Qing Xin Wan		
Constituent Substances		
Pinyin Name	**Pharmaceutical Name**	**% Composition**
Niu Huang	*Calculus Bovis*	8
Ling Yang Jiao	*Cornu Antelopis*	9
Dang Gui	*Radix Angelicae Sinensis*	6
Chuan Xiong	*Rhizoma Ligustici Wallichii*	6
Gan Cao	*Radix Glycyrrhizae Uralensis*	5
Bai Shao	*Radix Paeoniae Lactiflora*	5
Xi Jiao	*Cornu Rhinocerotis*	5
Ren Shen	*Radix Ginseng*	10
Rou Gui	*Cortex Cinnamomi Cassiae*	8
Fang Feng	*Herba Ledebouriellae Sesloidis*	6
A Jiao	*Gelatinum Corii Asini*	7
She Xiang	*Secretio Moschi Moschiferi*	5
Feng Mi	*Mel*	20

Composition and Rationale: *Niu Huang* clears heat and opens the heart portals; *Ling Yang Jiao* clears heat in the liver; *Dang Gui* supplements and moves blood; *Chuan Xiong* moves blood; *Gan Cao* is a catalyst for other herbs; *Bai Shao* relaxes muscles and smooths liver wind; *Xi Jiao* clears heat in the heart; *Ren Shen* supplements qi; *Rou Gui* warms the channels; *Fang Feng* stops wind; *A Jiao* strengthens yin and blood; and *She Xiang* opens the portals.

Zhong Guo Ji Ben Zhong Chen Yao (Fundamentals of Chinese Prepared Medicines, 1988) includes the following in its standardized formula for **Niu Huang Qing Xin Wan**: *Huang Qin, Bai Lian, Jie Geng, Xing Ren, Pu Huang, Chai Hu, Fu Ling, Bai Zhi, Gan Jiang, Da Zao, Shan Yao, Mai Don, Shen Qu, Da Dou Juan, Xiong Huang,* and *Zhu Sha.*

Niu Huang Jiang Ya Wan   6.6
牛黃降壓丸
Bovine Bezoar Hypotensor Pills

Primary Functions and Applications: **Niu Huang Jiang Ya Wan** clears heat in the heart and removes phlegm-heat accumulation, soothes the spirit, and reduces high blood pressure. It is used to treat ascendant hyperactivity of liver yang, resulting in liver wind affecting the head. Guiding symptoms include headache, dizziness, vertigo, impatience and irritability, high blood pressure, insomnia, a red face, and a bitter taste in the mouth. The tongue in such cases will be red, and the pulse wiry.

Niu Huang Jiang Ya Wan is also used to treat paralysis, limb numbness, aphasia, or coma due to phlegm-heat accumulation that has blocked the flow of qi in the channels. The pulse in such cases will be slippery and wiry.

Format and Administration: **Niu Huang Jiang Ya Wan** is produced by the Tientsin Da Ren Tang in 1.6 gram honey pills, 10 per box.

Recommended Dosage: One or two honey pills twice a day.

Niu Huang Jiang Ya Wan		
Constituent Substances		
Pinyin Name	Pharmaceutical Name	% Composition
Ling Yang Jiao	*Cornu Antelopis*	—
Niu Huang	*Calculus Bovis*	—
Zhen Zhu	*Margarita*	—
Bing Pian	*Borneolum*	—
Yu Jin	*Tuber Curcumae*	—
Huang Qi	*Radix Astragali*	—

Composition and Rationale: *Ling Yang Jiao* clears heat and reduces repletion of liver yang. *Niu Huang* clears heat in the heart and resolves fire toxin; *Zhen Zhu* calms the spirit; *Bing Pian* clears heat in the heart, opens the heart portals, and refreshes the spirit; *Yu Jin* moves stagnant liver qi and relieves depression; and *Huang Qi* strengthens spleen qi and prevents the other herbs from weakening the patient.

6.7

Bao Ying Dan †
保嬰丹
Infant-Safeguarding Elixir

Source: *Yao Dian (Chinese Pharmacopoeia).*

Primary Functions and Applications: **Bao Ying Dan** is primarily a children's medicine, used to clear heat, eliminate phlegm and extinguish liver wind due to excessive heat. It is used to treat high fever, and to resuscitate a semiconscious or unconscious patient. Copious phlegm may be present in the chest in such cases, and breathing may be difficult.

Format and Administration: **Bao Ying Dan** is produced by the Guangzhou Pharmaceutical Manufactory in powdered form.

Recommended Dosage, Powder: Each container of powder contains 0.3 grams of the medicine. For children younger than 1 month, use 0.1 gram, twice or 3 times per day. For children from 1 month to 1 year in age, use 0.3 grams twice or 3 times a day. For children older than 1 year, increase the dose accordingly, but do not exceed 0.9 grams, twice or 3 times per day. Use with a *yao yin* (herbal conductor) of *Dan Zhu Ye (Herba Lopatheri Gracilis)* and *Bo He (Herba Menthae)* in cases of acute pneumonia, acute bronchitis, asthma, and convulsions.

Recommended Dosage, Pill: Each pill contains 0.5 grams of the medicine. For children older than 1 year, administer 1 pill, 3 times per day. For children younger than 1 year, decrease the dose proportionately.

Bao Ying Dan		
Constituent Substances		
Pinyin Name	**Pharmaceutical Name**	**% Composition**
Niu Huang	*Calculus Bovis*	1.33
Dan Nan Xing	*Pulvis Arisaematis cum Felle Bovis*	33.22
Tian Zhu Huang	*Concretio Siliceae Bambusae*	11.63
Xiong Huang	*Realgar*	8.30
Jiang Can	*Bombyx Batryticatus*	9.97
Quan Xie	*Buthus Martensi*	4.98
Hu Po	*Succinum*	8.30
Zhu Sha	*Cinnabaris*	4.98
Fu Ling	*Sclerotium Poriae Cocus*	16.60
She Xiang	*Secretio Moschi Moschiferi*	0.66

Composition and Rationale: *Niu Huang* clears heat, resolves fire toxin and stops convulsions; *Dan Nan Xing, Zhu Huang,* and *Xiong Huang* clear phlegm-heat; *Jiang Can* and *Quan Xie* extinguish liver wind and stop convulsions; *Hu Po, Zhu Sha,* and *Fu Ling* calm the spirit and stop convulsions; and *She Xiang* opens the portals and resuscitates.

Hou Zao San [6.7a], a clinically related formula, contains *Hou Zao (Calculus Macacae Mulattae)* (monkey gallstone), which clears phlegm-heat in the lungs that may be causing heart portal blockage. This condition is seen in cases of pneumonia or bronchitis in children, and often results in high fever accompanied by convulsions. **Hou Zao San** is produced by the United Pharmaceutical Company as *Hou Tsao San*, available in small vials.

7

Heat-Clearing, Fire-Draining Formulae

To clear heat and dry damp

7.1 Niu Huang Shang Qing Wan
7.2 Huang Lian Shang Qing Wan Pian
7.3 Shuang Liao Hou Feng San
7.4 Yu Dai Wan

7.5 Huang Lian Su Pian
7.6 Jia Wei Xiang Lian Pian
7.7 Hua Tou Gao

To clear heat and reduce fire

7.8 Qing Yin Wan
7.9 She Xiang Xiong Dan
     Zhi Ling Gao
7.10 Niu Huang Jie Du Pian
7.11 Liu Shen Wan
7.12 Fu Fang Xi Gua Shuang
7.13 Long Dan Xie Gan Wan
7.14 Jiang Ya Ping Pian

7.15 Jiang Ya Wan
7.16 Du Zhong Pian
7.17 Huang Lian
     Yang Gan Wan
7.18 Li Gan Pian
7.19 Li Dan Pian
7.20 Hou Yan Wan
7.21 Dao Chi Pian

To clear heat and cool the blood

7.22 Huai Jiao Wan
7.23 Hua Zhi Ling Wan

7.24 Qiang Li Hua Zhi Ling
7.25 Zhi Wan

To resolve fire toxin and clear repletion heat

7.26 Chuan Xin Lian Kang Yan Pian
7.27 Niu Huang Xiao Yan Wan
7.28 Lian Qiao Bai Du Pian
7.29 Zi Jin Ding
7.30 Ji Gu Cao Wan

7.31 Hui Chun Dan
7.32 Jing Wan Hong
7.33 Fu Fang Tu Jin Pi Ding
7.34 Xi Huang Wan

Pattern Identification

The treatment of substantial heat and fire toxin in qi-aspect, construction-aspect, and blood-aspect heat patterns, as well as damp-heat and yang lesion patterns, primarily involves the methods of clearage and precipitation. Clearage includes heat clearage, fire draining, and fire toxin resolution. Precipitation (whereby the bowels are stimulated to expel repletion pathogens) includes draining precipitation, precipitation of depressed pulmogastric heat (sore throat, mouth and tongue lesions, agitation), and precipitation of upflaming liver fire.

Formulae Differentiation

Heat clearers are often combined with precipitators in a single formula. **Huang Lian Shang Qing Wan Pian [7.2]**, **Niu Huang Xiao Yan Wan [7.27]**, and **Lian Qiao Bai Tu Pian [7.28]**, all include draining precipitants among their constituents, though the therapeutic emphasis of each formulae is somewhat different.

In cases of qi heat clearage, attention is often paid to protection of the liquid (jin) by the inclusion of liquid safeguarders (such as *Tian Hua Fen*). This strategy is evident in the structure of **Niu Huang Xiao Yan Wan [7.27]**.

Formulae are included in this chapter whose primary objective is to drain liver fire. The presence of the liver-calming tetany-settling agent *Gou Teng (Ramulus et Uncus Uncariae)* (gambir vine) in **Jiang Ya Wan [7.15]**, and of the liver-clearing fire drainer, *Xia Ku Cao (Spica Prunellae)* in **Jiang Ya Wan [7.15]**, **Jiang Ya Ping Pian [7.14]** and **Du Zhong Pian [7.16]** point to the use of those formulae in conditions of upflaming liver fire. Note carefully the list of contraindications for use of **Jiang Ya Wan [7.15]**. **Huang Lian Yang Gan Wan [7.17]** has a somewhat specialized clinical application in the treatment of liver heat, especially as it affects the eyes. **Long Dan Xie Gan Wan [7.13]** and **Li Gan Pian [7.18]** cool the liver and reduce jaundice. **Long Dan Xie Gan Wan [7.13]** is a representative damp-heat formula, addressing upper body heat as well as lower, while **Li Gan Pian [7.18]** is a more specialized formula (of only two agents) for the expulsion of stones. **Li Dan Pian [7.19]** combines the specialized stone-eliminating properties of *Jin Qian Cao (Herba Jinqiancao)* with toxin resolvants, heat clearers, hepatocystic damp-heat agents, and the representative precipitant *Da Huang (Rhizoma Rhei)*.

Huai Jiao Wan [7.22] utilizes the blood-cooling and heat-draining properties of *Huai Jiao (Fructus Sophorae Japonicae)* and, with **Hua Zhi Ling Wan [7.23]**, **Qiang Li Hua Zhi Ling [7.24]** and **Zhi Wan [7.25]**, may be considered in cases of heat-caused bleeding disorders, particularly hemorrhoidal bleeding. **She Xiang Xiong Dan Zhi Ling Gao [7.9]** is also recommended for hemorrhoids, though its approach has greater emphasis on subduing the yang (with *Zhen Zhu [Concha Margaritafera]*); securing against desertion (with *Chi Shi Zhi [Halloysitum Rubrum]*); and resolving toxin, than on controlling bleeding.

Zi Jin Ding [7.29] and **Hui Chun Dan [7.31]** might have been included among the formulae that resuscitate and open the portals. **Zi Jin Ding [7.29]** might also be counted among the summerheat formulae of Chapter II. **Hui Chun Dan [7.31]** has been included here by virtue of its common, clinical application in China in the treatment of many of the digestive disorders and upper respiratory infections seen in children; only secondarily is it used in resuscitation.

Xi Huang Wan [7.34] emphasizes analgesic stasis transformation in the treatment of painful swellings.

Yu Dai Wan [7.4] drains damp-heat, and is specifically used in the treatment of leukorrhea.

7.1   # Niu Huang Shang Qing Wan †
牛黃上清丸
Bovine Bezoar Upper-Body-Clearing Pills

Source: *Yi Xue Ru Men (Elements of Medicine)*, Ming Dynasty (1368-1644).

Primary Functions and Applications: **Niu Huang Shang Qing Wan** clears heat, disperses fire, and reduces inflammation. It is used to treat sores and ulcers on the tongue, stomatitis (inflammation or infection in the mouth which may be viral) with or without fever, oral herpes, and wind-heat syndromes with the following symptoms: fever, sore throat, toothache, conjunctivitis, constipation and/or uneasiness due to heat in the heart.

Although **Niu Huang Shang Qing Wan** is similar in composition to **Huang Lian Shang Qing Pian [7.2]**, their therapeutic targets differ in certain respects. **Niu Huang Shang Qing Wan** contains four additional ingredients: *Niu Huang* and *Bing Pian* to clear heat and resolve fire toxin; and *Chi Shao* and *Dang Gui* to clear blood heat and move blood. This formula is indicated in cases with more fire toxin symptoms, such as swollen sore throat and carbuncles. **Huang Lian Shang Qing Pian [7.2]**, on the other hand, is more effective for expelling wind, and is indicated in cases of dizziness, vertigo, conjunctivitis, tongue or mouth ulcer, and constipation.

Format and Administration: **Niu Huang Shang Qing Wan** is produced by the Tientsin Drug Manufactory in pill format, 50 pills per bottle, and as honey pills, 10 per box.

Recommended Dosage: One honey pill, twice daily, or 10 coated pills once a day.

Niu Huang Shang Qing Wan		
Constituent Substances		
Pinyin Name	**Pharmaceutical Name**	**% Composition**
Niu Huang	*Calculus Bovis*	3.70
Huang Lin	*Rhizoma Coptidis*	2.93
Dang Gui	*Radix Angelicae Sinensis*	9.14
Bing Pian	*Borneolum*	1.83
Da Huang	*Rhizoma Rhei*	14.63
Ju Hua	*Flos Chrysanthemi Indicae*	7.31
Jie Geng	*Radix Platycodonis Grandiflori*	2.93
Lian Xin	*Plumula Nelumbinis*	0.91
Gan Cao	*Radix Glycyrrhizae Uralensis*	1.83
Chuan Xiong	*Rhizoma Ligustici Wallichii*	2.93
Jing Jie	*Flos Schizonepetae Tenuifoliae*	2.93
Huang Qin	*Radix Scutellaria*	9.14
Shi Gao	*Gypsum*	14.63
Bai Zhi	*Radix Angelicae*	2.93
Lian Qiao	*Fructus Forsythiae Suspensae*	9.14
Huang Bai	*Cortex Phellodendri*	1.83
Bo He	*Herba Menthae*	5.48
Shan Zhi Zi	*Fructus Gardeniae Jasminoidis*	9.14
Sheng Di Huang	*Radix Crudae Rehmanniae Glutinosae*	11.70
Chi Shao	*Radix Paeoniae Rubrae*	2.93

Composition and Rationale: *Niu Huang, Huang Qin, Bing Pian, Huang Lian, Huang Bai* and *Lian Qiao* clear heat and disperse fire; *Ju Hua* and *Bo He* clear wind-heat; *Ju Hua* clears heat in the liver; *Lian Xin* clears heat in the heart; *Shi Gao* clears heat in the lungs; *Da Huang* clears heat through precipitation (promoting fecal flow) and *Zhi Zi* clears heat through urination; *Dang Gui* moves the blood; *Bing Pian* opens the portals and awakens the spirit; *Jie Geng* opens the lung, soothes the throat, and discharges pus; and *Gan Cao* harmonizes the constituents.

7.2 ## Huang Lian Shang Qing Pian
黃連上清片
Coptis Upper-Body-Clearing Tablets

Source: *Wan Bing Hui Chung, (Recovery of Ten Thousand Patients),* Ming Dynasty (1368-1644).

Primary Functions and Applications: **Huang Lian Shang Qing Pian** relieves fire and dispels wind-heat. It differs in therapeutic effect from the previous formula, **Niu Huang Shang Qing Wan [7.1],** in its ability to clear wind, primarily in the upper and middle burners. In addition, **Huang Lien Shang Qing Wan** helps promote bowel movement. It is used to treat fever, headache, dizziness, ear or mouth ulcers, swollen gums, sore throat, conjunctivitis, toothache, constipation, and tinnitus associated with common cold or influenza, tonsillitis, parotitis, otitis media, infections (sores, carbuncles, boils) bronchitis (acute), pneumonia (early stages), and pulmonary abscess. It may also be used in cases of hypertension with dizziness, especially when accompanied by such wind-heat signs as red eyes, flushed face, and headache.

Format and Administration: **Huang Lian Shang Qing Wan Pian** is produced by the Tientsin Drug Manufactory in tablet format, 8 tablets per vial, 12 vials per box.

Recommended Dosage: Four pills, twice a day.

Contraindication: **Do not use Huang Lian Shang Qing Wan during pregnancy.**

Huang Lian Shang Qing Wan Pian		
Constituent Substances		
Pinyin Name	Pharmaceutical Name	% Composition
Huang Lian	*Rhizoma Coptidis*	7.6
Chuang Xiong	*Rhizoma Ligustici Wallichi*	3.05
Jing Jie	*Flos Schizonepetae Tenuifoliae*	6.11
Fang Feng	*Herba Ledebouriellae Sesloidis*	3.05
Huang Qin	*Radix Scutellariae*	6.11
Jie Geng	*Radix Platycodonis Grandiflori*	6.11
Shi Gao	*Gypsum*	3.05
Ju Hua	*Flos Chrysanthemi Indicae*	12.21
Bai Zhi	*Radix Angelicae*	6.11
Gan Cao	*Radix Glycyrrhizae Uralensis*	3.05
Da Huang	*Rhizoma Rhei*	24.43
Man Jing Zi	*Fructus Viticis*	6.11
Lian Qiao	*Fructus Forsythiae Suspensae*	6.11
Xuan Fu Hua	*Flos Inulae*	1.53
Huang Bai	*Cortex Phellodendri*	3.05
Bo He	*Herba Menthae*	3.05
Shan Zhi Zi	*Fructus Gardeniae Jasminoidis*	6.11

Composition and Rationale: **Huang Lian Shang Qing Wan Pian** is constructed in the same manner as the previous formula, **Niu Huang Shang Qing Wan [7.1]**, except for the absence of *Niu Huang, Bing Pian, Chi Shao*, and *Dang Gui*. The constituents function similarly. In addition, *Xuan Fu Hua* acts as a counterflow downbearer, bringing down counterflow qi and eliminating phlegm.

7.3 Shuang Liao Hou Feng San
雙料喉風散
Double-Ingredient Throat Wind Powder

Primary Functions and Applications: **Shuang Liao Hou Feng San** clears heat, eliminates inflammation and soothes sore throat pain. It is used to treat oral infections or disorders (such as stomatitis, tonsillitis, pharyngitis, mouth ulcers, canker sores, toothache, scarlet fever, and other throat disorders caused by heat); nasal infections or disorders (such as runny nose, sinus headache, and yellow, pus-like nasal secretions caused by sinusitis); ear infections or disorders (such as ear pain accompanied by pus-like discharges, and diminished hearing, caused by otitis media); and skin infections (such as carbuncles, open boils and skin blisters).

Format and Administration: **Shuang Liao Hou Feng San** is produced by the Meizhou City Pharmaceutical Manufactory, Guangdong, China, as *Superior Sore Throat Powder.* It is used topically.

Recommended Dosage:

• *For mouth infections:* Blow one sixth of a vial onto the infected area three times a day.

• *For nasal infections:* Sniff one tenth of a vial into the nostril three times a day.

• *For ear infections:* Use H_2O_2 (hydrogen peroxide) to wash the ear. Then blow one tenth of a vial into the ear once a day.

• *For skin infections:* Wash the area first with a strong black tea (as an astringent), then apply an appropriate amount of the powder to the open wound once a day.

Shuang Liao Hou Feng San		
Constituent Substances		
Pinyin Name	Pharmaceutical Name	% Composition
Niu Huang	*Calculus Bovis*	5
Bing Pian	*Borneolum*	25
Gan Cao	*Radix Glycyrrhizae Uralensis*	15
Qing Dai	*Indigo Puloverata Levis*	5
Zhen Zhu	*Margarita*	5
Huang Lian	*Rhizoma Coptidis*	30
Shan Dou Gen	*Radix Sophora Subprostrata*	15

Composition and Rationale: Niu Huang, Huang Lian, and *Shan Dou Gen* clear heat and resolve fire toxin; *Bing Pian* clears heat and relieves pain; *Qing Dai* clears heat in the blood and resolves fire toxin; *Gan Cao* clears heat; *Zhen Zhu* calms a spirit agitated by heat, relieves pain, and promotes healing; *Shan Dou Gen* clears heat, and specifically benefits the throat.

Yu Dai Wan † 7.4
愈帶丸
Vaginal-Discharge-Curing Pills

Source: Zheng Zhi Zhuen Shen (Regulations of Diagnosis and Treatment), Ming Dynasty.

Primary Functions and Applications: **Yu Dai Wan** clears damp-heat in the lower burner and treats leukorrhea. In such cases, damp has already combined with heat, and the leukorrhea is yellow, possibly malo-derous, and may be accompanied by itching. In severe cases, blood may be present in the discharge. Damp heat in the lower burner is often accompanied by burning urination, abdominal pain, a bitter taste in the mouth, and a dry throat.

Format and Administration: **Yu Dai Wan** is produced by the Lanzhou Fo Ci Pharmaceutical Factory as *Yudai Wan,* in bottles of 100 pills.

Recommended Dosage: Eight to 10 pills three times a day.

Contraindications: Do not use **Yu Dai Wan** in cases where spleen qi depletion has produced damp, and where the damp has not combined with heat. In such cases, the discharge will be clear or white, with a minimum of odor. **Qian Jin Zhi Dai Wan [12.11]** is the formula of choice in such cases.

Yu Dai Wan		
Constituent Substances		
Pinyin Name	**Pharmaceutical Name**	**% Composition**
Shou Di Huang	*Radix Rehmanniae Glutinosa Conquitae*	12.5
Bai Shao	*Radix Paeoniae Rubra*	15.62
Dang Gui	*Radix Angelicae Sinensis*	9.37
Chuan Xiong	*Radix Ligustici Wallichi*	3.13
Huang Bai	*Cortex Phellodendri*	6.25
Chun Gen Pi	*Cortex Ailanthi*	46.88
Gao Liang Jiang	*Rhizoma Alpiniae Officinari*	6.25

Composition and Rationale: Shou Di Huang, Bai Shao, Dang Gui, and *Chuan Xiong* comprise the formula *Si Wu Tang*, a representative blood-supplementing formula and a standard medicine for liver-blood insufficiency and menstrual disorders. *Huang Bai* is a damp-heat agent, fire clearer, and depletion-heat clearer. *Chun Gen Pi* is an astringent, which acts to clear leukorrhea and to dry damp. *Gao Liang Jiang* is a warming agent as well as a cold-pain dissipator; it is carbonized to enhance its property of arresting hemorhage.

Yu Dai Wan is a modification of the original formula **Chun Pi Wan**, which contained four of the seven herbs included here *(Bai Shao, Huang Bai, Chun Gen Pi,* and *Gao Liang Jiang.)*

Zhong Guo Ji Ben Zhong Chen Yao (Fundamentals of Chinese Prepared Medicines, 1988) describes a significantly different formula under the name **Yu Dai Wan**. Its clinical focus is wider than the formula presented here, and includes irregular menstruation (especially delayed menses, scanty flow, cold pain) and hypermenorrhea among its indications. The formula contains *Shou Di Huang, Bai Shao, Dang Gui, Huang Bai, Shao Yao Hua, Niu xi, Ai Ye Tan, Zong Lu Tan, Gan Jiang, Bai Cao Shuang, Pu Huang, Rou Gui, Mu Xiang, Xiang Fu, Zhi Mu, Ji Huan Hua,* and *Gan Cao.*

Huang Lian Su Pian
黃連素片
Coptis Extract Tablets

Primary Functions and Applications: **Huang Lian Su Pian** reduces inflammation and resolves fire toxin. It is used to treat intestinal infection and inflammation, and dysentery. Guiding symptoms include frequent bloody or watery stool, abdominal pain, vomiting, and fever. It is also effective in the treatment of carbuncles and sores on the skin with pus, as well as for the treatment of conjunctivitis.

In China, the active ingredient Coptine is extracted chemically and sold in drug stores as well as in herb shops. This medicine is very effective, and quite popular in China.

Format and Administration: **Huang Lian Su Pian** is produced by the Min-Kang Drug Manufactory, I-Chang, China, in tablet format, 12 tablets per vial, 12 vials per box.

Recommended Dosage: Two to three tablets each time, 3 times a day. For children, ½ to 1 tablet, 3 times a day with warm water.

Huang Lian Su Pian		
Constituent Substances		
Pinyin Name	**Pharmaceutical Name**	**% Composition**
Huang Lian	*Rhizoma Coptidis*	100

Composition and Rationale: Huang Lian clears heat and resolves fire toxin.

Laboratory research in China has shown the function of this medicine to be similar to that of a broad-spectrum antibiotic. It is effective in reducing bacterial counts for bacillus dysenteriae, staphlococcus, pneumococcus, meningococcus, corynebacterium diptheriae, streptococcus, mycobacterium tuberculosis Var. hominis and leptospira.

7.6 Jia Wei Xiang Lian Pian
加味香連片
Supplemented Saussurea and Coptis Tablets

Source: From experience in the Chinese military. The formula is described in the text *He Li Jiu Fang (Formularies of the People's Welfare Pharmacies)*, Song Dynasty (960-1279).

Primary Functions and Applications: **Jia Wei Xiang Lian Pian** clears heat, dries damp, promotes qi circulation, and removes qi stagnation. It is used to treat acute bacillary dysentery due to damp-heat, with such symptoms as fever (in very serious cases where shock is present, fever may be absent), abdominal pain, urgent sensation to have a bowel movement several times in one day, and diarrhea with blood and pus.

Format and Administration: The original name for this formula was *Jia Wei Xiang Lian Wan*, produced in pill format with the same ingredients. The present formula is produced in a convenient, higher-potency tablet form. **Jia Wei Xiang Lian Pian** is manufactured by the Beijing Pharmaceutical Manufactory as *Chia Wei Hsiang Lien Pian*. It is available in tablet format, 8 tablets per tube, 12 tubes per box.

Recommended Dosage: Two tablets, twice to 4 times a day with warm water.

Jia Wei Xiang Lian Pian		
Constituent Substances		
Pinyin Name	**Pharmaceutical Name**	**% Composition**
Mu Xiang	*Radix Saussureae*	10.81
Bin Lang	*Semen Arecae Acacia seu Catechu*	5.40
Zhi Qiao	*Fructus Citri seu Ponciri*	10.81
Hou Po	*Cortex Magnoliae Officinalis*	10.81
Wu Zhu Yu	*Fructus Evodiae*	5.40
Huang Lian	*Rhizoma Coptidis*	16.22
Huang Bai	*Cortex Phellodendri*	5.40
Huang Qin	*Radix Scutellaria*	10.81
Yan Hu Suo	*Tuber Corydalis Yanhusuo*	5.40
Bai Shao	*Radix Paeoniae Lactiflora*	10.81
Dang Gui	*Radix Angelicae Sinensis*	5.40
Gan Cao	*Radix Glycyrrhizae Uralensis*	2.70

Composition and Rationale: *Mu Xiang, Bin Lang, Zhi Qiao, Hou Po* and *Wu Zhu Yu* promote intestinal qi circulation, remove intestinal qi stagnation, dry damp, and relieve pain; *Huang Lian, Huang Bai* and *Huang Qin* clear heat, resolve fire toxin, and eliminate damp; *Yuan Hu, Bai Shao,* and *Dang Gui* regulate blood circulation and relieve pain; and *Gan Cao* regulates the middle burner, relieves pain, and harmonizes the other herbs.

This formula is a modification of **Xiang Lian Wan [7.6a]**. In 1955, a study was reported in the *Journal of Traditional Chinese Medicine* in which **Xiang Lian Wan [7.6a]** was used to treat bacillary dysentery. In this study with 38 patients, **Xiang Lian Wan [7.6a]** was found to control the fever for an average of 32.5 hours, to control the diarrhea in four days, and to produce negative cultures by the third day. C.f., *Journal of Traditional Chinese Medicine* 8 (1955). The modified formula presented above, **Jia Wei Xiang Lian Pian**, is more effective in treating the dysentery.

Hua Tou Gao
華佗膏
Hua Tou's Paste

Primary Functions and Applications: **Hua Tou Gao** expels wind, eliminates damp and relieves itching. It is used to treat athlete's foot (tinea pedis) or fungal infection of the hand. The skin in such conditions may be rough, thick, and peeling, and itching may be present. **Hua Tou Gao** is also used to treat dermatitis (eczema). Guiding symptoms include superficial inflammation of the skin characterized by vesicles (when acute), redness, edema, oozing, crusting, scaling, and itching.

Format and Administration: Wash the affected area with warm water. Apply the ointment to the skin twice a day, morning and evening. If the ointment is applied between the toes, place a cotton ball between the toes during the day and at night. When treating skin infection on the palm, or where the surface is thick and rough, soak the area in warm water to soften the skin surface before application. If there is no effect after using this ointment for a few days, it is recommended that the patient soak the affected area in the following herbal solution twice a day before applying the ointment:

Simmer 15 grams each of *Fang Feng (Herba Ledebouriellae Sesloidis), Jing Jie (Flos Schizonepetae Tenuifoliae),* and *Ming Fan (Alumen)* in 2 cups of water for 30 minutes, or until one cup remains. Let cool slightly, and, leaving the herbs in the liquid, soak the affected area. Apply the **Hua Tou Gao** without rinsing the solution from the skin. The solution should be refrigerated, and may be reheated and reused for three days.

Use a solution of baking soda, or black tea, rather than soap and water, to remove the ointment from the skin.

Contraindications: While using **Hua Tou Gao** on the skin, do not use soap, lysol, H_2O_2 (hydrogen peroxide), alcohol, tincture of iodine or sulphur. These may cause irritation.

Hua Tou Gao		
Constituent Substances		
Pinyin Name	**Pharmaceutical Name**	**% Composition**
—	*Salicylic Acid*	5
—	*Benzoic Acid*	10
—	*Cera Chinensis*	2
—	*Camphora*	2
—	*Vaseline*	80
—	*Chimonanthus Praecox-Link Oil*	1

Qing Yin Wan †
清音丸
Voice-Clearing Pills

7.8

Source: Lan Tai Gui Fan, Qing Dynasty (1644-1911).

Primary Functions and Applications: **Qing Yin Wan** enriches the yin and clears heat in the lungs, promotes the production of body fluid, promotes salivation, and quenches thirst. It is a very common medicine used to treat throat diseases due to wind-heat or fire pathogen that has accumulated in the lungs, preventing the lung qi from opening. It is effective in cases of swollen, painful throat associated with tonsillitis, scarlet fever, or early stages of febrile diseases; throat narrowing (Vincent's angina); and hoarseness, throat swelling and pain, and dry mouth due to lung problems. It is indicated in cases of hoarseness or discomfort that may follow speaking or singing.

Format and Administration: Three manufacturers produce **Qing Yin Wan**, and each uses a different formula. The formula discussed here is produced by the Beijing Tung Ren Tang in honey pill format, 10 pills per box.

The formula produced in Tianjin contains *Yuan Shen, Jie Geng, Shan Dou Gen, Pang Da Hai, Bo He, Pang Sha, Jin Guo Lan, She Gan, Huang Lian, Jin Yin Hua, Mai Men Tong, He Zi Rou, Huang Qing, Zhi Zi, Jin Deng*

Long, Chuan Bei Mu and *Gan Cao*, and is effective in the treatment of lung heat and stomach heat that has damaged the yin and body fluid.

A third formula, produced in Shanghai, is made even more cooling through the addition of minerals.

Zhong Guo Ji Ben Zhong Chen Yao (Fundamentals of Chinese Prepared Medicines, 1988) includes the following as its standardized formula for **Qing Yin Wan**: *Jie Geng, Han Shui Shi, Bo He, Gan Cao, Wu Mei, Qing Dai, Peng Sha, Bing Pian*, and *Ke Zi Rou*.

Recommended Dosage: One honey pill, twice a day. Dissolve the pill slowly in the mouth, or take with warm water. While taking this medicine, do not eat greasy, spicy food.

Qing Yin Wan		
Constituent Substances		
Pinyin Name	**Pharmaceutical Name**	**% Composition**
Ge Gen	*Radix Puerariae Lobetae*	15
Ke Zi Rou	*Fructus Terminaliae Chebule*	15
Feng Mi	*Mel*	25
Tian Hua Fen	*Radix Tricosanthis*	20
Chuan Bei Mu	*Bulbus Fritillariae Cirrhosae*	25

Composition and Rationale: *Ge Gen* increases the flow of body fluid to the upper half of the body to clear heat, particularly in the neck and throat; *He Zi Rou* soothes the throat; and *Feng Mi* moistens the throat, as does *Chuan Bei*, which also opens the lung.

7.9   She Xiang Xiong Dan Zhi Ling Gao
射香熊膽痔靈膏
Musk and Bear's Gall Hemorrhoid Paste

Primary Functions and Applications: **She Xiang Xiong Dan Zhi Ling Gao** clears heat, resolves fire toxin, reduces inflammation, reduces pain, and controls bleeding. It is used to treat hemorrhoids with inflammation and bleeding, for treatment of anal fistulae, and to treat other skin sores such as carbuncles with or without open wounds and pus.

Format and Administration: **She Xiang Xiong Dan Zhi Ling Gao** is produced as *Hemorrhoid's Ointment for External Use* by the Chung-Lien Drug Works, Hankow, China in 4-gram and 10-gram tubes.

Recommended Dosage: For external use only. Apply ointment on the affected anal region. The area should be clean before the ointment is applied. Apply 1-3 times per day.

She Xiang Xiong Dan Zhi Ling Gao		
Constituent Substances		
Pinyin Name	Pharmaceutical Name	% Composition
Xiong Dan	*Vesica Fel Ursi*	2.7
Bing Pian	*Borneolum*	1.6
Zhen Zhu	*Margarita*	2.7
Chi Shi Zhi	*Halloysitum Rubrum*	13.84
She Xiang	*Secretio Moschi Moschiferi*	0.16

Composition and Rationale: *Xiong Dan*, *Bing Pian* and *Zhen Zhu* clear heat and resolve fire poison; *Chi Shi Zhi* controls bleeding and eliminates mucus and inflammation; and *She Xiang* promotes blood circulation and reduces swelling.

Niu Huang Jie Du Pian †   7.10
牛黃解毒片
Bovine Bezoar Toxin-Resolving Tablets

Source: *Bian Zheng Zhun Sheng Fu Yu Ji (Differentiation Standards from Volume on Gynecology and Pediatrics)*, Ming Dynasty (1368-1644).

Primary Functions and Applications: **Niu Huang Jie Du Pian** is a popular, commonly used medicine for early-stage seasonal febrile disorder with fever and sore throat. It clears heat, reduces inflammation, and resolves fire toxin. It is effective in the treatment of repletion fire in the upper burner, with such symptoms as mouth dryness, throat dryness, tongue ulcer, mouth ulcer, toothache with or without swollen gums, and headache. It is also used to treat tonsillitis and pharyngitis (with symptoms such as fever, throat pain and swollen tonsils, with or without pus); conjunctivitis; parotitis (mumps); ear pain due to fire; constipation caused by excess heat (*not* constipation from yin depletion); and skin infections, including sores, carbuncles, and boils.

Format and Administration: **Niu Huang Jie Du Pian** is produced by at least three major manufacturers. Beijing Tung Ren Tang produces an uncoated tablet, 8 per vial. Tianjing Drug Manufactory and Shanghai Chinese Medicine Works produce a coated tablet in bottles of 20. A honey-pill format is also available.

Recommended Dosage: Two tablets, twice a day. Dose may be increased for more serious cases. For the 3-gram honey pill, administer 1-2 pills, twice a day. It is common to simultaneously prescribe **Yin Qiao Jie Du Pian [1.6]**. p. 168

Contraindications: **Niu Huang Jie Du Pian contains** *Da Huang,* **a strong precipitant and blood mover, and should not be used during pregnancy.** Do not use for cases of depletion; use in cases of repletion heat only. Because of the purgative ingredients contained in this formula, bowel movements may occur frequently during its use.

Niu Huang Jie Du Pian		
Constituent Substances		
Pinyin Name	Pharmaceutical Name	% Composition
Niu Huang	*Calculus Bovis*	2.5
Huang Lian	*Rhizoma Coptidis*	14.0
Bing Pian	*Borneolum*	7.5
Jin Yin Hua	*Flos Lonicerae Japonicae*	20.0
Bo He	*Herba Menthae*	7.0
Huang Qin	*Radix Scutellaria*	14.0
Bai Zhi	*Radix Angelicae*	8.0
Shan Zhi Zi	*Fructus Gardeniae Jasminoidis*	10.0
Da Huang	*Rhizoma Rhei*	10.0
Chuan Xiong	*Rhizoma Ligustici Wallichii*	7.0

Zhong Guo Ji Ben Zhong Chen Yao (Fundamentals of Chinese Prepared Medicines, 1988) lists the following as its standardized formula for **Niu Huang Jie Du Pian**: *Niu Huang, Bing Pian, Huang Qin, Da Huang. Xiong Dan, Shi Gao, Jie Geng,* and *Gan Cao.*

Composition and Rationale: Niu Huang and *Jin Yin Hua* clear heat and resolve fire toxin; *Huang Lian* clears heat, disperses replete fire, and dries damp; *Bing Pian* clears heat, opens the portals, and resuscitates; *Bo He* expels wind-heat; *Huang Qin* clears heat, resolves fire toxin, and dries damp; *Bai Zhi* expels wind, discharges pus, reduces swelling, and relieves pain; *Zhi Zi* clears heat and calms the patient; *Da Huang* clears intestinal heat and moves the bowels; and *Chuan Xiong* relieves pain and reduces wind.

Liu Shen Wan †   7.11
六神丸
Six-Spirit Pills

Source: Zhong Guo Yi Xue Da Ci Dian (Dictionary of Chinese Medicine), published in the 1930's.

Primary Functions and Applications: **Liu Shen Wan** resolves fire toxin, reduces inflammation, and relieves pain. It is used in cases of severe swollen sore throat (as seen, for example, in scarlet fever), for the treatment of stomatitis or parotitis, and in certain external skin disorders such as carbuncles, sores, and boils.

Although a common medication in China, because of its relative expense and potency it is not the first medicine chosen for the treatment of the common sore throat. Rather, its use is generally reserved for cases in which the first choice medicine has proven ineffective. It should be considered for administration in cases unaffected by medicines such as **Niu Huang Jie Du Pian [7.10]**.

Zhong Guo Ji Ben Zhong Chen Yao (Fundamentals of Chinese Prepared Medicines, 1988) reports a 1976 lab report (appearing in *Zhong Yi Yao Yen Jiu San Gao, #5*) that establishes the synergistic effects of *She Xiang*

(Secretio Moschi Moschiferi), Niu Huang (Calculus Bovis), and *Chan Su (Secretio Bufonia),* especially when combined in the proportion 2:3:2.

Format and Administration: **Liu Shen Wan** is produced by the Shanghai Chinese Medicine Works, and is available in boxes of 100 tiny, 0.3 gram pills. The pills should be allowed to dissolve in the mouth, although they may be swallowed with warm water. During therapy with this medication, avoid such throat-irritating habits as smoking, drinking, and the consumption of hot, spicy, pungent food.

Recommended Dosage: Adults, 10 pills, once a day. Children, 3 years and younger, 1 pill per year of age, once a day. Children 4-8 years, 5-6 pills, once a day; 9-15 years, 8 pills, once a day.

For External Use: Dissolve 10 pills in cold water or vinegar, make a paste and spread on the skin several times daily, keeping it damp until the condition is relieved.

Contraindications: **Do not use Liu Shen Wan during pregnancy.**

Liu Shen Wan		
Constituent Substances		
Pinyin Name	**Pharmaceutical Name**	**%Composition**
Niu Huang	*Calculus Bovis*	20.0
She Xiang	*Secretio Moschi Moschiferi*	20.0
Zhen Zhu	*Margarita*	20.0
Chan Su	*Secretio Bufonia*	13.3
Bing Pian	*Borneolum*	13.3
Xiong Huang	*Realgar*	13.3

Composition and Rationale: The six herbs in **Liu Shen Wan** (the "Six Spirits" from which it derives its name) are somewhat unusual and relatively expensive. The formula is comprised solely of animal parts and minerals, and contains no vegetable products. Each substance contributes toward a single focus: resolving fire toxin. In addition, *She Xiang* reduces inflammation, *Zhen Zhu* promotes tissue regeneration, *Chan Su* relieves pain, and *Xiong Huang* reduces swelling.

Fu Fang Xi Gua Shuang   7.12
復方西瓜霜
Compound Formula Watermelon Frost

Source: *Yang Yi Da Quan (The Complete Works for the Treatment of Sores)*, Qing Dynasty (1644-1911).

Primary Functions and Applications: **Fu Fang Xi Gua Shuang** eliminates swelling and relieves pain. It is used in the treatment of diseases of the mouth, including mouth sores, stomatitis, and ulcers in the mouth or on the tongue. It cools blood heat and soothes the throat. Used topically, it is effective in the treatment of toothache and throat infections. It may also be used effectively to treat burns of the skin.

Format and Administration: **Fu Fang Xi Gua Shuang** is produced by the Kweilin Drug Manufactory, Kwangsi, China, as *Water Melon Frost*, in 2-gram vials, 6 vials per box. The primary ingredient in this formula, watermelon "frost," is produced by a special process. An entire watermelon is cut into small pieces, mixed with Na_2SO_4 and $NaNO_3$, and sealed inside a clay jar, which is then placed in a well ventilated area. In time, the liquid from the mixture seeps through the clay jar, forming crystals on the jar's outer surface. These crystals, called *Xi Gua Shuang*, are scraped off as they accumulate until the crystallization process has ceased.

Each vial contains 2 grams. When used internally, take 1-2 grams with water twice or 3 times a day. To apply topically, the powder may be blown through a short straw or rubber atomizer every 2 or 3 hours. Alternatively, mix 2 vials of powder with cooking oil and apply topically for a few days until the burn is healed. Topical and internal use may be administered concurrently. Do not eat greasy, oily food when taking this medication.

Fu Fang Xi Gua Shang		
Constituent Substances		
Pinyin Name	**Pharmaceutical Name**	**% Composition**
Xi Gua Shuang	*Mirabilitum Praeparatum Citrulli*	50
Chuan Bei Mu	*Bulbus Fritillariae Cirrhosae*	12
Huang Bai	*Cortex Phellodendri*	8
Bo He Nao	*Herba Menthae (Crystal)*	4
Huang Lian	*Rhizoma Coptidis*	12
Huang Qin	*Radix Scutellaria*	8
Bing Pian	*Borneolum*	4
Zhu Sha	*Cinnabaris*	2

Zhong Guo Ji Ben Zhong Chen Yao (Fundamentals of Chinese Prepared Medicines, 1988) lists a related, though simpler, medicine, **Xi Gua Shang**, as its standardized formulae formula for **Fu Fang Xi Gua Shuang**.

Composition and Rationale: Xi Gua Shuang relieves pain and reduces swelling. *Huang Bai, Bo He Nao, Huang Lian* and *Huang Qin* clear heat and resolve fire toxin. *Chuan Bei Mu* clears heat and moistens the lungs. *Bing Pian* relieves pain and *Zhu Sha* clears heat and calms the spirit.

7.13

Long Dan Xie Gan Wan †
龍膽瀉肝丸
Gentian Liver-Draining Pills

Source: Yi Zong Jin Jian (The Golden Mirror of Medicine), Qing Dynasty (1644-1911).

Primary Functions and Applications: **Long Dan Xie Gan Wan** discharges hepatocystic damp-heat accumulation and replete liver fire, and may be used to drain liver fire in the upper portion of the body. Guiding symptoms include red, swollen eyes, headache, a bitter taste in the mouth, earache and sudden deafness. Pain in the hypochondriac region may also be present. Due to damp-heat accumulation, the urine may be dark and scanty. When signs of liver fire repletion and damp-heat accumulation are present, **Long Dan Xie Gan Wan** is effective in cases of acute conjunctivitis, acute otitis media, acute nasal furuncle, acute furuncle in the external auditory canal, hypertension due to upflaming liver fire, acute hepatitis with jaundice, acute cholecystitis, acute pyelonephritis, acute cystitis, acute urethritis, acute pelvic inflammatory disease, acute vulvitis, and prostatitis.

Format and Administration: **Long Dan Xie Gan Wan** is available in pill form, 100 per bottle.

Contraindications: Most substances in this formula have a bitter taste (cold property), and, if used for a long period of time, may damage the spleen or stomach. Therefore, use of **Long Dan Xie Gan Wan** should be stopped promptly following recovery.

Recommended Dosage: Ten pills, 3 times a day.

Long Dan Xie Gan Wan		
Constituent Substances		
Pinyin Name	**Pharmaceutical Name**	**% Composition**
Long Dan Cao	*Radix Gentianae*	15.38
Shan Zhi Zi	*Fructus Gardeniae Jasminoidis*	7.69
Huang Qin	*Radix Scutellaria*	7.69
Mu Tong	*Caulis Mutong*	7.69
Che Qian Zi	*Semen Plantaginis*	7.69
Zi Xie	*Buthus Martensi*	15.00
Chai Hu	*Radix Bupleuri*	15.30
Dang Gui	*Radix Angelicae Sinensis*	7.69
Sheng Di Huang	*Radix Crudae Rehmanniae Glutinosae*	7.69
Gan Cao	*Radix Glycyrrhizae Uralensis*	7.69

Composition and Rationale: The formula used in this medicine is particularly well-organized. Included are the sovereign medicine *(Long Dan Cao)*; minister medicines *(Zhi Zi, Huang Qin, Zi Xie, Mu Tong,* and *Che Qian Zi)*; assistant medicines *(Chai Hu, Dang Gui,* and *Shen Di Huang)*; and a guide medicine *(Gan Cao)*. Whenever herbs are used to discharge damp-heat, additional herbs are also used to supplement the blood and enrich the yin to prevent possible side effects from the strong cooling medicines.

Long Dan, Zhi Zi, and *Huang Qin* discharge damp-heat repletion in the liver and gallbladder; the assistant herbs *Quan Xie, Ze Hie, Mu Tong*, and *Che Qian Zi* clear heat, promote urination and discharge accumulated damp-heat; *Quan Xie*, and *Chai Hu* smooth and regulate liver qi; *Quan Xie, Dang Gui*, and *Sheng Di Huang* strengthen the blood and nourish the liver; *Quan Xie* and *Gan Cao* harmonize the other herbs.

7.14 Jiang Ya Ping Pian
降壓平片
Hypotensor and Normalizing Tablets

Primary Functions and Applications: **Jiang Ya Ping Pian** clears liver heat, settles replete liver yang, and reduces internal wind. It is primarily used to treat atherosclerosis, and will lower high cholesterol levels in the blood. It is indicated in cases of hypertension, especially in its early stages, when the blood vessels are not yet very hard (i.e., the atherosclerosis is not yet severe). In such cases, the high blood pressure will not yet have affected the function of the heart, brain, or kidney. Reduction in blood pressure should be observed within two weeks of treatment, and such symptoms as dizziness, headache, tinnitus, and irritability will all improve during that time.

Format and Administration: **Jiang Ya Ping Pian** is produced by the Liao Yuan Pharmaceutical Works as *Hypertension Repressing Tablets* in coated tablet format, 12 tablets per tube, 12 tubes per box.

Recommended Dosage: Four tablets, 3 times a day over at least 3 two-week courses. After the first course, the high blood pressure should be reduced. After the second and third courses, the blood pressure should be within normal limits. If blood pressure has not been reduced sufficiently after three courses, continue for a few more courses. This medicine can be taken as long as necessary, even for several years, with no negative side effects.

Jiang Ya Ping Pian		
Constituent Substances		
Pinyin Name	Pharmaceutical Name	% Composition
Xia Ku Cao	*Spica Prunellae*	25
Huang Qin	*Radix Scutellaria*	25
Di Long	*Lumbricus*	20
Ju Hua	*Flos Chrysanthemi Indicae Morifolii*	15
Huai Hua	*Flos Sophorae Japonicae*	15

Composition and Rationale: *Xia Ku Cao* clears liver heat, disperses liver fire and decreases blood pressure; *Huang Qin* clears heat, disperses fire, lowers blood pressure, and calms the patient; *Di Long* clears liver heat, calms wind and lowers blood pressure; *Ju Hua* clears liver heat, extinguishes wind and dilates the coronary arteries; *Huai Hua* cools the blood, lowers blood pressure, treats atherosclerosis, and reduces the fragility of small blood vessels.

Jiang Ya Wan
降壓丸
Hypotensor Pills

7.15

Source: This formula was developed by Dr. Shih Chinmo, a 20th-century physician.

Primary Functions and Applications: **Jiang Ya Wan** clears heat from yang repletion, lowers high blood pressure in cases with yang repletion, calms internal wind, and promotes blood circulation. It is used to treat hypertension due to repletion heat or internal wind, and is indicated in the presence of such symptoms as hypertension with dizziness, uneasiness, neck stiffness, distention-type headaches, and red face. It may also be used to treat hypertensive patients of an excessive type who are in a pre-stroke condition, having already had one or more transient ischemic attacks resulting in temporary neurological symptoms such as facial or limb paralysis, diminished visual field, and abnormal sensations in the face or limbs.

Jiang Ya Wan may be used for patients who are in either early or more developed stages of hypertension. It is effective for the hypertensive patient who has developed such central nervous system disorders as headache, dizziness, facial paralysis, numbness, and speech problems.

Contraindications: **Do not use Jiang Ya Wan during pregnancy.** Use this herb formula in yang repletion cases only. It contains herbs to promote blood circulation, remove stasis, and resolve counterflow qi. Use of **Jiang Ya Wan** should be suspended temporarily if the patient experiences an invasion of exogenous wind-cold, since the formula contains herbs of a cold nature. This medicine may cause loose stools.

Format and Administration: **Jiang Ya Wan** is produced by the Beijing Tong Ren Tang in pill format, 200 pills per bottle.

Recommended Dosage: Twenty pills, twice a day, with warm water.

Jiang Ya Wan		
Constituent Substances		
Pinyin Name	**Pharmaceutical Name**	**% Composition**
Chong Yu Zi	*Semen Leonuri Heterophylli*	15
Huang Lian	*Rhizoma Coptidis*	3
Ling Yang Jiao	*Cornu Antelopis*	3
Gou Teng	*Ramulus et Uncus Uncariae*	7
Hu Po	*Succinum*	3
Dang Gui	*Radix Angelicae Sinensis*	8
Chen Xiang	*Lignum Aquilariae*	5
Chuan Xiong	*Rhizoma Ligustici Wallichii*	5
Tian Ma	*Rhizoma Gastrodiae Elatae*	4
Da Huang	*Rhizoma Rhei*	4
Sheng Di Huang	*Radix Crudae Rehmanniae Glutinosae*	10
A Jiao	*Gelatinum Corii Asini*	10
Xia Ku Cao	*Spica Prunellae*	5
Mu Dan Pi	*Cortex Radicis Mouton*	5
Niu Xi	*Radix Achyranthes Bidentatae*	13

Composition and Rationale: *Chong Yu Zi* clears liver heat and promotes blood circulation; *Huang Lian* clears heat; *Ling Yang Jiao* clears liver heat and extinguishes liver wind; *Gou Teng* clears liver heat, extinguishes liver wind, clears the channels, and reduces blood pressure; *Hu Po* calms the spirit, promotes blood circulation, and promotes urination;

Dang Gui supplements the blood and removes blood stasis; *Chen Xiang* moves stagnant qi; *Chuan Xiong* promotes blood circulation and relieves headache; *Tian Ma* expels liver wind and clears the channels; *Da Huang* clears heat and relieves constipation; *Sheng Di Huang* clears heat and cools the blood; *A Jiao* nourishes the blood and yin; *Xia Ku Cao* clears liver heat and lowers blood pressure; *Mu Dan Pi* clears heat, promotes blood circulation, and lowers blood pressure; *Niu Xi* removes blood stasis, promotes blood circulation, and lowers blood pressure.

Du Zhong Pian
杜仲片
Eucommia Tablets

7.16

Primary Functions and Applications: **Du Zhong Pian** nourishes kidney yang, lowers high blood pressure in cases of kidney yang depletion, lowers blood cholesterol levels, reduces hardening of the arteries, and calms the spirit and the mind. It is used to treat earlier stages of high blood pressure in cases of kidney yang depletion, with such symptoms as pale face, sensations of coldness, and lumbago. Limb numbness and/or edema may also be present. In addition, **Du Zhong Pian** is used to treat earlier stages of high blood pressure in cases with liver-wind repletion syndrome. Symptoms in such cases will include agitation, uneasiness, insomnia, and excessive anger.

Format and Administration: **Du Zhong Pian** is produced by the Kweichow United Pharmaceutical Manufactory as *Compound Cortex Eucommia Tablets*, available as coated tablets, 100 per bottle.

Recommended Dosage: Five tablets, 3 times a day with warm water. It is common to combine this medicine with anti-hypertensive Western medicine. With its use, the amount of Western medicine may be reduced or eliminated. However, it is important to carefully monitor the blood pressure during treatment. **Reduction of medications should only be accomplished in consultation with the prescribing physician.** This herbal formula will have a gradual effect in reducing the blood pressure. It has no side effects and may be prescribed for an extended period of time.

Du Zhong Pian		
Constituent Substances		
Pinyin Name	**Pharmaceutical Name**	**% Composition**
Du Zhong	*Cortex Eucommiae Ulmoidis*	50
Gou Teng	*Ramulus et Uncus Uncariae*	20
Huang Qin	*Radix Scutellaria*	10
Xia Ku Cao	*Spica Prunellae Vulgaris*	20

Composition and Rationale: Du Zhong strengthens the liver and kidneys, lowers blood pressure, and calms the spirit; *Gou Teng* calms liver wind, lowers blood pressure, and tranquilizes the spirit; *Huang Qin* clears heat, calms the spirit, and lowers blood pressure; and *Xia Ku Cao* lowers blood pressure and clears liver heat and liver yang repletion.

7.17　Huang Lian Yang Gan Wan †
黃連羊肝丸
Coptis and Goat's Liver Pills

Source: Tai Ping Hui Ming He Ji Ju Fang *(Formularies of the People's Welfare Pharmacies),* Song Dynasty, 960-1279.

Primary Functions and Applications: **Huang Lian Yang Gan Wan** disperses liver fire and brightens the eyes. It is used to treat eye disorders due to upflaming liver fire, with such symptoms as poor vision (especially at night), photophobia, pterygium, headache, dizziness, bitter taste in the mouth, restlessness, and redness of the eyes. It is important to note that this formula is effective for eye disorders such as glaucoma, cataracts, or nightblindness only when they are accompanied by upflaming liver fire or ascendant hyperactivity of liver yang.

Format and Administration: **Huang Lian Yang Gan Wan** is produced by the Beijing Tung Ren Tang as 9-gram honey pills.

Recommended Dosage: One honey pill, twice a day.

Huang Lian Yang Gan Wan		
Constituent Substances		
Pinyin Name	Pharmaceutical Name	% Composition
Huang Lian	*Rhizoma Coptidis*	3.23
Mi Meng Hua	*Flos Buddleiae Officinalis*	6.45
Jue Ming Zi	*Semen Cassiae Torae*	6.45
Shi Jue Ming	*Concha Haliotidis*	6.45
Chong Wei Zi	*Semen Leonuri Heterophylli*	6.45
Ye Ming Sha	*Excrementum Vespertilionis*	6.45
Long Dan Cao	*Radix Gentianae*	3.23
Huang Bai	*Cortex Phellodendri*	3.23
Huang Qin	*Radix Scutellaria*	6.45
Hu Huang Lian	*Radix Picrorhizae*	6.45
Chai Hu	*Radix Bupleuri*	6.45
Qing Pi	*Pericarpium Citri Reticulatae Viride*	6.45
Mu Zei	*Herba Equiseti Hieinalis*	6.45
Yang Gan	*Iecur Caprae seu Ovis*	25.81

The standardized formula for **Huang Lian Yang Gan Wan** in *Zhong Guo Ji Ben Zhong Chen Yao (Fundamentals of Chinese Prepared Medicines, 1988)* contains *Huang Lian, Mi Meng Hua, Jue Ming Zi, Shi Jue Ming, Long Dan Cao, Chai Hu,* and *Yang Gan.*

Composition and Rationale: *Huang Lian* clears heat and resolves fire toxin; *Mi Meng Hua* and *Chong Wei Zi* cool the liver, brighten the eyes, and remove pterygium; *Jue Ming Zi* clears heat in the liver and large intestine, brightens the eyes, and moves bulk in the intestinal tract; *Shi Jue Ming* clears liver heat, reduces liver yang repletion, and brightens the eyes; *Ye Ming Sha* clears heat, nourishes the eyes, and improves night vision (due to high levels of vitamin A); *Long Dan Cao* clears liver heat; *Hu Huang Lian, Huang Qin,* and *Huang Bai* clear heat and resolve fire toxin; *Chai Hu* smoothes the liver and frees binding depression of liver qi; *Qing Pi* treats depression; *Mu Zei* expels wind-heat and reduces pterygium; and *Yang Gan* nourishes liver yin and improves vision.

7.18

Li Gan Pian
利肝片
Liver-Disinhibiting Tablets

Primary Functions and Applications: **Li Gan Pian** clears heat, soothes the liver, and clears the bile ducts. It is used to treat acute hepatitis with or without jaundice, and to treat chronic hepatitis and chronic cholecystitis, while ameliorating symptoms by relieving pain in the region of the liver.

Format and Administration: **Li Gan Pian** is produced by the Zhenjiang Chinese Medicine Works as *Liver-Strengthening Tablets*, available 100 per bottle.

Recommended Dosage: Two to 4 pills, 3 times a day after meals.

Li Gan Pian		
Constituent Substances		
Pinyin Name	**Pharmaceutical Name**	**% Composition**
Jin Qian Cao	*Herba Jinqiancao*	70
Niu Dan	*Fellis Bovis*	30

Composition and Rationale: *Jin Qian Cao* clears heat, reduces jaundice, promotes urination, and expels urinary tract or biliary stones; and *Niu Dan* clears heat, reduces liver and gallbladder inflammation, and assists in the digestion of fat.

Li Dan Pian †

利膽片

Gallbladder-Disinhibiting Tablets

7.19

Primary Functions and Applications: **Li Dan Pian** clears the bile ducts and reduces inflammation. It is used to treat acute jaundice from hepatocystic damp-heat (yang jaundice), and acute or chronic inflammation in the bile ducts and cholecystitis. In the treatment of gallstones (cholecystolithiasis), it helps expel stones less than 1 cm in diameter.

Format and Administration: **Li Dan Pian** is produced by the Tsingtao Pharmaceutical Works, Tsingtao, China, as tablets, 120 per bottle.

Recommended Dosage: Four to 6 pills, 3 times a day.

Li Dan Pian		
Constituent Substances		
Pinyin Name	**Pharmaceutical Name**	**% Composition**
Huang Qin	*Radix Scutellaria*	30
Mu Xiang	*Radix Muhsiang*	16
Jin Qian Cao	*Herba Jinqiancao*	10
Jin Yin Hua	*Flos Lonicerae Japonicae*	10
Yin Chen Hao	*Folium Artemisiae Capillaris*	10
Chai Hu	*Radix Bupleuri*	10
Da Qing Ye	*Folium Ta Ch'ing Yeh*	10
Da Huang	*Rhizoma Rhei*	4

The standardized formula for **Li Dan Pian** in *Zhong Guo Ji Ben Zhong Chen Yao (Fundamentals of Chinese Prepared Medicines, 1988)* contains *Bai Shao, Mu Xiang, Yin Chen Hao, Da Qing Ye,* and *Da Huang.*

Composition and Rationale: *Huang Qin* and *Da Qing Ye* clear heat, reduce inflammation, and resolve fire toxin; *Mu Xiang* moves stagnant qi and relieves pain; *Jin Qian Cao* clears heat, reduces jaundice, promotes urination, and expels urinary tract or biliary stones; *Jin Yin Hua* clears heat and reduces inflammation; *Yin Chen* clears damp heat and reduces jaundice; *Chai Hu* frees bound liver qi and clears bile ducts; and *Da Huang* clears intestinal heat and promotes bowel movement.

7.20 Hou Yan Wan †
喉炎丸
Laryngitis Pills

Primary Functions and Applications: **Hou Yan Wan** clears heat, resolves fire toxin, and relieves pain. It is used to treat spasms or seizures from high fever or central nervous system infection in children. It is used both internally and externally in the treatment of furuncles or carbuncles of the skin, especially when they are red, swollen, and without pus.

Hou Yan Wan was developed in the 1960's as a substutute for **Liu Shen Wan (7.11)** due to the expense and shortage of *She Xiang (Secretio Moschi Moschiferi)*.

Format and Administration:

Recommended Dosage, Internal: Adults, ten pills with warm water, 3 times a day.

Children, with warm water, three times a day: 1 year old, 1 pill each time; 2 years old, 2 pills each time; 3 years old, 3-4 pills each time; 4-8 years old, 5-6 pills each time; 9-15 years of age, 7-9 pills each time.

Recommended Dosage, External: Mix at least 10 pills in a small amount of cold water or vinegar, and apply the resultant mixture to the outer edge of the red and swollen area. Cover the affected area with gauze moistened with a saline solution. It is important to keep the area wet, otherwise the herbal medicine will not be absorbed. Store the unused solution in the refrigerator. Apply several times a day until the swelling and infection have disappeared.

Contraindications: **Do not use Hou Yan Wan during pregnancy.** Do not apply topically if the furuncle or carbuncle has become an open wound with pus.

Hou Yan Wan		
Constituent Substances		
Pinyin Name	**Pharmaceutical Name**	**% Composition**
Xi Jiao	*Cornu Rhinocerotis*	--
Xiong Dan	*Vesica Fel Ursi*	--
Niu Huang	*Calculus Bovis*	--
Huang Lian	*Rhizoma Coptidis*	--
Peng Sha	*Borax*	--

The standardized formula for **Huo Yan Wan** in *Zhong Guo Ji Ben Zhong Chen Yao (Fundamentals of Chinese Prepared Medicines, 1988)* contains *Xi Jiao, Xiong Dan, Niu Huang, Zhen Zhu,* and *She Xiang.*

Dao Chi Pian 7.21
導赤片
Red-Abducting Tablets

Source: *Xiao Er Yao Zheng Zhi Jue (Pediatric Pharmaceutics),* Song Dynasty (960-1279).

Primary Functions and Applications: **Dao Chi Pian** clears heat, reduces repletion heat, and promotes bowel movement and urination. It is used to treat symptoms of repletion heat in the heart channel, including swollen and sore throat, mouth or tongue sores (stomatitis), swollen gums with toothache, conjunctivitis, and difficult, burning, or painful passing of dark yellow urine. It is also indicated in cases of repletion heat in the stomach or large intestine, causing constipation, and in the treatment of bacterial infection of the urinary tract, including cystitis, urethritis, or pyelitis.

The word red (*chi*) in the name of this herbal formula refers to the heart, by association with its color in classical Chinese medical theory. *Dao* literally means "to abduct," and refers to the removal of pathogens after they have been dispersed. Thus, the formulae name **Dao Chi Pian**,

"Heat-Abducting Tablets," harkens to its primary function of clearing the heart and draining fire in the heart channel. Further, since the heart is paired with the small intestine, and the small intestine relates to the general function of the urinary tract, *Dao Chi* indicates the formula's applicability in the treatment of the disorder known as "heat pouring down from the heart into the small intestine," a category of urinary tract infection.

Format and Administration: **Dao Chi Pian** is produced by the Tianjin Drug Manufactory as *Tao Chih Pien (for Babies)* in tubes of 8 tablets. It was originally available as a 3 gram honey-pill.

Recommended Dosage: One honey-pill, or 3-5 tablets, twice a day.

In cases of urinary tract infection with bleeding, an herbal conductor (*yao yin*) of *Bai Mao Gen (Rhizoma Imperatae Cylindricae)* should be taken. Simmer 30 grams of the herb in 1 cup of water until ½ cup remains, and drink warm.

Contraindication: **Do not use Dao Chi Pian during pregnancy.** Do not use with a weak patient or a patient who has diarrhea.

Dao Chi Pian		
Constituent Substances		
Pinyin Name	Pharmaceutical Name	% Composition
Sheng Di Huang	*Radix Rehmanniae Glutinosae*	15.69
Da Huang	*Rhizoma Rhei*	29.41
Mu Tong	*Caulis Mutong*	7.84
Shan Zhi Zi	*Fructus Gardeniae Jasminoidis*	23.53
Fu Ling	*Sclerotium Poriae Cocus*	7.84
Hua Shi	*Talcum*	7.84
Gan Cao	*Radix Glycyrrhizae Uralensis*	7.84

Composition and Rationale: *Sheng Di Huang* clears heat, nourishes yin and reduces heart fire; *Da Huang* clears heat, resolves fire toxin, and promotes fecal flow; *Mu Tong, Zhi Zi, Fu Ling,* and *Hua Shi* clear heat in the heart, relieve painful urination, and discharge heat through urination; and *Gan Cao* harmonizes the other herbs, clears heat and relieves painful urination.

Huai Jiao Wan †
槐角丸
Sophora Fruit Pills

Source: Dan Xi Xin Fa (Methods of Dr. Dan Xi), Yuan Dynasty.

Primary Functions and Applications: **Huai Jiao Wan** clears damp in the large intestine, and is used to control intestinal bleeding where there is fresh blood with or without stool, and to control hemorrhoidal bleeding. It is effective in the treatment of intestinal bleeding with repletion heat symptoms, such as burning sensations around the anus, constipation or incomplete sensation following bowel movement (indicative of damp heat in the large intestine), thirst, and a rapid pulse.

Format and Administration: **Huai Jiao Wan** is produced by the Min-Kang Drug Manufactory as *Fructus Sophorae Japonicae.* It is available in pill format, 100 per bottle.

Recommended Dosage: Nine pills, twice a day.

Huai Jiao Wan		
Constituent Substances		
Pinyin Name	**Pharmaceutical Name**	**% Composition**
Huai Jiao	*Fructus Sophorae Japonicae*	28.5
Zhi Qiao	*Fructus Citri seu Ponciri*	14.3
Dang Gui	*Radix Angelicae Sinensis*	14.3
Di Yu	*Radix Sanguisorbae Officinalis*	14.3
Fang Feng	*Herba Ledebouriellae Sesloidis*	14.3
Huang Qin	*Radix Scutellaria*	14.3

Composition and Rationale: *Huai Jiao* clears heat and controls bleeding; *Zhi Qiao* moves stagnant qi and reduces distension; *Dang Gui* supplements the blood and regulates blood function; *Di Yu* cools the blood and controls bleeding; *Fang Feng* eliminates wind in the large intestine and controls bleeding; and *Huang Qin* clears heat and reduces swelling.

7.23   Hua Zhi Ling Wan
化痔靈丸
Hemorrhoidal Pills

Primary Functions and Applications: **Hua Zhi Ling Wan** clears heat, cools blood, reduces swelling, and relieves pain. It is used to treat hemorrhoids from damp-heat collecting in the lower warmer, with such symptoms as swelling, redness, and severe pain. It controls hemorrhoidal bleeding, and reduces the bleeding, pain, and swelling of anal prolapse.

Format and Administration: **Hua Zhi Ling Wan** is produced by the United Pharmaceutical Manufactory as *Fargelin for Piles*, and is available as coated tablets, 60 per bottle.

Recommended Dosage: Four to six pills, 3 times a day.

Hua Zhi Ling Wan		
Constituent Substances		
Pinyin Name	**Pharmaceutical Name**	**% Composition**
Wen Ge	*Concha Meretricis*	30
Shi Liu Pi	*Flos et Pericarpium Punicae Granati*	30
Huang Lian	*Rhizoma Coptidis*	10
Tian Qi	*Radix Pseudoginseng*	17
Xiong Dan	*Vesica Fel Ursi*	3
Hu Po	*Succinum*	10
Huai Hua	*Flos Sophorae Japonicae*	—
Wu Bei Zi	*Galla Rhi Chinensis et Potaninii*	—
Xiong Huang	*Realgar*	—

Some formulae omit *Huai Hua, Wu Bei Zi* and *Xiong Huang*.

Composition and Rationale: *Wen Ge* and *Shi Lin Pi* are astringents, and control bleeding and prolapse; *Huang Lian* clears heat and resolves fire toxin; *Tian Qi* controls bleeding and reduces pain; *Xiong Dan* clears heat and cools blood; *Hu Po* disperses static blood and aids in tissue regeneration; *Huai Hua* controls intestinal bleeding and clears heat; *Wu Bei Zi* has an astringent effect and reduces prolapse; and *Xiong Huang* resolves fire toxin in the intestines.

Qiang Li Hua Zhi Ling

7.24

強力化痔靈
Extra Strength Hemorrhoidal

Primary Functions and Applications: **Qiang Li Hua Zhi Ling** clears heat, relieves pain, and controls bleeding. It is a stronger medicine than the previous formula, **Hua Zhi Ling Wan (7.23)**, and contains more hemostatic herbs. It is used to treat internal and/or external hemorrhoids and anal prolapse, and will help control bleeding, reduce pain, and prevent infection.

Format and Administration: **Qiang Li Hua Zhi Ling** is produced by the United Pharmaceutical Manufactory as *High Strength Fargelin for Piles* in coated tablet format, 30 per bottle.

Recommended Dosage: Three to four pills, 3 times a day. For serious cases, double the dose. For best results, use for at least 3 days.

Qiang Li Hua Zhi Ling		
Constituent Substances		
Pinyin Name	**Pharmaceutical Name**	**% Composition**
Hu Po	*Succinum*	15
Xiong Dan	*Vesica Fel Ursi*	5
Tian Qi	*Radix Pseudoginseng*	20
Huang Qin	*Radix Scutellaria*	15
Yan Hu Suo	*Tuber Corydalis Yanhusuo*	5
Di Yu	*Radix Sanguisorbae Officinalis*	10
Huai Hua	*Flos Sophorae Japonicae*	15
Zi Zhu Cao	*Folium Callicarpae Pedunculatae*	15

Composition and Rationale: *Hu Po* disperses static blood and aids in tissue regeneration; *Xiong Dan* clears heat and cools blood; *Tian Qi* controls bleeding and relieves pain; *Huang Qin* clears heat and resolves fire toxin; *Yuan Hu* relieves pain; *Di Yu* controls bleeding; *Huai Hua* controls bleeding and cools the blood; and *Zi Zhu Cao* controls bleeding and reduces inflammation.

7.25

Zhi Wan
痔丸
Hemorrhoid Pills

Source: *Yang Yi Da Chuen (Complete Book of Dermatology)*, Qing Dynasty, 1644-1911.

Primary Functions and Applications: **Zhi Wan** clears heat and reduces swelling. It is used to reduce infected hemorrhoids, to control hemorrhoidal bleeding, and to reduce inflammed, bleeding, infected anal abscesses by discharging the pus and regenerating the tissue. It is especially effective in the treatment of hardened, thrombosed hemorrhoids (i.e., hemorrhoids containing clotted blood.) Pain is primary in these conditions. In addition to pain accompanying bowel movement, there is pain when sitting, walking, or coughing. When the hemorrhoid is examined, it will appear hard, with a round, purple-colored node.

Format and Administration: **Zhi Wan** is produced by the Min-Kang Drug Manufactory in pill format, 100 pills per bottle.

Recommended Dosage: Six pills, twice to 3 times a day.

Zhi Wan		
Constituent Substances		
Pinyin Name	Pharmaceutical Name	% Composition
Ci Wei Pi	*Corium Erinacei seu Hemiechini*	18.8
Chuan Shan Jia	*Squama Manitisg*	1.5
Jin Yin Hua	*Flos Lonicerae Japonicae*	18.8
Hong Hua	*Flos Carthami Tinctorii*	3.7
Huai Hua	*Flos Sophorae Japonicae*	18.8
Bin Lang	*Semen Arecae Acacia seu Catechu*	4.7
Ru Xiang	*Gummi Olibanum*	2.8
Mo Yao	*Myrrha*	1.5
Bai Zhi	*Radix Angelicae*	2.8
—	*Unspecified substances*	to 100%

Composition and Rationale: *Ci Wei Pi* controls hemorrhoidal bleeding; *Chuan Shan Jia* moves static blood and reduces swelling; *Jin Yin Hua* clears heat and resolves fire toxin; *Hong Hua* moves the blood and eliminates swelling; *Huai Hua* controls bleeding and cools the blood; *Bin Lang* moves stagnant qi; *Mo Yao* and *Ru Xiang* promote blood circulation, relieve pain, and reduce the hemorrhoidal swelling; and *Bai Zhi* reduces swelling, relieves pain, and expels pus.

Chuan Xin Lian Kang Yan Pian 7.26
川心蓮抗炎片
Andrographis Anti-Inflammatory Tablets

Primary Functions and Applications: **Chuan Xin Lian Kang Yan Pian** clears heat and reduces inflammation in the upper, middle, and lower burners. It is used to treat upper-warmer inflammation in common colds and flu, and to clear lung heat, relieving such symptoms as yellow sputum with cough and/or chronic asthma, pulmonary abscess, pneumonia, tuberculosis, and other infections.

In addition, **Chuan Xin Lian Kang Yan Pian** clears heat and eliminates damp associated with damp-heat urinary tract infection, diarrhea, or dysentery.

Pharmacological research in China suggests that this herbal formula inhibits the growth of bacillus dysentery virus, streptococcus bacteria, staphlococcus bacteria, and diplococcus bacteria (as seen in pneumonia).

Format and Administration: **Chuan Xin Lian Kang Yan Pian** is produced by the United Pharmaceutical Manufactory, Guangzhou, China, as *Chuan Xin Lian Antiphlogistic Tablets*, and are available as coated tablets, 36 per bottle.

Recommended Dosage: Two to three pills, 3 times a day.

Chuan Xin Lian Kang Yan Pian		
Constituent Substances		
Pinyin Name	Pharmaceutical Name	% Composition
Chuan Xin Lian	*Herba Andrographis Paniculatae*	50
Pu Gong Ying	*Herba cum Radice Taraxaci Mongolici*	25
Ban Lan Gen	*Radix Isatidis seu Baphicanthi*	25

Composition and Rationale: *Chuan Xin Lian* clears heat; *Pu Gong Ying* and *Ban Lan Ge* clear heat and resolve fire toxin; and *Ban Lan Gen* clears blood heat.

7.27 Niu Huang Xiao Yan Wan
牛黃消炎丸
Bovine Bezoar Anti-Inflammatory Pills

Primary Functions and Applications: **Niu Huang Xiao Yan Wan** clears heat and relieves inflammation and fever due to fire toxin. Often used as a substitute for **Liu Shen Wan (7.11)**, it is recommended in cases of serious tonsillitis and pharyngitis, with throat swelling and pain associated with fire toxin. Pus may be present in these cases. It is also commonly used in cases of such skin infections as carbuncles and sores, and for the treatment of mastitis.

Format and Administration: **Niu Huang Xiao Yan Wan** is produced by the Kiangsu Soochow Chinese Medicine Works as tiny pills, 60 per vial, 10 vials per box.

Recommended Dosage: Ten pills, 3 times a day for adults. Children under 5 years, use one quarter the dose or less; over 5 years, one half the dose or less.

For External Use: Crush the pills into powder and use directly, or mix with a small amount of vinegar and place on the sore once a day. Cover affected area with a sterile dressing.

Contraindications: **Do not use Niu Wan Xiao Yan Wan during pregnancy.** This formula may be used by nursing mothers, but may cause diarrhea in the child.

Niu Huang Xiao Yan Wan		
Constituent Herbs		
Pinyin Name	Pharmaceutical Name	% Composition
Niu Huang	*Calculus Bovis*	9.61
Jen Zhu Mu	*Concha Margaritifera Usta*	19.23
Tian Hua Fen	*Radix Tricosanthis*	19.23
Da Huang	*Rhizoma Rhei*	19.23
Qing Dai	*Indigo Puloverata Levis*	7.69
Xiong Huang	*Realgar*	19.81

Composition and Rationale: Niu Huang, Tian Hua Fen, Qing Dai, and *Xiong Huang* clear heat and resolve fire toxin. *Jen Zhu Mu* clears liver heat and calms the spirit. *Tian Hua Fen* reduces swelling and helps discharge pus. *Da Huang* disperses heat through bowel movement. *Qing Dai* clears heat in the blood and reduces throat swelling. *Xiong Huang* reduces inflammation.

Lian Qiao Bai Du Pian † 7.28
連翹敗毒片
Forsythia Toxin-Vanquishing Tablets

Source: Zheng Zhi Zhun Sheng (Standards for Diagnosis and Treatment), Ming Dynasty, 1368-1644.

Primary Functions and Applications: **Lian Qiao Bai Tu Pian** clears heat, reduces inflammation, eliminates swelling, and relieves pain. It is primarily used for carbuncles in their early stages, where the skin is red but has not yet erupted, and in the presence of pain. If pus is present, this medicine will help in its discharge. **Lian Qiao Bai Tu Pian** will effectively clear wind-heat, and may be used to treat skin infections, inflammations (including carbuncles, boils, and poison ivy), and eruptions (such as itchy skin caused by allergies and wind-heat psoriasis).

Format and Administration: **Lian Qiao Bai Tu Pian** is produced by the Tientsin Drug Manufactory as *Lienchiaopaitu Pien* available in both syrup (for children) and pill form.

Recommended Dosage: Four to five tablets, or 2 teaspoons, 3 times a day.

Contraindications: **Do not use Lian Qiao Bai Tu Pian during pregnancy.** Avoid greasy, spicy food while taking this medication.

Lian Qiao Bai Du Pian		
Constituent Substances		
Pinyin Name	Pharmaceutical Name	% Composition
Jin Yin Hua	*Flos Lonicerae Japonicae*	13.78
Shan Zhi Zi	*Fructus Gardeniae Jasminoidis*	10.34
Huang Qin	*Radix Scutellaria*	10.34
Chi Shao Yao	*Radix Paeoniae Rubra*	10.34
Bai Xian Pi	*Dictamni Dasycarpi Radicis, Cortex*	10.34
Lian Qiao	*Fructus Forsythiae Suspensae*	13.78
Chan Tui	*Periostracum Cicadae*	6.96
Fang Feng	*Herba Ledebouriellae Sesloidis*	10.34
Da Huang	*Rhizoma Rhei*	13.78

The standardized formula for **Lian Qiao Bai Du Pian** in *Zhong Guo Ji Ben Zhong Chen Yao (Fundamentals of Chinese Prepared Medicines, 1988)* adds the following herbs: *Pu Gong Ying, Zhe Bei Mu, Jie Geng, Bai Zhi, Mu Tong, Tian Hua Fen, Bai Zhi, Di Ding, Xuan Shen*, and *Gan Cao.*

Composition and Rationale: *Jin Yin Hua, Zhi Zi, Huang Qin*, and *Lian Qiao* clear heat and resolve fire toxin; *Chi Shao Yao* clears heat, cools the blood, and disperses blood stasis; *Bai Xian Pi* and *Fang Feng* expel wind and stop itching, *Bai Xian Pi* eliminates damp heat; *Chan Tui* expels wind; and *Da Huang* discharges fire toxin through the bowels.

Zi Jin Ding † 7.29
紫金錠
Purple Gold Nugget

Source: Wai Ke Zheng Zong (Orthodox Manual of Surgery), Ming Dynasty (1368-1644).

Primary Functions and Applications: **Zi Jin Ding** is used to treat summerheat strike with abdominal distension, abdominal pain, diarrhea, and semi-consciousness; children's pneumonia and bronchitis; and to treat the early stages of skin infections (such as carbuncles).

Format and Administration: The standard format is a 0.3 gram *ding.* Though the medicine is used both internally and externally, external application is far more common.

Recommended Dosage: Internally: Administer 0.6 to 1.5 grams, once or twice a day. The medication should be dissolved in warm water before swallowing, or broken into pieces and swallowed with warm water. Reduce the dose for children.

Externally: Use vinegar or cold water to soften the ding and apply the paste to the affected area. The area may then be covered.

Contraindication: **Do not use Zi Jin Ding internally during pregnancy, or for elderly or weak patients.**

Zi Jin Ding		
Constituent Substances		
Pinyin Name	**Pharmaceutical Name**	**% Composition**
She Xiang	*Secretio Moschi Moschiferi*	4.68
Shan Ci Gu	*Rhizoma vel Bulbus Shangtzuku*	31.25
Xiong Huang	*Realgar*	3.13
Da Ji	*Radix Euphorbiae seu Knoxiae*	23.44
Qian Jin Zi	*Semen Euphorbiae Lathyris*	15.63
Wu Bei Zi	*Galla Rhi Chinensis Potaninii*	15.63
Zhu Sha	*Cinnabaris*	6.25

Composition and Rationale: *She Xiang* opens the heart portal, resolves fire toxin due to summer-season exogenous pathogen, moves the blood, and removes heat accumulation (carbuncles); *Shan Ci Gu* discharges heat, removes accumulation, and reduces swelling; *Xiong Huang* resolves fire toxin and treats carbuncles; *Da Ji* is a water expellant which removes intestinal accumulation; *Qian Jin Zi Shuang* removes intestinal accumulation and reduces swelling; *Wu Bei Zi* as an astringent controls diarrhea; and *Zhu Sha* calms the spirit and tranquilizes.

7.30   Ji Gu Cao Wan
雞骨草丸
Fructus Abri Pills

Primary Functions and Applications: **Ji Gu Cao Wan** clears liver heat, clears the bile ducts, resolves fire toxin, reduces inflammation, and relieves pain. It is used to treat acute hepatitis with or without jaundice, to treat chronic hepatitis or chronic cholecystitis associated with damp-heat, and to treat liver heat syndrome and eliminate liver fire, with symptoms such as dizziness, vertigo, tinnitus, ear pain, and burning urination.

Format and Administration: **Ji Gu Cao Wan** is produced by the Yulin Drug Manufactory as *Jigucao Wan*. It is available in pill format, 50 per bottle.

Recommended Dosage: Four pills, 3 times a day, after meals.

Ji Gu Cao Wan		
Constituent Substances		
Pinyin Name	**Pharmaceutical Name**	**% Composition**
Ji Gu Cao	*Fructus Abri*	40
She Dan	*Agkistrodon*	15
Zhen Zhu	*Margarita*	3
Niu Huang	*Calculus Bovis*	10
Dang Gui	*Radix Angelicae Sinensis*	10
Gou Qi Zi	*Fructus Lycii Chinensis*	7
Dan Shen	*Radix Salviae Miltiorrhizae*	15

Composition and Rationale: *Ji Gu Cao* and *Niu Huang* clear heat and resolve fire toxin; *She Dan* clears heat and clears the bile ducts; *Zhen Zhu* nourishes the heart and calms the spirit; *Dan Shen* and *Dang Gui* nourish the blood and promote blood circulation; and *Gou Qi Zi* nourishes the liver and the blood.

Hui Chun Dan †   7.31
回春丹
Return-to-Spring Elixir

Source: The formula was developed by Qian Shu-tian, an herbalist of the Qing Dynasty (1644-1911).

Primary Functions and Applications: **Hui Chun Dan** clears heat, resolves fire toxin, eliminates phlegm, and opens the heart portals, reducing agitation and resuscitating unconscious patients. In China, this is a medicine commonly used to treat many of the digestive disorders and upper respiratory infections seen in children. It is used to treat syndromes caused by phlegm-heat in the lung in children, with such symptoms as fever, cough, and phlegm congestion in the lungs, with difficulty breathing. Wheezing may be present in such cases. In serious cases, there may be agitation, loss of consciousness, or convulsions due to the fever.

Hui Chun Dan may be used to regulate the splenogastric system, where dysfunction has caused qi stagnation with phlegm-heat. Symptoms in such cases include regurgitation and vomiting of milk, nighttime crying, abdominal pain, or diarrhea.

When the child exhibits the above symptoms of phlegm-heat in the lung, or splenogastric symptoms where qi stagnation has combined with phlegm-heat, **Hui Chun Dan** may be used for acute bronchitis, pneumonia, acute encephalitis, acute cerebro-spinal meningitis, and acute or chronic gastroenteritis.

In classical Chinese medical theory, pediatric diseases are often caused by the combination of exogenous pathogens and poor digestion of milk, a situation that may produce internal phlegm-heat. The development of this phlegm-heat may cause gastric disorders, such as vomiting and diarrhea, which may later develop into acute convulsions. Sometimes the regurgitation, vomiting and diarrhea are the primary signs indicating the presence of phlegm-heat. This may later develop into high-grade fever and convulsions. **Hui Chun Dan** is composed of agents that address these basic pathological developments: heat, phlegm, wind, and convulsions.

Format and Administration: **Hui Chun Dan** is produced by the United Pharmaceutical Company in vials of approximately 2.5 grams of powder.

In addition to this original formula, several similar formulae of the same name have been produced by different manufactories. The formula made in Shanghai contains more ingredients to expel wind and stop convulsions. The formula made in Suzhou contains more ingredients to clear heat and open the portals.

Zhong Guo Ji Ben Zhong Chen Yao (Fundamentals of Chinese Prepared Medicines, 1988) lists this medicine as *Wu Li Hui Chun Dan*. The standardized formula is significantly different than that presented here: of the 24 constituents, only five (*Niu Huang, Chuan Bei Mu, Dan Nan Xing, Jiang Can,* and *Chen Pi*) are common to both. The remaining constituents are *Xi Jiao, Jin Yin Hua, Lian Qiao, Zhu Ye, Chi Shao, Fang Feng, Qiang Huo, Sang Ye, Bo He, Chan Tui, Nui Bang Zi, Huo Po, Zhen Ju, She Xiang, Bing Pian, Ling Yang Jiao, Xing Ren, Fu Ling,* and *Gan Cao*.

Recommended Dosage: Children younger than 1 year, one third vial; 1-5 years, 1 vial; 6-12 years, 1½ vials, with warm water. *Lu Gen* is often used as an herbal conductor (*yao yin*).

Hui Chun Dan		
Constituent Substances		
Pinyin Name	Pharmaceutical Name	% Composition
Niu Huang	*Calculus Bovis*	1.4
Tian Zhu Huang	*Concretio Siliceae Bambusae*	4.4
Chuan Bei Mu	*Bulbus Fritillariae Cirrhosae*	4.4
Dan Nan Xing	*Pulvis Arisaematis cum Felle Bovis*	6.9
Gou Teng	*Ramulus et Uncus Uncariae*	27.7
Tian Ma	*Rhizoma Gastrodiae Elatae*	4.4
Quan Xie	*Buthus Martensi*	4.4
Jiang Can	*Bombyx Batryticatus*	4.4
Da Huang	*Rhizoma Rhei*	6.9
Chen Pi	*Pericarpium Citri Reticulatae*	4.4
Fan Ban Xia	*Rhizoma Pinelliae Ternatae*	4.4
Bai Dou Kou	*Fructus Amomi Cardamomi*	4.4
Zhi Qiao	*Fructus Citri seu Ponciri*	4.4
Mu Xiang	*Radix Muhsiang*	4.4
Chen Xiang	*Lignum Aquilariae*	4.4
Tan Xiang	*Lignum Santali Albi*	4.4
Zhu Sha	*Cinnabaris*	

Composition and Rationale: *Niu Huang* clears heat in the heart and relieves fire toxin; *Tian Zhu Huang, Chuan Bei Mu,* and *Dan Nan Xing* clear heat and eliminate phlegm; *Gou Teng, Tian Ma, Quan Xie,* and *Jiang Can* calm liver wind; *Da Huang* clears heat, eliminates fire toxin, and clears intestinal fire; *Chen Pi* and *Fan Ban Xia* regulate stomach qi and eliminate phlegm; *Bai Dou Kou, Zhi Qiao, Mu Xiang, Chen Xiang,* and *Tan Xiang* move stagnant qi in the stomach and intestines, eliminate phlegm, and prevent the accumulation of phlegm heat; *Gan Cao* clears heat and harmonizes; *Zhu Sha* calms the spirit.

7.32

Jing Wan Hong †
京萬紅
Capital Myriad Red

Primary Functions and Applications: **Jing Wan Hong** relieves pain, reduces inflammation, resolves toxins, and promotes regeneration of burned tissue. It is used to treat burns caused by steam, hot water, flame, hot oil, chemicals, nuclear radiation (including burns from radiation therapy), sunburn, and electrical burns. In addition, it may be used to treat such disorders as hemorrhoids and bedsores.

Format and Administration: **Jing Wan Hong** is produced by the Tientsin Drug Manufactory as *Ching Wan Hung*, and is available in tubes of 30 and 500 grams.

Recommended Dosage: For first or second degree burns, and for third degree burns without infection, clean the area, apply the ointment to the burn, and cover the area with gauze. Change dressing daily. For third-degree burns with infection, the wound should be cleaned every day, and larger amounts of the ointment used. Keep the wound covered at all times.

Composition and Rationale: The ingredients of **Jing Wan Hong** have been unpublished since its origination. Recently, however, samples of the ointment have entered the U.S. with a list of the following ingredients attached to the outer box: *Mu Gua, Di Yu, Ru Xiang, Ban Bian Lian, Mo Yao, Hong Hua, Dang Gui,* and *Bing Pian.*

7.33

Fu Fang Tu Jin Pi Ding
復方土槿皮酊
Medicinal Compound Nugget

Primary Functions and Applications: **Fu Fang Tu Jin Pi Ding** resolves fire toxin and relieves itching. It is used to treat skin infection caused by fungi, tinea, or Sarcoptes scabiei (scabies), which causes itching on the skin at the site of the irritation.

Format and Administration: **Fu Fang Tu Jin Pi Ding** is produced by the United Pharmaceutical Manufactory, Guangzhou, China, in 15 cc bottles.

Recommended Dosage: For external use only. Each day, rub the liquid onto the skin once or twice until the skin is healed. It is not necessary to cover the skin, since the liquid will dry quickly.

Fu Fang Tu Jin Pi Ding		
Constituent Substances		
Pinyin Name	**Pharmaceutical Name**	**Composition**
Mu Jin Hua	*Flos Hibisci Syriaci*	6.0 cc
Ben Jia Suan	*Benzoic Acid*	1.8 cc
Xue Yang Suan	*Salycilic Acid*	0.9 cc
	Ethyl alcohol	9.0 cc

Composition and Rationale: **Fu Fang Tu Jin Pi Ding** is structured to clear heat, eliminate damp, and treat fungal infection.

The standardized formula for **Fu Fang Tu Jin Pi Ding** presented in *Zhong Guo Ji Ben Zhong Chen Yao (Fundamentals of Chinese Prepared Medicines, 1988)* includes *Di Yu, Shan Zhi Zi, Da Huang, Chuan Shen Jia,* and *Bing Pian.*

Xi Huang Wan †
犀黃丸
Rhinoceros Bezoar Pills

7.34

Source: Wai Ke Chuen Sheng Ji (Volume on Surgery for the Entire Lifespan [Children and Adults]), Qing Dynasty (1644-1911).

Primary Functions and Applications: **Xi Huang Wan** reduces swelling, resolves fire toxin, moves blood stasis and phlegm accumulation, and relieves pain. It is used to treat carbuncles and abscesses from heat or fire toxin, including pulmonary abscess, breast abscess, intestinal abscess (such as acute or chronic appendicitis, suppurative peritonitis, and suppurative colitis). It is also indicated in the treatment of abscesses due to phlegm accumulation, including abscesses associated with scrofula, lymphadenitis, breast cancer, and osteomyelitis.

Format and Administration: **Xi Huang Wan** is produced by the Sichuan Chengdu Traditional Pharmaceutical Factory in vials of small pills.

Recommended Dosage: One vial, twice a day.

Contraindication: **Do not use Xi Huang Wan during pregnancy.**

Xi Huang Wan		
Constituent Substances		
Pinyin Name	**Pharmaceutical Name**	**% Composition**
Niu Huang	*Calculus Bovis*	1.38
She Xiang	*Secretio Moschi Moschiferi*	6.88
Ru Xiang	*Gummi Olibanum*	45.87
Mo Yao	*Myrrha*	45.87

Composition and Rationale: *Niu Huang* clears heat and resolves fire toxin; *She Xiang*, by virtue of its strong aroma, promotes circulation of qi in the channels. It also reduces accumulation of static blood, reduces accumulation of static phlegm, and reduces swelling; *Ru Xiang* is an analgesic stasis remover that promotes qi and blood circulation; and *Mao Yao*, another analgesic stasis remover, promotes tissue regeneration.

Xing Xiao Wan (7.24a) substitutes *Xiong Huang (Realgar)* for *Niu Huang*. It is used for carbuncles without pus, whereas **Xi Huang Wan** is used for carbuncles with or without pus. *Xing* means "to wake up"; *Xiao* means "to disappear." Hence, it "works overnight."

8

Interior-Warming Formulae

To warm the center and dissipate cold
8.1   Fu Zi Li Zhong Wan

Pattern Identification and Formula Differentiation

Warming the center and dissipating cold is but one of several subsets of the general treatment method, "warming." Salvaging yang and eliminating inversion frigidity, warming yang and disinhibiting water, and warming the channels and dissipating cold, all call for warming strategies. However, Chinese prepared formulae with such therapeutic targets are not commonly available. Practitioners rely instead on custom-made, whole-herb decoctions and powders to achieve such clinical effects.

Fu Zi Li Zhong Wan [8.1], the only formula in this section, is a representative formula for warming the center and dissipating cold. It is used to supplement constitutional yang, to warm and supplement the spleen, and to warm the center following penetration of exogenous cold.

8.1

Fu Zi Li Zhong Wan †
附子理中丸
Aconite Center-Rectifying Pills

Source: *He Ji Ju Fang* (Formularies of the People's Welfare Pharmacies), 1151. This is a modification of the original formula, *Li Zhong Wan*, which appeared in the *Shang Han Lun*.

Primary Functions and Applications: **Fu Zi Li Zhong Wan** warms the middle burner, dispels internal cold, and nourishes splenogastric qi. The principal formula for the treatment of taiyin disorders with pronounced interior cold, it is used to nourish middle burner yang that has been damaged by cold. Symptoms in such cases are characteristic of splenic depletion qi stagnation and cold: vomiting, loose stool, diarrhea, abdominal pain, clear urine, cold limbs, deep, thin pulse, and pale tongue without much fur. Stomachache and middle burner distension alleviated by warmth are also indications of middle burner yang depletion. When coldness in the middle burner is apparent, **Fu Zi Li Zhong Wan** may be prescribed to address acute gastroenteritis, gastric ulcer, duodenal ulcer, colitis, gastroptosis, and cholera.

Format and Administration: **Fu Zi Li Zhong Wan** is produced by the United Pharmaceutical Manufactory, Guangzhou, China, as large honey pills, 10 per box, and by the Lanchow Chinese Medicine Works in pill format, 100 per bottle.

Recommended Dosage: Five smaller pills, or 1 honey pill, twice a day.

Fu Zi Li Zhong Wan		
Constituent Substances		
Pinyin Name	**Pharmaceutical Name**	**% Composition**
Gan Jiang	*Rhizoma Exsiccatum Zingiberis Officinalis*	21.74
Bai Zhu	*Rhizoma Atractylodis Macrocephalae*	21.74
Dang Shen	*Radix Codonopsis Pilosulae*	21.74
Gan Cao	*Radix Glycyrrhizae Uralensis*	21.74
Fu Zi	*Radix Aconiti Carmichaelii*	13.04

Composition and Rationale: *Gan Jiang* warms the middle burner and fortifies the yang; *Bai Zhu* fortifies the spleen and dries dampness; *Dang Shen* fortifies the middle burner qi; *Gan Cao* warms the middle burner and harmonizes the other herbs; and *Fu Zi* fortifies the yang and relieves pain.

9

Digestate Accumulation Dispersing Formulae

To treat splenogastric depletion with ingesta damage complications
9.1 Jian Pi Wan 9.2 Qi Xing Cha
To relieve gastrointestinal accumulation through precipitation
9.3 Run Chang Wan

Pattern Identification

Digestate accumulations are generally subdivided into three distinct patterns of disharmony: *ingesta damage, gastrointestinal accumulation* and *splenogastric depletion complicated by ingesta damage.* The first two patterns refer to overeating or inappropriate dietary practices. Gastrointestinal accumulation is considered somewhat more serious than ingesta damage, and is most frequently distinguished by the presence of palpable masses in the abdomen. While ingesta damage is usually handled by the application of abduction-dispersing agents such as *Liu Qu (Massa Fermentata), Shan Zha (Fructus Crataegi),* and *Ji Nei Jin (Endothelium Gigeriae Galli),* gastrointestinal accumulation requires the use of such offensive precipitants (purgatives) as *Da Huang (Rhizoma Rhei).*

Digestate accumulations are often accompanied by phlegm-damp and qi stagnation. Similarly, splenogastric depletion and binding depression of liver qi often give rise to digestate accumulation complications. Thus, when the pathological syndrome involves digestive disorders in general, the practitioner will find it useful to cross-reference this chapter with Chapter 11 (Qi-Rectifying, Liver-Coursing, and Harmonizing Formulae).

Formula Differentiation

Jian Pi Wan [9.1] contains a combination of cereal and meat digestate dispersers, gastrosplenic supplementers, abductive dispersers, and appetite-increasing digestate dispersers. It is thus used as a generalized formula for indigestion and digestate accumulation.

Qi Xing Cha [9.2] is a popular pediatric formula for clearing heat while dispersing digestate accumulation. It contains a water disinhibitor, a qi-aspect damp-heat disinhibitor, and a cereal digestate disperser. The presence of the liver-clearing wind extinguisher, *Gou Teng (Ramulus et Uncus Uncariae),* is an interesting addition to this formula, as is the cool-natured wind-dissipator *Chan Tui (Periostracum Cicadae).*

The therapeutic emphasis of **Run Chung Wan [9.3]** is restoration of fecal flow through precipitation and intestinal lubrication. It is thus appropriate for cases of gastrointestinal accumulation.

Jian Pi Wan
健脾丸
Spleen-Fortifying Pills †

Source: Zheng Zhi Zhun Sheng *(Standards for Diagnosis and Treatment)*, 1602.

Primary Functions and Applications: **Jian Pi Wan** strengthens the spleen, eliminates damp, regulates the qi of the stomach and spleen, and moves food mass. It is used to treat symptoms caused by spleen qi depletion, with both splenogastric and intestinal symptoms. Splenogastric symptoms include frequently occurring accumulation of food mass, poor appetite, stomach distension, low energy, pale face, and weak pulse. Intestinal symptoms include frequent diarrhea or loose stools from damp, a symptom associated with spleen qi depletion.

Format and Administration: **Jian Pi Wan** is produced by the Lanchow Chinese Medicine Works as *Ginseng Stomachic Pills*, in bottles of 200 pills.

Recommended Dosage: Adults, 8 pills, 3 times a day, 30 minutes to one hour after meals.

Formulae with the same name and similar function, though slightly different in composition, are available.

Contraindications: Because the herb *Mai Ya (Fructus Hordei Germinatus)* has the additional function of restraining lactation, **Jian Pi Wan** should not be administered to nursing mothers.

Jian Pi Wan		
Constituent Substances		
Pinyin Name	Pharmaceutical Name	% Composition
Dang Shen	*Radix Codonopsis Pilosulae*	16
Shan Zha	*Fructus Crataegi*	12
Bai Zhu	*Rhizoma Atractylodis Macrocephalae*	16
Zhi Shi	*Fructus Ponciri*	24
Chen Pi	*Pericarpium Citri Reticulatae*	16
Mai Ya	*Fructus Hordei Germinatus*	16

Composition and Rationale: Dang Shen strengthens the spleen and supplements the qi; *Shan Zha* moves food mass and strengthens the spleen; *Bai Zhu* supplements the spleen and the stomach and dries damp; *Zhi Shi* moves stagnant qi and food mass; *Chen Pi* regulates stomach qi, strengthens the spleen, dries damp and relieves vomiting or nausea; and *Mai Ya* dissolves food mass and strengthens the stomach.

The standardized formulae for **Jian Pi Wan** presented in *Zhong Guo Ji Ben Zhong Chen Yao (Fundamentals of Chinese Prepared Medicines, 1988)* includes, in addition to the substances listed here, *Ren Shen, Dou Kou, Zhi Qiao, Gan Cao, Shan Yao, Mu Xiang, Yi Yi Ren, Bai Bian Dou, Chen Shi, Lian Zi Xin, Ching Pi, Shen Qu,* and *Dang Gui.* It is listed in that source as *Ren Shen Jian Pi Wan.*

9.2

Qi Xing Cha
七星茶
Seven-Star Tea

Primary Functions and Applications: In China, **Qi Xing Cha** is a common household item, used especially for children. It is safe and gentle, with a wide variety of uses for treating disorders in their early stages. It is especially useful in treating digestive disorders both in their early stages (without symptoms of heat) or later stages (with symptoms of heat).

Qi Xing Cha supplements the spleen and improves digestion, clears heat, and calms uneasiness. It is used to treat indigestion in babies and children, with such symptoms as poor appetite, regurgitation and vomiting of milk, breath odor associated with poor digestion, weight loss due to poor digestion, and loose stools. It is also used to calm uneasiness (as evidenced by sleep disturbed by several periods of wakefulness during the night), and excessive crying.

Finally, it is used in cases of oral inflammation, including oral ulcer, which may be due to yeast or other infection. In this condition, the urine may be a darker or reddish color.

Format and Administration: **Qi Xing Cha** is produced by the Sin-Kyn Drug House, Canton, China, as *Chi-Sing-Char*, in 100 ml bottles.

Recommended Dosage: For children 1 to 2 years old, use 5 ml, twice a day. For children 2 to 12 years old, use 10-20 ml, twice a day. Dilute in warm water before administration.

Qi Xing Cha		
Constituent Substances		
Pinyin Name	Pharmaceutical Name	Composition
Dan Zhu Ye	*Herba Lopatheri Gracilis*	19.58
Yi Yi Ren	*Semen Coicis Lachryma-Jobi*	26.04
Gu Ya	*Fructus Oryzae Germinatus*	26.04
Gou Teng	*Ramulus et Uncus Uncariae*	10
Chan Tui	*Periostracum Cicadae*	2
Shan Zha	*Fructus Crataegi*	13.02
Gan Cao	*Radix Glycyrrhizae Uralensis*	3.25

Composition and Rationale: *Dan Zhu Ye* clears heat and promotes urination; *Yi Ren* clears heat, promotes urination, strengthens the spleen, and relieves diarrhea; *Gu Ya* strengthens the spleen and removes food mass; *Gou Teng* clears heat and stops nighttime crying; *Chan Tui* clears heat, expels wind, and calms uneasiness; *Shan Zha* removes food mass and improves digestion; and *Gan Cao* clears heat and harmonizes the other herbs.

9.3   Run Chang Wan
潤腸丸
Intestine-Moistening Pill

Primary Functions and Applications: **Run Chang Wan** clears intestinal heat, moistens the stool, and promotes bowel movement. It is used to treat constipation due to excessive internal heat or insufficiency of body fluid caused by depletion heat and yin depletion.

Format and Administration: **Run Chang Wan** is produced by the Lanchow Chinese Medicine Works as *Fructus Persica Compound Pills*, available as small pills in bottles of 200.

Recommended Dosage: Four pills, 3 times a day. The dose may be increased to 8 pills, 3 times a day, if the regular dose produces no effect.

Run Chang Wan		
Constituent Substances		
Pinyin Name	**Pharmaceutical Name**	**% Composition**
Huo Ma Ren	*Semen Cannabis Sativae*	28.6
Tao Ren	*Semen Persicae*	28.6
Qiang Huo	*Rhizoma et Radix Notopterygii*	14.3
Dang Gui	*Radix Angelicae Sinensis*	14.3
Da Huang	*Rhizoma Rhei*	14.3

Composition and Rationale: *Huo Ma Ren* moistens the intestines (these seeds are 31% oil); *Tao Ren* moistens dryness and lubricates the intestines; *Qiang Huo* and *Dang Gui* moisten the intestines, move the stool, and supplement the yin and blood; and *Da Huang* clears large intestine heat and promotes bowel movement.

10

Damp-Dispersing Formulae

To treat dysuria
10.1   Shi Lin Tong Pian

Pattern Identification and Formulae Differentiation

The single formula in this section has a relatively specialized function: softening calculi and relieving bladder damp-heat. It is a medicine composed of a single agent, *Jin Qian Cao (Herba Jinqiancao)*, which itself is credited with the ability to disperse (by softening hardness) and to dislodge damp-heat.

Formulae associated with the treatment of damp-heat (such as **Li Dan Pian [7.19]**, **Yu Dai Wan [7.4]**, and **Ji Gu Cao Wan [7.30]** will be found among the heat-clearing, fire-draining formulae of Chapter 7.

10.1   Shi Lin Tong Pian
石淋通片
Stone Strangury Tablets

Source: This medicine has been in common use for at least 25 years.

Primary Functions and Applications: **Shi Lin Tong Pian** promotes diuresis (especially in cases of difficult urination) and clears damp-heat in the lower burner. It is used to treat various diseases caused by heat or damp-heat in the urinary system. Guiding symptoms include frequent scanty urination, with or without blood, and painful urination. Dysfunctions addressed with **Shi Lin Tong Pian** include urinary stones (including kidney stones), urinary tract infection or inflammation, pyelonephritis, gallstone, hepatitis with jaundice, cirrhosis of the liver with ascites, and edema associated with nephritis.

Format and Administration: **Shi Lin Tong Pian** is produced by the Swatow United Medicinal Factory in pill format, 100 pills per bottle.

Recommended Dosage: Six tablets, 3 times a day. For serious cases, 8 or 9 tablets per dose is recommended.

Shi Ling Tong Pian		
Constituent Substances		
Pinyin Name	**Pharmaceutical Name**	**% Composition**
Jin Qian Cao	*Herba Jinqiancao*	100

Composition and Rationale: *Jin Qian*, the only herb in this formula, eliminates dampness, promotes urination, clears damp-heat, and reduces jaundice.

Te Xiao Pai Shi Wan [10.1a], produced by the Mai Yun Shan Pharmaceutical Manufactory in bottles of 120 pills, is used in a similar fashion as **Shi Lin Tong Pian** in the treatment of kidney stones and gallstones. **Te Xiao Pai Shi Wan** is produced as *Specific Drug Passwan*.

11

Qi-Rectifying, Liver-Coursing, and Harmonizing Formulae

Pattern Identification and Formulae Differentiation

Though qi rectifying is the primary objective of the formulae in this section, liver coursing and harmonization figure in their therapeutic actions prominently enough to warrant inclusion in this chapter. The stomach, the liver (by virtue of its governance of free coursing), and the spleen (by virtue of its sensitivity to binding liver qi depression) are implicated in a set of syndromes characterized primarily by gastric disorders and their variations.

Generally, the formulae in Chapter 11 address the following conditions:

• Splenic qi depletion with stomach qi dysfunction: **Xiang Sha Liu Jun Zi Wan [11.4].**

• Hepatosplenic disharmony: **Xiao Yao San [11.9].**

• Binding depression of liver qi: **Shu Gan Wan [11.1].** When binding depression of liver qi is accompanied by disorders of the penetrating *(dai)* and conception *(ren)* channels: **Xiao Yao San [11.9].** When binding depression of liver qi is accompanied by signs of ingesta damage: **Mu Xiang Shun Qi Wan [11.2].**

• Insufficiency of stomach yin: **Xiang Sha Yang Wei Pian [11.5].**

• Gastric hyperacidity and stomach ulcers: **Wei Te Ling [11.6]**, **Sai Mei An (11.7)**, and **Wei Yao (11.8).**

Chapter 9, *Digestate Accumulation Dispersing Formulae*, should be consulted for additional formulae for the treatment of gastric disorders.

Shu Gan Wan †
舒肝丸
Liver-Soothing Pills

11.1

Source: Ming Dynasty (1368-1644) physician Zhu Tianbi.

Primary Functions and Applications: **Shu Gan Wan** soothes the liver, smoothes depressed liver qi, aids digestion, disperses digestate accumulation, and relieves pain in the middle burner. It is used to treat liver qi stagnation, and is indicated in the presence of such symptoms as distension and pain in the hypochondrium, or abdominal pain in the region of the liver or gallbladder (which may be reflected to the shoulder or lower abdomen).

Shu Gan Wan is also indicated for splenogastric syndromes associated with stagnant liver qi. Guiding symptoms include poor digestion, a sensation of fullness in the stomach especially after eating, nausea, burping, vomiting, and regurgitation associated with hyperacidity.

This formula is indicated in the treatment of chronic hepatitis, chronic cholecystitis and/or gallstones, acute or chronic gastritis and idiopathic, functional or hysteria-related digestive disorders when associated with liver qi stagnation, or splenogastric syndromes.

Format and Administration: **Shu Gan Wan** is produced by the Lanchow Chinese Medicine Works as *Shu Kan Wan (Hepatico-Tonic Pills)* in bottles of 100 pills.

Recommended Dosage: Eight pills, 3 times a day.

Contraindications: **Do not use Shu Gan Wan during pregnancy.**

Though this formula is effective when used alone, it is commonly used as an adjunctive, supportive formula with other medicines for digestive disorders or liver/gallbladder problems.

Shu Gan Wan		
Constituent Substances		
Pinyin Name	**Pharmaceutical Name**	**% Composition**
Chuan Lian Zi	*Fructus Meliae Toosendan*	14.02
Jiang Huang	*Rhizoma Curcumae Longae*	9.35
Chen Xiang	*Lignum Aquilariae*	8.41
Yan Hu Suo	*Tuber Corydalis Yanhusuo*	8.41
Mu Xiang	*Radix Saussureae seu Vladimiriae*	6.54
Dou Kou	*Semen Myristicae*	4.67
Bai Shao	*Radix Paeoniae Lactiflora*	13.08
Fu Ling	*Sclerotium Poriae Cocus*	9.35
Zhi Qiao	*Fructus Citri seu Ponciri*	8.41
Chen Pi	*Pericarpium Citri Reticulatae*	6.54
Sha Ren	*Fructus Amomi Cardamomi*	6.54
Hou Po	*Cortex Magnoliae Officinalis*	4.67

Composition and Rationale: *Chuan Lian Zi* and *Mu Xiang* move stagnant qi and relieve pain; *Jiang Huang* smoothes depressed liver qi and treats mental depression; *Chen Xiang* lowers adverse rising qi and relieves pain; *Yuan Hu* promotes blood circulation and relieves pain; *Dou Kou* moves stagnant qi in the stomach and disperses digestate accumulation; *Bai Shao* smoothes the liver and supplements liver yin; *Fu Ling* fortifies the spleen, discharges damp, and promotes urination; *Zhi Qiao* moves qi and disperses stagnation; *Chen Pi* regulates stomach qi and disperses digestate accumulation; *Sha Ren* regulates stomach qi and stops vomiting; and *Hou Po* moves stagnant qi and lowers adverse rising qi.

Zhong Guo Ji Ben Zhong Chen Yao (Fundamentals of Chinese Prepared Medicines, 1988) includes *Zhu Sha,* and omits *Sha Ren* in its standardized formula for **Shu Gan Wan.**

A similar formula called **Shu Kan Wan (condensed)** is produced by the Lanchow Chinese Medicine Works, Lanchow, China. It omits *Chuan Lian Zi (Fructus Meliae Toosendang)* and *Fu Ling (Sclerotium Poriae Cocus)* from the original formula, and adds eight additional herbs, *Xiang Fu (Rhizoma Cyperi Rotundi), Gan Cao (Radix Glycyrrhizae Uralensis), Dan Pi (Caulis Mutong), Chai Hu (Radix Bupleuri), Fo Shou (Flos Citri Sarcodactylis), Qing Pi (Pericarpium Citri Reticulatae), Xiang Yuan (Fructus Citri Medicae)* and *Tan Xiang (Lignum Santali Albi).* Although the primary function of both formulae is the same, **Shu Kan Wan (condensed)** is more effective in moving stagnant liver qi.

216

Mu Xiang Shun Qi Wan † 11.2
木香順氣飲
Saussurea Qi-Normalizing Powder

Source: *Shen Shi Zun Sheng Shu (Respect of Life Book)*, by Dr. Shen, Qing Dynasty (1644-1911).

Primary Functions and Applications: **Mu Xiang Shun Qi Wan** moves stagnant qi in the middle burner, relieves pain, fortifies the stomach, and disperses digestate accumulation. It is used to treat feelings of fullness in the chest, diaphragm, and hypochondrium caused by stagnant liver qi or digestate accumulation, and to increase peristalsis and remove digestate accumulation in the stomach due to poor eating habits. In such cases, the patient may have a foul smell in the mouth and foul belching, a symptom sometimes associated with gastric hypoacidity. It is indicated in cases of chronic hepatitis, cirrhosis of the liver in its early stages, chronic gastritis and intestinal spasms (abdominal pain).

Format and Administration: **Mu Xiang Shun Qi Wan** is produced by the Lanchow Pharmaceutical Works as *Aplotaxis Carminative Pills*, in bottles of 200 pills.

Recommended Dosage: Eight pills, twice a day.

Mu Xiang Shun Qi Wan		
Constituent Substances		
Pinyin Name	**Pharmaceutical Name**	**% Composition**
Mu Xiang	*Radix Saussureae seu Vladimiriae*	6.15
Dou Kou	*Semen Myristicae*	6.15
Cang Zhu	*Radix Atractylodis*	4.62
Shen Jiang	*Rhizoma Drynariae*	6.15
Qing Pi	*Pericarpium Citri Reticulatee Viride*	6.15
Chen Pi	*Pericarpium Citri Reticulatae*	6.15
Fu Ling	*Sclerotium Poriae Cocus*	6.15
Chai Hu	*Radix Bupleuri*	4.62
Hou Po	*Cortex Magnoliae Officinalis*	6.15
Bin Lang	*Semen Arecae Acacia seu Catechu*	6.15
Zhi Qiao	*Fructus Citri seu Ponciri*	6.15
Wu Yao	*Radix Linderae Strychnifoliae*	6.15
Lai Fu Zi	*Semen Raphani Sativi*	6.15
Shan Zha	*Fructus Crataegi*	6.15
Shen Qu	*Massa Medica Fermentata*	6.15
Mai Ya	*Fructus Hordei Germinatus*	6.15
Gan Cao	*Radix Glycyrrhizae Uralensis*	4.62

Composition and Rationale: *Mu Xiang* moves stagnant qi and relieves pain; *Dou Kou* moves stagnant qi in the stomach and disperses digestate accumulation; *Can Zhu* fortifies the spleen and dries damp; *Shen Jiang* warms the middle burner and relieves nausea and vomiting; *Qing Pi* moves stagnant liver qi and decreases distension; *Chen Pi* regulates stomach qi and fortifies the spleen; *Fu Ling* fortifies the spleen, discharges damp, and promotes urination; *Chai Hu* moves stagnant liver qi; *Hou Po* moves stagnant qi and lowers adverse rising qi; *Bin Lang* reduces middle burner abdominal distension; *Zhi Qiao* moves qi and disperses stagnation; *Wu Yao* moves stagnant qi and relieves pain; *Lai Fu Zi* moves stagnant qi in the stomach and disperses digestate accumulation; *Shan Zha* disperses digestate accumulation and increases acid in the stomach; *Shen Qu* and *Mai Ya* strengthen the stomach and disperse digestate accumulation; and *Gan Cao* warms the middle burner and harmonizes the other herbs.

Zhong Guo Ji Ben Zhong Chen Yao (Fundamentals of Chinese Prepared Medicines, 1988) includes *Sha Ren* and *Xiang Fu*, and omits *Dou Kou, Fu Ling, Chai Hu, Wu Yao, Lai Fu Zi, Shan Zha, Shen Qu,* and *Mai Ya* in its standardized formula for **Mu Xiang Shun Qi Wan**.

Chen Xiang Hua Qi Wan
沉香化氣丸
Aquilaria Qi-Rectifying Pills †

Source: Yu Yao Yuan Fang (Imperial Pharmacy Formula), Yuan Dynasty (1279-1368).

Primary Functions and Applications: **Chen Xiang Hua Qi Wan** moves stagnant qi, lowers adverse rising qi, and removes food stagnation in the stomach. It is used to treat abdominal distension and to reduce the sensation of fullness and pain in the hypochondrium and chest areas. **Chen Xiang Hua Qi Wan** is also recommended in the treatment of gastric disorders such as masses of food in the stomach due to poor diet, that has given rise to such symptoms as poor or no appetite, belching, and sour regurgitation. It is thus effective in cases of chronic hepatitis, gastritis, stomach ulcer, duodenal ulcer, intestinal obstruction, and chronic cholecystitis.

Format and Administration: **Chen Xiang Hua Qi Wan** is produced by the Min-Kang Drug Manufactory, I-Chang, China, in bottles of 100 pills.

Recommended Dosage: Nine pills, twice a day, half an hour before or after meals.

Contraindications: **Do not use in cases of yin depletion. This formula contains herbs with slightly warming properties.**

Che Xiang Hua Qi Wan		
Constituent Substances		
Pinyin Name	**Pharmaceutical Name**	**% Composition**
Chen Xiang	*Lignum Aquilariae*	3.60
Bin Lang	*Semen Arecae Acacia seu Catechu*	4.86
Cao Dou Kou	*Semen Alpiniae Katsumadai*	4.86
Sha Ren	*Fructus Amomi Cardamomi*	2.43
Xiang Fu	*Rhizoma Cyperi Rotundi*	7.20
Hou Po	*Cortex Magnoliae Officinalis*	7.20
Fu Ling	*Sclerotium Poriae Cocus*	7.20
Chen Pi	*Pericarpium Citri Reticulatae*	7.20
Lai Fu Zi	*Semen Raphani Sativi*	4.86
Gan Cao	*Radix Glycyrrhizae Uralensis*	2.43
—	*Unspecified substances*	to 100%

Composition and Rationale: **Chen Xiang** lowers adverse rising qi, moves stagnant qi, and relieves pain; *Bin Lang* moves stagnant qi and disperses digestate accumulation; *Cao Dou Kou* fortifies the spleen, dries damp, and aids digestion; *Sha Ren* moves qi, relieves pain, fortifies the stomach, and dries damp; *Xiang Fu* smoothes the liver, regulates the liver and stomach qi, and relieves pain; *Hou Po* moves qi and lowers adverse rising qi; *Fu Ling* fortifies the spleen, harmonizes the middle burner, promotes tranquility, and promotes urination; *Chen Pi* moves middle burner qi, fortifies the spleen, lowers adverse rising qi, and controls vomiting; *Lai Fu Zi* disperses digestate accumulation and relieves distension; and *Gan Cao* fortifies the middle burner and relieves stomachache.

Zhong Guo Ji Ben Zhong Chen Yao (Fundamentals of Chinese Prepared Medicines, 1988) includes *Mu Xiang, Huo Xiang, E Zhu, Shen Qu,* and *Mai Ya,* and omits *Bin Lang, Cao Dou Kou, Hou Po, Fu Ling,* and *Lai Fu Zi* in its standardized formula for **Che Xiang Hua Qi Wan**.

Xiang Sha Liu Jun Zi Wan † 11.4
香砂六君子丸
Saussurea and Cardomom Six Nobles Pills

Primary Functions and Applications: **Xiang Sha Liu Jun Zi Wan** nourishes the spleen and stomach, supplements qi, relieves pain, and eliminates phlegm. It is used as a simple, though highly effective tonic for reinforcing the splenogastric system, and can be used to treat any symptoms caused by a depletion of qi in those organs. Guiding symptoms include improper digestion with nausea, vomiting, burping, regurgitation, stomach gurgling, borborygmus, distension in the middle burner, stomachache, chronic diarrhea, pale face, pale tongue, weak or slow pulse, and phlegm retention due to splenic qi depletion. It is thus applicable in cases of gastric or duodenal ulcer, acute or chronic gastritis, chronic diarrhea and Crohn's disease.

Format and Administration: **Xiang Sha Liu Jun Zi Wan** is produced by the Lanchow Chinese Medicine Works as *Aplotaxis-Amomum Pills* in bottles of 100.

Recommended Dosage: Twelve pills 3 times a day before meals. Avoid cold or raw food during therapy to enhance efficacy.

Xiang Sha Liu Jun Zi Wan		
Constituent Substances		
Pinyin Name	**Pharmaceutical Name**	**% Composition**
Dang Shen	*Radix Codonopsis Pilosulae*	17.2
Bai Zhu	*Rhizoma Atractylodis Macrocephalae*	17.2
Fu Ling	*Sclerotium Poriae Cocus*	17.2
Ban Xia	*Rhizoma Pinelliae Ternatae*	17.2
Chen Pi	*Pericarpium Citri Reticulatae*	8.6
Mu Xiang	*Radix Saussureae seu Vladimiriae*	6.9
Sha Ren	*Fructus Amomi Cardamomi*	6.9

Composition and Rationale: *Dang Shen* supplements the middle burner and fortifies the qi; *Bai Zhu* and *Fu Ling* strengthen the spleen and dry damp; *Ban Xia* dries damp, eliminates phlegm and controls vomiting; *Chen Pi* regulates middle burner qi, controls vomiting and nausea, and dries damp; *Mu Xiang* moves stagnant qi and relieves pain; and *Sha Ren* moves middle burner qi, eliminates damp, and controls diarrhea.

Zhong Guo Ji Ben Zhong Chen Yao (Fundamentals of Chinese Prepared Medicines, 1988) includes *Gan Jiang* and *Da Zao* in its standardized formula for **Xiang Sha Liu Jun Zi Wan**.

The classical, representative formula for spleen fortification and stomach harmonization is *Si Jun Zi Tang (Four Nobles Soup)*, which is composed of *Ren Shen (Radix Ginseng)*, *Bai Zhu (Radix Atractylodis Macrocephalae)*, *Gan Cao (Radix Glycyrrhizae Uralensis)* and *Fu Ling (Sclerotium Poriae Cocus)*. With the addition to these ingredients of *Dang Shen (Radix Codonopsis Pilosulae)* and *Ban Xia (Rhizoma Pinelliae Ternatae)*, the formula **Liu Jun Zi Pian [11.4a]**, *Six Nobles Pills*, is produced. **Liu Jun Zi Pian [11.4a]** is produced as a prepared formula by the Sing-kyn Drug House in bottles of 96 tablets. Containing neither *Mu Xiang (Radix Saussureae)* nor *Sha Ren (Fructus Amomi Cardamomi)*, **Liu Jun Zi Pian [11.4a]** is not as effective in moving stagnant qi in the stomach as **Xiang Sha Liu Jun Zi Wan**. However, it is somewhat more effective in fortifying the spleen and drying the damp of spleen qi depletion, and for relieving vomiting.

11.5   Xiang Sha Yang Wei Pian †
香砂養胃片
Saussurea and Cardamom Stomach-Nourishing Tablets

Source: *Wen Bing Hui Chun (Recovery of Ten Thousand Diseases)*, Ming Dynasty (1368-1644).

Primary Functions and Applications: **Xiang Sha Yang Wei Pian** nourishes qi, fortifies the stomach, disperses digestate accumulation, and relieves stomachache. It is indicated for the weaker patient with a splenogastric depletion syndrome, accompanied by such symptoms as lethargy, poor appetite, and gastric discomfort, especially following a meal (stomach distension, burping, heartburn, stomachache, nausea, loose stools or diarrhea). It is used in cases of acute or chronic gastritis (including idiopathic) and with gastric or duodenal ulcer.

Format and Administration: **Xiang Sha Yang Wei Pian** is produced by the Tientsin Drug Manufactory as *Hsiang Sha Yang Wei Pien* in bottles of 60 uncoated tablets.

Recommended Dosage: Four tablets, twice a day.

Xiang Sha Yang Wei Pian		
Constituent Substances		
Pinyin Name	**Pharmaceutical Name**	**% Composition**
Bai Zhu	*Rhizoma Atractylodis Macrocephalae*	21.3
Mu Xiang	*Radix Saussureae seu Vladimiriae*	5.7
Sha Ren	*Fructus seu Semen Amomi*	5.7
Bai Dou Kou	*Fructus Amomi Cardamomi*	8.5
Dang Shen	*Radix Codonopsis Pilosulae*	24.2
Mai Ya	*Fructus Hordei Germinatus*	8.5
Chen Pi	*Pericarpium Citri Reticulatae*	14.2
Gan Cao	*Radix Glycyrrhizae Uralensis*	3.4
Shen Qu	*Massa Medica Fermentata*	8.5

Composition and Rationale: *Bai Zhu* fortifies the spleen and stomach and dries spleen damp; *Mu Xiang* regulates qi, moves stagnation, and relieves pain; *Sha Ren* regulates stomach qi; *Bai Dou Kou* regulates stomach qi and warms the middle burner; *Dang Shen* supplements the middle burner and fortifies spleen qi; *Mai Ya* disperses digestate accumulation and fortifies the spleen; *Chen Pi* regulates stomach qi and dries spleen damp; *Gan Cao* warms the middle burner and harmonizes the other herbs; *She Qi* disperses digestate accumulation and regulates the stomach.

Zhong Guo Ji Ben Zhong Chen Yao (Fundamentals of Chinese Prepared Medicines, 1988) lists this formula as **Xiang Sha Yang Wei Wan**, and includes *Xiang Fu, Huo Xiang, Fu Ling, Hou Po, Ban Xia Qu,* and *Chi Shi*, while omitting *Dang Shen, Mai Ya,* and *Shen Qu*.

11.6

Wei Te Ling
胃特靈
Special Stomachic

Primary Functions and Applications: **Wei Te Ling** fortifies the stomach, relieves stomachache, and neutralizes excess stomach acid. It is used to treat stagnant splenogastric qi that manifests as stomachache, heartburn, burping, stomach distension, and gas. It is especially effective for the treatment of gastric and duodenal ulcers, and is used to treat gastritis with hyperacidity.

Format and Administration: **Wei Te Ling** is produced by the Tsingtao Medicine Works, Tsingtao, China, as *Stomach Sedative*, in bottles of 120 coated tablets.

Recommended Dosage: Four to 6 pills, 3 times a day, before meals or during periods of pain or heartburn.

Though **Wei Te Ling** is a simple formula, it is most effective in relieving stomach pain and reducing stomach acid. If burping, distension, and gas are significant, additional herbal formulae, such as **Xiang Sha Yang Wei Pian [11.5]** or **Mu Xiang Shun Qi Wan [11.2]** may be simultaneously prescribed.

Wei Te Ling		
Constituent Substances		
Pinyin Name	**Pharmaceutical Name**	**% Composition**
Wu Zei Gu	*Os Sepia seu Sepelliae*	40
Yan Hu Suo	*Tuber Corydalis Yanhusuo*	30
Feng Mi	*Mel*	30

Composition and Rationale: The astringent properties of *Wu Zei Gu (Os Sepia seu Sepelliae)* neutralize excess stomach acid and promote the healing of ulcers; *Yuan Hu Suo (Tuber Corydalis Yanhusuo)* relieves pain; and *Feng Mi (Mel)* fortifies the middle burner and promotes tissue regeneration.

Sai Mei An 11.7
賽霉安
(Name of Manufacturer)

Source: Developed by the Sai Mei An Medicine Factory, Quanzhou, China.

Primary Functions and Applications: **Sai Mei An** decreases excess stomach acid, controls bleeding, protects the mucosa of the stomach, and relieves stomachache. A primary application of this formula is in the treatment of gastric and duodenal ulcers caused by gastric hyperacidity. In addition, it is recommended for acute or chronic gastritis with hyperacidity in the stomach. Finally, it may be used topically to treat stomatitis or ulcers in the mouth.

Format and Administration: **Sai Mei An** is available in capsule format, 50 per bottle.

Recommended Dosage: Three pills, 3 times a day. It is important to administer on an empty stomach only, at least one half hour before a meal, to give the medicine a chance to form a membrane and line the stomach wall and protect the ulcer from contact with food and gastric secretions. Continue taking for at least 2 weeks after symptoms are gone, to help the tissues regenerate.

In cases of stomatitis or mouth ulcers, apply a small amount of the powder topically, 3 or 4 times a day.

Contraindications: Do not take this along with antacids, as the alkalinity would reduce the membrane-producing effect.

Sai Mei An		
Constituent Substances		
Pinyin Name	Pharmaceutical Name	% Composition
Zhong Ru Shi	*Stalactitum*	10
Han Shui Shi	*Gypsum Rubrum et Calcitum*	20
Bing Pian	*Borneolum*	10
Zhen Zhu	*Margarita*	2
Wa Leng Zi	*Concha Arcae*	20
Bai Cao Shuang	*Fuligo Herbarum Ustarum*	15
Hai Ge Ke	*Concha Cyclinae Sinensis*	23

Composition and Rationale: Zhong Ru Shi, Han Shiu Shi, Zhen Zhu, Wa Leng Zi and Hai Ge Ke neutralize hyperacidity in the stomach; Bing Pian clears heat and relieves pain; and Bai Cao Shuang controls bleeding in the stomach.

11.8 Wei Yao
胃藥
Stomach Medicine

Primary Functions and Applications: **Wei Yao** fortifies the spleen and stomach and neutralizes excess stomach acid, thus reducing stomach pain. It is used to move stagnant qi in the stomach manifesting as stomach pain; to decrease distension, reduce gas, relieve stomach pain, and reduce burping and regurgitation of stomach acid. **Wei Yao** may thus be recommended in cases of acute or chronic gastritis (due only to excessive stomach acid), and to treat gastric or duodenal ulcer. It will reduce acidity, reduce stomach pain, and promote tissue regeneration in the stomach mucosa and muscles.

Format and Administration: **Wei Yao** is produced by the Zhenjiang Chinese Medicine Works, Kiang Su, China, as *Gastropathy Capsules* in bottles of 42 capsules.

Recommended Dosage: Three pills, 3 times a day before meals, or during periods of pain or heartburn.

Wei Yao		
Constituent Substances		
Pinyin Name	**Pharmaceutical Name**	**% Composition**
Yan Hu Suo	*Tuber Corydalis Yanhusuo*	21.1
Wu Zei Gu	*Os Sepia seu Sepelliae*	10.5
Qing Mu Xiang	*Radix Vladimiriae Cantharis*	10.5
Zhen Zhu Mu	*Concha Margaritifera Usta*	21.1
Ming Fan	*Alumen*	15.8
Feng Huang Yi	*Membrana Follicularis Ovi*	21.1

Composition and Rationale: *Yuan Hu* relieves pain; *Wu Zei Gu,* an astringent, neutralizes excess stomach acid and promotes the healing of ulcers; *Qing Mu Xiang* clears heat, resolves fire toxin, and reduces swelling; *Zhen Zhu Mu* neutralizes excessive stomach acid; *Ming Fan* stops bleeding (by virtue of its astringent property); and *Feng Huang* neutralizes excess stomach acid.

Xiao Yao Wan † 11.9
逍遙丸
Free Wanderer Pills

Source: *He Ji Ju Fang (Formularies of the People's Welfare Pharmacies),* Song Dynasty (960-1279).

Primary Functions and Applications: **Xiao Yao Wan** moves stagnant liver qi, fortifies the spleen, and nourishes the blood. It is used to treat liver stagnation due to liver blood depletion. Guiding symptoms include bilateral hypochondriac pain, headache, vertigo, dry mouth, dry throat, fatigue, poor appetite, moodiness, possible alternating feelings of hot and cold, possible irregular menstruation, and breast distension. The tongue in such cases will be slightly red, and the pulse will be wiry and empty. In the presence of these symptoms, **Xiao Yao Wan** is indicated for such gynecological disorders as irregular menstruation, pre-menstrual syndrome with abdominal pain, and neurasthenia associated with meno-pause. **Xiao Yao Wan** is commonly prescribed in combination with other formulae when treating menstrual disorders.

Xiao Yao Wan is also used in cases of chronic hepatitis, pleurisy, and cystic hyperplasia of the breast.

Clinical research in China, completed in 1960, was conducted on 253 cases of chronic hepatitis manifesting symptoms such as distension and pain in the hypochondrium, swelling of the liver and/or spleen, fatigue, vertigo, insomnia, nightmares, palpitations, shortness of breath, irregular bowel movements, lumbago, and low-grade fever. Liver tests returned normal readings in 36 cases, and showed improvement in 139 cases, a 68.8% effective rate (*Guang Dong Zhong Yi* 8: 1960).

Format and Administration: **Xiao Yao Wan** is produced by the Lanzhou Fo Ci Pharmaceutical Factory as *Hsiao Yao Wan (Bupleurum Sedative Pills)*, in bottles of 200 pills.

Recommended Dosage: Eight to 10 pills, 3 times a day.

Xiao Yao Wan		
Constituent Substances		
Pinyin Name	**Pharmaceutical Name**	**% Composition**
Chai Hu	*Radix Bupleuri*	14.28
Dang Gui	*Radix Angelicae Sinensis*	14.28
Bai Zhu	*Rhizoma Atractylodis Macrocephalae*	14.28
Bai Shao	*Radix Paeoniae Lactiflora*	14.28
Fu Ling	*Sclerotium Poriae Cocus*	14.28
Gan Cao	*Radix Glycyrrhizae Uralensis*	11.42
Sheng Jiang	*Rhizoma Recens Zingiberis Officinalis*	14.28
Bo He	*Herba Menthae*	2.85

Composition and Rationale: *Chai Hu* clears heat; *Dang Gui* sup-plements liver blood and moves blood; *Bai Zhu* fortifies the spleen and dries spleen damp; *Bai Shao* nourishes liver yin and fortifies the blood; *Fu Ling* fortifies the spleen and calms the spirit; *Gan Cao* regulates the mid-dle burner qi and harmonizes; *Shen Jiang* regulates stomach qi and warms the middle; and *Bo He* smooths the liver and reduces liver wind-heat.

12

Blood-Regulating Formulae

To move static blood
12.1   Fu Fang Dan Shen Pian
12.2   Yan Hu Su Zhi Tong Pian
12.3   Qi Li San
12.4   She Xiang Die Da Gao
12.5   Die Da Zhi Tong Gao
12.6   Zheng Gu Shui
12.7   Die Da Wan Hua You
12.8   Gu Zhe Cuo Shang San
12.9   Mao Dong Qing
To control bleeding
12.10   Yun Nan Bai Yao
To regulate menstruation
12.11   Qian Jin Zhi Dai Wan
12.12   Wu Ji Bai Feng Wan
12.13   Wu Jin Wan
12.14   Dang Gui Su
12.15   Fu Ke Zhong Zi Wan
12.16   Bu Xue Tiao Jing Pian

Pattern Identification and Formulae Differentiation

Two treatment methods are represented by the formulae in this section: *securing astriction* (specifically arresting hemorrhage and securing the menses); and *dispersion* (specifically transformation of static blood). Disorders addressed by these formulae thus include traumatic injury, gynecologic disorders, and circulatory dysfunction (specifically coronary artery disease).

Blood stasis patterns are treated by quickening the blood, by transforming stasis, and by blood breaking. *Dan Shen (Radix Salviae Miltiorhizae)*, which comprises 75% of the formulae **Fu Fang Dan Shen Pian [12.1]**, is a representative blood quickening agent; the formulae is thus prescribed when blood flow must be stimulated, specifically in cases of coronary artery disease.

Blood breakers are among the most potent agents for transformation of static blood, and appear infrequently in prepared formulae. The plaster **Die Da Zhi Tong Gao** contains the blood breaker *Tu Bie Chong (Eupolyphaga seu Opishoplatia)*, and the gynecologic formula **Wu Jin Wan [12.13]** contains the blood breaking agent *San Leng (Rhizoma Sparganni)*.

Yan Hu Su Zhi Tong Pian [12.2] is structured around the analgesic stasis transformer *Yan Hu Suo (Rhizoma Corydalis)*, and is used when pain relief is uppermost in the therapeutic strategy. See Chapter 4 for information on formulae such as **Ji Xue Teng Qin Gao Pian [4.2]**, which emphasizes the transformation of static blood as well as the freeing of bi (obturation) patterns, and **Xiao Huo Luo Dan [4.7]**, which features analgesic stasis transformers.

The six gynecologic formulae used to regulate menstruation include formulae for the treatment of dysmenorrhea as well as leukorrhea. Note, however, that **Qian Jin Zhi Dai Wan [12.11]** might well have been included in the chapter on astringents.

Yun Nan Bai Yao [12.10] is a well-known antihemorrhagic, used in daily and emergency care of such trauma as gunshot and knife wounds.

The plasters **She Xiang Die Da Gao [12.4]** and **Die Da Zhi Tong Gao [12.5]** are used for sports injuries and traumatic injuries such as bruising, strains, and sprains, as is the liniment **Die Da Wan Hua You [12.7]** (which may also be applied to bleeding cuts and abrasions). The liniment **Zheng Gu Shui [12.6]** is used specifically for the treatment of broken bones.

Fu Fang Dan Shen Pian †   12.1
復方丹參片
Compound Formula Salvia Tablets

Primary Functions and Applications: **Fu Fang Dan Shen Pian** promotes blood circulation, transforms static blood, and eliminates sensations of uneasiness. It is used specifically to treat symptoms related to coronary artery disease from blood stasis. Symptoms in such cases usually include strong, fixed, stabbing, and sharp pain (which may be worse at night), often accompanied by heart palpitations. The tongue will likely be dark purple, and the pulse deep and choppy. **Fu Fang Dan Shen Pian** is also prescribed to reduce high blood pressure.

Format and Administration: **Fu Fang Dan Shen Pian** is produced by the Shanghai Chinese Medical Works in bottles of 50 tablets.

Recommended Dosage: Two tablets, 3 times a day.

Fu Fang Dan Shen Pian		
Constituent Substances		
Pinyin Name	**Pharmaceutical Name**	**% Composition**
Dan Shen	*Radix Salviae Miltiorhizae*	75
Bing Pian	*Borneolum*	25

Composition and Rationale: *Dan Shen* invigorates the blood, disperses static blood, and tranquilizes the spirit. *Bing Pian* is aromatic, and opens the heart portals and relieves chest pain.

Zhong Guo Ji Ben Zhong Chen Yao (Fundamentals of Chinese Prepared Medicines, 1988) includes *She Xiang* in its standardized formula for **Fu Fang Dan Shen Pian**.

Fu Fang Dan Shen Pian is a modification of the original formula **Dan Shen Pian [12.1a]**, a tablet composed solely of *Dan Shen* extract. Though both formulae have similar effects in the treatment of coronary artery disease, **Dan Shen Pian [12.1a]** is also used to resolve blood stasis in cases of dysmenorrhea or amenorrhea, as well as for bruises.

Laboratory research in China has shown that **Dan Shen Pian [12.1a]** may be used to improve heart muscle contraction and to distend the coronary arteries, thus increasing the heart's blood supply while decreasing heart rate. Clinical research trials in China showed that 80% of subjects with heart disease to whom *Dan Shen* was administered for one month had remission of such symptoms as chest fullness and angina. Electrocardiograms indicated improvement in 30-50% of those subjects, and higher rates of improvement in subjects who took *Dan Shen* for one year.

12.2   Yan Hu Su Zhi Tong Pian †
延胡索止痛片
Corydalis Extract Pain-Relieving Tablets

Primary Functions and Applications: **Yan Hu Su Zhi Tong Pian** promotes blood circulation, relieves pain, and relaxes smooth and striated muscle spasms. It is used to treat pain due to blood stasis and qi stagnation, and is appropriate in cases of dysmenorrhea, post-partum uterine pain, and other gynecological disorders with pain, stomachache including gastric or duodenal ulcer, abdominal pain, hypochondrium pain that may be associated with hepatitis or gallbladder problems, chest pain that may be associated with angina, and generalized pain due to rheumatism or injury. It is especially effective in the treatment of dull pain. By its gentle tranquilizing effect, **Yan Hu Su Zhi Tong Pian** is also indicated in cases of uneasiness, agitation, and insomnia, especially when caused by pain. The formula inhibits the reticular activating system but does not act directly on the cortex or on the periaqueductal grey matter (Bensky & Gamble, 1986).

Yan Hu Su Zhi Tong Pian is effective in relaxing striated muscle spasms, and is thus useful in relaxing tremors and spasms. The most effective ingredient in **Yan Hu Su**, tetrahydropalmatine ($C_{21}H_{25}O_4N$), has a synergistic effect with Dilantin in reducing seizures. (1960: "Pharmacological research on yan hu su: The effect of tetrahydropalmatine on the central nervous system." *Sheng Li Xue Bao, Physiology Journal* 24(2):110-120.)

Finally, it is used to treat chronic headache, especially when associated with insomnia.

Format and Administration: **Yan Hu Su Zhi Tong Pian** is produced by the Sing-Kyn Drug House, Guangzhou, China, as *Coryanalgine Tetrahydropalmatine Sulfas* in vials of 12 tablets. Each tablet contains 50 mg of the extract tetrahydropalmatine.

An herbal formula with a very similar name, **Yan Hu Suo Zhi Tong Pian [12.2a]**, is produced by the Chongqing Chinese Medicine Factory, Chongqing, Szechuan, China, as *Corydalis Yanhusu Analgesic Tablets*. In addition to the herb *Yan Hu Suo*, this formula contains *Bai Zhi (Radix Angelicae)*, and can be used to treat headache caused by wind-cold. **Yan Hu Suo Zhi Tong Pian [12.2a]** contains botanicals exclusively; **Yan Hu Su Zhi Tong Pian** contains the extract from the *Yan Hu Suo* herb, tetrahydropalmatine.

Recommended Dosage: For pain, take 1 to 2 tablets, twice or 3 times a day. For insomnia, take 1 to 3 tablets before bedtime.

Yan Hu Su Zhi Tong Pian		
Constituent Substances		
Pinyin Name	**Pharmaceutical Name**	**% Composition**
Yan Hu Suo	*Tuber Corydalis Yanhusuo*	100

Zhong Guo Ji Ben Zhong Chen Yao (Fundamentals of Chinese Prepared Medicines, 1988) lists this medicine as *Yan Hu Zhi Tong Pian,* and includes *Bai Zhi* in its standardized formula.

12.3

Qi Li San †
七厘散
Seven Pinches Powder

Source: *Liang Fang Ji Ye (Collection of Fine Formulas)*, Qing Dynasty (1644-1911).

Primary Functions and Applications: **Qi Li San** promotes blood circulation, transforms static blood, reduces swelling, and relieves pain. It is used to treat sports and other traumatic injuries, including open wounds, broken bones, and soft tissue injuries such as sprains, strains, and bruises; and to treat skin infections, including carbuncles and sores, ulcers (with or without infection), first or second degree burns caused by fire or hot water, and herpes zoster (shingles).

Because this formula transforms static blood, opens the portals, and relieves pain, some researchers have begun to use it to treat coronary artery disease and myocarditis, and to treat patients with chronic hepatitis who suffer from severe pain in the region of the liver due to blood stasis.

Format and Administration: **Qi Li San** is produced by the Beijing Tong Ren Tang, in vials containing 1.5 grams of powder.

Topical Application: For contusions, fractures, sprains, strains, bruises, and burns, apply a paste of **Qi Li San** and white wine to the affected area. Cover with a sterile dressing and re-apply once a day. For open wounds, sprinkle the powder over the wound, cover with a sterile dressing and re-apply once a day. Topical application may be combined with internal administration.

Internal: Two tenths to 9 tenths of a gram with warm water or wine, once to 3 times a day. The powder may also be placed in gelatin capsules and swallowed.

Contraindication: **Do not use Qi Li San during pregnancy.**

Qi Li San		
Constituent Substances		
Pinyin Name	**Pharmaceutical Name**	**% Composition**
Xue Jie	*Sanguis Draconis*	52.4
Hong Hua	*Flos Carthami Tinctorii*	8.7
Ru Xiang	*Gummi Olibanum*	8.7
Mo Yao	*Myrrha*	8.7
She Xiang	*Secretio Moschi Moschiferig*	0.7
Bing Pian	*Borneolum*	0.7
Zhu Sha	*Cinnabaris*	7.0
Er Cha	*Acacia seu Catechu*	13.1

Composition and Rationale: Xue Jie and Hong Hua move the blood and disperse stagnation; *Ru Xiang* and *Mo Yao* remove stagnation of qi and blood, reduce swelling, and relieve pain; *She Xiang* and *Bing Pian* promote circulation of qi and blood, open the portals, clear the channels, and relieve pain; *Zhu Sha* tranquilizes the heart and calms the spirit; and *Er Cha* clears heat and controls bleeding.

Die Da Yao Jin [12.3a], a liniment version of **Qi Li San** produced by the Tientsin Drug Manufactory as *Tieh Ta Yao Gin*, may be used in the same manner as the powder.

Jin Gu Die Shang Wan [12.3b], produced by the Tientsin Drug Manufactory in bottles of 120 pills, adds *San Qi (Radix Pseudoginseng)* to the **Qi Li San** formula, thus increasing its antihemorrhagic effect. It is used for traumatic injury accompanied by bleeding.

She Xiang Die Da Gao
麝香跌打膏
Musk Impact Trauma Plaster

12.4

Primary Functions and Applications: **She Xiang Die Da Gao** promotes blood circulation, transforms static blood, and relieves pain. It is used to treat contusions, sprains, strains, sports injuries, or other traumatic injuries. This formula is especially effective in reducing swelling and relieving pain, and will help regenerate injured tissue.

Format and Administration: **She Xiang Die Da Gao** is produced by the Tianjin Drug Manufactory, Tian Jin, China, as *Musk Anti-Contusion Plasters* in boxes of 6 plasters.

The therapeutic benefits of plasters are enhanced if application follows a warm bath. Wash the affected area first with gentle soap and warm water. Peel the plaster from the cellophane and place it over the affected area, using as many plasters as necessary for adequate coverage. The plaster(s) may be left in place for 2 days, during which time they must be kept dry.

Contraindication: **Do not use She Xiang Die Da Gao during pregnancy.** Discontinue use if redness, itching, or allergic skin reaction develops.

Only the seven primary ingredients are listed below.

She Xiang Die Da Gao		
Constituent Substances		
Pinyin Name	Pharmaceutical Name	% Composition
She Xiang	*Secretio Moschi Moschiferig*	—
Ru Xiang	*Gummi Olibanum*	—
Mo Yao	*Myrrha*	—
Hong Hua	*Flos Carthami Tinctorii*	—
Ding Xiang	*Flos Caryophylli*	—
Chuan Xiong	*Rhizoma Ligustici Wallichii*	—
Long Bao	*Borneolum Camphor*	—

Composition and Rationale: *She Xiang* moves static blood and relieves pain; *Ru Xiang* and *Mo Yao* promote blood circulation and relieve pain; *Hong Hua* promotes blood circulation and transforms static blood; *Ding Xiang* moves stagnant qi and relieves pain; *Chuan Xiong* promotes blood circulation and moves stagnant qi; and *Long Bao* reduces swelling and relieves pain.

Die Da Zhi Tong Gao
跌打止痛膏
Impact Injury Pain-Relieving Plaster

Primary Functions and Applications: **Die Da Zhi Tong Gao** promotes blood circulation, relaxes sinews and muscles, transforms static blood, and relieves pain. It is used to treat sports or traumatic injuries with bruising and swelling; to treat sprains and fractures; to treat lumbar area backache due to over-exertion; and to treat neuralgia and chronic arthritis.

Format and Administration: **Die Da Zhi Tong Gao** is produced by the United Pharmaceutical Manufactory as *Plaster for Bruise and Analgesic* in boxes of 10 plasters. Measuring 10 cm x 28 cm in size, this herbal plaster is one of the largest available. It may be used either whole, or cut into pieces for appropriate coverage. Press the plaster firmly to form a tight seal with the skin. If the plaster does not stick tightly to the skin, as may happen especially in the winter, use gauze or tape to secure it. This herbal plaster will be effective for 2 days. Keep the plaster dry, if possible.

Contraindications: Discontinue use if redness, itching, or allergic skin reaction occurs. Do not use on an open wound.

Die Da Zhi Tong Gao		
Constituent Substances		
Pinyin Name	**Pharmaceutical Name**	**% Composition**
Hong Hua	*Flos Carthami Tinctorii*	9.17
Mo Yao	*Myrrha*	6.25
Xue Jie	*Sanguis Draconis*	4.17
Er Cha	*Acacia seu Catechu*	6.25
Tu Bie Chong	*Eupolyphaga seu Opisthoplatia*	10.42
Xu Duan	*Radix Dispaci*	4.17
Gu Sui Bu	*Rhizoma Drynariae*	4.17
Long Gu	*Os Draconis*	10.42
Da Huang	*Rhizoma Rhei*	8.33
Pu Gong Ying	*Herba cum Radice Taraxaci Mongolici*	8.33
Bo He	*Herba Menthae*	20.00
Dong Qing Yu	*Wintergreen Oil*	8.32

Composition and Rationale: Hong Hua, Mo Yao, Xue Jie, Er Cha, and *Tu Bie Chong* promote blood circulation, transform stagnation and relieve pain; *Xu Duan*, *Gu Sui Bu* and *Long Gu* promote blood circulation, relieve pain, promote the healing of broken bones, and relax sinews and muscles; *Da Huang* and *Pu Gong Ying* transform static blood, clear heat, and reduce swelling; and *Bo He* and *Dong Qing Yu* disperse stagnant qi and relieve pain.

12.6   Zheng Gu Shui
正骨水
Bone-Correcting Water

Primary Functions and Applications: **Zheng Gu Shui** promotes blood circulation, reduces swelling, relieves pain, promotes regeneration of broken bone tissue, and promotes healing of fractures. It is used to treat fractures and dislocated joints from sports or other traumatic injuries.

Format and Administration: **Zheng Gu Shui** is produced by the Tulin Drug Manufactory, Kwangsi, China, in 50 ml and 100 ml bottles.

Although a single application of **Zheng Gu Shui** may be useful as an analgesic before a fracture is set or a dislocation re-positioned, daily application should not begin until after such procedures have been performed by a medical professional using hospital facilities. After the bone is set, apply a cotton ball soaked with the **Zheng Gu Shui** to the affected area. Two or three soaked cotton balls may be used to "surround" the fractured area. Lightly wrap the soaked cotton balls with gauze. Leave the soaked cotton balls on the area for one hour if the fracture is on an upper limb, or for 1½ hours if the fracture is on a lower limb. The cotton balls will be dry when they are removed, and there will be no need to wipe the skin. Follow this procedure twice a day until complete recovery has taken place.

Contraindications: This solution is for external use only. Keep away from children. When used for children, reduce application time. When for adults, do not leave the soaked cotton ball in place for more than the indicated period of time. If the patient has a serious skin reaction to the solution (blistering or rash), discontinue use. Do not apply this solution to an open wound. The solution is flammable; keep the bottle tightly closed.

Zheng Gu Shui		
Constituent Substances		
Pinyin Name	**Pharmaceutical Name**	**% Composition**
San Qi	*Radix, Folium et Flos Pseudoginseng*	25
Bai Zhi	*Radix Angelicae*	13
Ji Gu Xiang	*Radix Crotonis Crassifolii*	15
Bo He Nao	*Herba Menthae (Crystal)*	3
Zhang Nao	*Camphora*	2
Wu Ma Xun Cheng	*Semen Tiglii*	18
Qian Jin Ba	*Radix Moghaniae Philippinensis*	12
Da Li Wang	*Inula Cappa*	12

Composition and Rationale: *San Qi* and *Bai Zhi* eliminate bruising, control bleeding, reduce swelling, relieve pain, and transform static blood; *Ji Gu Xiang*, *Bo He Nao*, and *Zhang Nao* move stagnant qi, open portals, and relieve pain; and *Wu Ma Xun Cheng*, *Qian Jin Ba*, and *Da Li Wang* strengthen the bones and sinews, help regenerate damaged tissues, reduce swelling, and relieve pain.

Die Da Wan Hua You
跌打萬花油
Myriad Flowers Impact Trauma Oil

12.7

Primary Functions and Applications: **Die Da Wan Hua You** promotes blood circulation, disperses stagnation, reduces swelling, relaxes sinews, relieves pain, and promotes regeneration of damaged tissues. It is used to treat sports or traumatic injuries, with or without open wounds; to treat sprains and strains of muscles and sinews; to treat burns due to flames or hot liquid; and to treat bleeding cuts on the skin (including those resulting from martial arts practice.)

Format and Administration: **Die Da Wan Hua You** is produced by the United Pharmaceutical Manufactory, Guangzhou, China, in 15 ml bottles. For sports or traumatic injuries without open wounds, rub the injured area with a cotton ball soaked with this oil, two or three times per day. For burns and cuts, soak a cotton ball, apply to the injured area, and wrap the area with gauze. Change the soaked cotton ball daily.

Die Da Wan Hua You		
Constituent Substances		
Pinyin Name	**Pharmaceutical Name**	**% Composition**
San Qi	*Radix, Folium et Flos Pseudoginseng*	22
Gu Sui Bu	*Rhizoma Drynariae*	11.76
Hong Hua	*Flos Carthami Tinctorii*	11.76
Xue Jie	*Sanguis Draconis*	8.82
Ru Xiang	*Gummi Olibanum*	8.82
Mo Yao	*Myrrha*	8.82
Wu Ming Yi	*Pyrolusitum*	8.82
La Mei Hua	*Flos Chimonanthus*	8.82
Lu Hui	*Herba Aloes*	11.76

Composition and Rationale: *San Qi* and *Gu Sui Bu* control bleeding, disperse static blood, strengthen the bones, and promote regeneration of injured tissues; *Hong Hua, Xue Jie, Ru Xiang, Mo Yao, Wu Ming Yi*, and *La Mei Hua* promote blood circulation, reduce swelling, and relieve pain; and *Lu Hui* heals burns and wounds.

Gu Zhe Cuo Shang San † 　　12.8
骨折挫傷散
Fracture and Contusion Powder

Primary Functions and Applications: **Gu Zhe Cuo Shang San** promotes blood circulation, aids regeneration of bone tissue, soothes muscles and sinews, reduces swelling and relieves pain. It is used to aid in the healing of broken bones, bruises, contusions, sprains, strains, and other tissue injuries associated with trauma, including sports injuries.

Format and Administration: **Gu Zhe Cuo Shang San** is produced by the Kiamusze Chinese Medicine Works, Kiamusze, China, as *Fractura Pulvis* in bottles of 50 capsules.

Recommended Dosage: Seven capsules, three times a day, with warm water or warm wine. Reduce the dosage proportionately with children.

Contraindication: **Do not use Gu Zhe Cuo Shang San during pregnancy.**

Gu Zhe Cuo Shang San		
Constituent Substances		
Pinyin Name	**Pharmaceutical Name**	**% Composition**
Ye Zhu Gu	*Cranium Suis Scrofae*	45
Huang Gua Zi	*Semen Cucumeris Sativae*	37
Dang Gui	*Radix Angelicae Sinensis*	3
Hong Hua	*Flos Carthami Tinctorii*	5
Xue Jie	*Sanguis Draconis*	2
Da Huang	*Rhizoma Rhei*	
Ru Xiang	*Gummi Olibanum*	2
Mo Yao	*Myrrha*	2
Tu Bie Chong	*Eupolyphaga seu Opishoplatia*	1

Composition and Rationale: Ye Zhu Gu and *Huang Gua Zi* strengthen and regenerate bones; *Dang Gui, Hong Hua, Xue Jie,* and *Da Huang* nourish and move blood; *Ru Xiang, Mo Yao,* and *Tu Bie Chong* act as analgesics, move static blood, and reduce swelling.

Zhong Guo Ji Ben Zhong Chen Yao (Fundamentals of Chinese Prepared Medicines, 1988) includes *Zi Ran Tong (Pyritum)* in its standardized formula for **Gu Zhe Cuo Shang San.**

12.9

Mao Dong Qing
毛冬青
Ilex Root Formula

Primary Functions and Applications: **Mao Dong Qing** promotes blood circulation, transforms static blood, clears heat, and resolves fire toxin. It generally improves the function of the heart, and is used primarily to treat coronary artery disease, angina pectoris, and such related symptoms as headache, dizziness, and numbness. **Mao Dong Qing** has been shown to produce positive effects within one month of therapy (*Xin Yi Xue,* 1972, 5:12-16.)

Mao Dong Qing is effective in the treatment of Buerger's Disease (thromboangilitis obliterans), a condition of intravascular clot formation, with attendant inflammation of the vessel wall. In such cases, clinical results will be better for patients with local or general heat signs, including swelling, redness, pain, sensations of warmth, thirst, constipation, rapid pulse, and yellow tongue coating.

Mao Dong Qing is also used to treat patients with a history of transient ischemic attacks and arteriosclerosis. Clinical reports show that this medicine will improve blood circulation (1972: *Xin Yi Xue* 2:37).

Finally, **Mao Dong Qing** may be used to treat infections that may be associated with pharyngitis, bronchitis, and tonsillitis.

Format and Administration: **Mao Ding Qing** is produced by the Kwanchow Pharmaceutical Industry Company as *Maodungching*, in bottles of thirty 500 mg capsules.

Recommended Dosage: Three capsules, 3 times a day for 7 days, followed by a 3 day hiatus.

Contraindications: In some patients, slight nausea, abdominal cramping, dizziness, or headaches may occur with the administration of large doses of **Mao Dong Qing**. In a small number of cases, administration of **Mao Dong Qing** will produce symptoms associated with the presence of blood thinners, especially easy bruising.

Patients with low platelet counts or internal bleeding problems (such as bleeding ulcers) or hypermenorrhea should use this medicine with caution.

Mao Dong Qing		
Constituent Substances		
Pinyin Name	**Pharmaceutical Name**	**% Composition**
Mao Dong Qing	*Radix Ilicis Pubescentis*	100%

Yun Nan Bai Yao †   12.10
雲南白藥
Yunnan White

Primary Functions and Applications: **Yun Nan Bai Yao** controls bleeding and relieves pain (transforms static blood). It is used to control bleeding from open wounds (including severe bleeding associated with gunshot wounds), and to control internal bleeding from such sources as:

1. *Gastric system bleeding,* including the serious bleeding associated with vomiting of blood due to stomach ulcer, stomach cancer, or cirrhosis of the liver; and intestinal bleeding with blood in the stools as a result of such disorders as colitis.

2. *Pulmonary system bleeding,* including the serious hemoptysis accompanying pulmonary tuberculosis, bronchiectasis, and lung cancer.

3. *Nasal bleeding (epistaxis),* including serious nose bleeding associated with hypertension, leukemia, hemophilia, and thrombocytopenia.

In addition, **Yun Nan Bai Yao** is used internally to treat soft tissue sports injuries, such as sprains and strains of the joints and muscles, with symptoms such as pain, swelling, and bruising; and to treat gynecological disorders caused by blood stasis, such as dysmenorrhea, amenorrhea, hypermenorrhea, and postpartum hemorrhaging.

According to the December 30, 1985 issue of the Hong Kong newspaper, *South China Morning Post*, Dr. James Ma, an organic chemist who specializes in spectroscopy at the Chemistry Department of Chinese University, Hong Kong, has conducted research into the chemical components of **Yun Nan Bai Yao**. He reports there are 21 components, four of which are classified as being active in arresting hemorrhage. Both *in vitro* and *in vivo* studies have been carried out regarding the clotting time for blood when **Yun Nan Bai Yao** was used. The clotting time for human blood in a test tube was observed to be reduced by 33 percent. In animal studies where the actual rate of hemorrhage was examined, it was cut by 54 per cent. Dr. Ma states that the herb stimulates a physiological mechanism significantly different from anything found in Western medicine. He has sent the pure compound to a world authority in Sweden who predicted that it could possibly have anti-cancer properties. Some Chinese medical authorities have also said **Yu Nan Bai Yao** could be useful in the treatment of leukemia.

During the Vietnam war, **Yun Nan Bai Yao** was often discovered in a tiny bottle on the bodies of dead Vietcong soldiers. Wounded soldiers sprinkled it on their injuries to control severe bleeding while waiting for emergency medical treatment.

Other work on **Yun Nan Bai Yao** has been conducted in Taiwan, Japan, and India, as well as in the state of Wisconsin. It is grown primarily in Yunnan Province and in Nepal, and is now being grown on herb farms in China.

Format and Administration: **Yun Nan Bai Yao** is produced by the Yunnan Paiyao Factory, Yunnan, China, in bubble-packs of 16 capsules, or in small 4 gram bottles. This medicine is also sometimes called *Bai Yao* (white medicine). Each package of 12 capsules, and each bottle, contains one small red "emergency" pill called *Bao Xian Zi*. This pill is used only as a first-aid emergency measure to prevent shock following severe bleeding or injury. For best results, the pill should be taken with wine. The contents of the *Bao Xian Zi* are different from the **Yun Nan Bai Yao** powder. The *Bao Xian Zi* contains analgesics and portal-opening agents, but does not reduce bleeding, as does the **Yun Nan Bai Yao** that accompanies it.

Recommended Dosage, Internal Use: Adults, 0.25 to 0.5 grams of powder, or 1 to 2 capsules, 4 times a day. The powder can be swallowed with liquid or put into gelatin capsules and swallowed with liquid.

Children: Age 2 to 5 years: use one-fourth the adult dose, 4 times a day. Age 5 to 12 years: use one-half the adult dose, 4 times a day.

For bleeding injuries, the powder should be taken with water. For injuries that are not bleeding (sprain or strain of joint or muscle), the powder should be taken with wine. For gynecological disorders, the powder should be taken with wine, but if heavy bleeding is present, the powder should be taken with water.

When the red "emergency" pill must be used, never exceed 1 pill per day.

Recommended Dosage, Topical Use: Sprinkle the powder onto the open wound and apply pressure until bleeding has stopped.

Contraindication: **Do not use Yun Nan Bai Yao during pregnancy.** Do not eat fish or shellfish, lima beans, or cold or sour foods during therapy that includes **Yun Nan Bai Yao**.

Yun Nan Bai Yao		
Constituent Substances		
Pinyin Name	Pharmaceutical Name	% Composition
San Qi	*Radix, Folium et Flos Pseudoginseng*	—
—	*Unlisted Addidiontal Ingredients*	—

Composition and Rationale: San Qi transforms static blood, controls bleeding, reduces swelling, and relieves pain.

12.11   Qian Jin Zhi Dai Wan †
千金止帶丸
Thousand Gold Piece Vaginal Discharge Pills

Source: *Ji Yin Gang Mu (Compendium of Therapy for Women's Diseases),* Qing Dynasty (1644-1911).

Primary Functions and Applications: **Qian Jin Zhi Dai Wan** regulates qi and blood, adjusts menstruation, and is appropriate for the treatment of leukorrhea in cases of depletion.

It will be recalled that spleen qi depletion, the most common form of splenic transformation failure, may be manifested as an accumulation of damp. Dampness retention, fundamental in the etiology of leukorrhea, will in turn produce such signs as lumbar ache, abdominal distension, fatigue, and poor appetite. The tongue coating in such cases will be white and greasy, and the pulse slippery.

Qian Jin Zhi Dai Wan is indicated in the treatment of dysmenorrhea and amenorrhea (from qi and/or blood stagnation, or kidney depletion), providing relief from menstrual cramps through the use of herbs that move stagnant liver qi and reduce pain.

Format and Administration: **Qian Jin Zhi Dai Wan** is produced by the Tientsin Drug Manufactory as *Chien Chin Chih Tai Wan* in pill form, 120 pills per bottle.

Recommended Dosage: Ten pills, once or twice a day.

Qian Jin Zhi Dai Wan		
Constituent Substances		
Pinyin Name	**Pharmaceutical Name**	**% Composition**
Dang Gui	*Radix Angelicae Sinensis*	10
Bai Zhu	*Rhizoma Atractylodis Macrocephalae*	5
Xiao Hui Xiang	*Fructus Foeniculi Vulgaris*	5
Yan Hu Suo	*Tuber Corydalis Yanhusuo*	10
Mu Xiang	*Radix Saussureae seu Vladimiriae*	10
Xu Duan	*Radix Dispaci*	10
Dang Shen	*Radix Codonopsis Pilosulae*	12
Mu Li	*Concha Ostreae (fired)*	12
Qing Dai	*Indigo Pulverata Levis*	16

Composition and Rationale: Dang Gui nourishes the blood, promotes blood circulation and regulates menstruation; *Bai Zhu* supplements the spleen and eliminates dampness; *Xiao Hui Xiang* regulates qi, warms the yang and alleviates pain; *Yan Hu Suo* promotes blood circulation and alleviates pain; *Mu Xiang* moves stagnant qi and relieves pain; *Xu Duan* strengthens the liver and kidney and controls bleeding; *Dang Shen* strengthens the spleen and supplements the qi; *Mu Li* controls leukorrhea and hypermenorrhea (functioning as an astringent); and *Qing Dai* clears damp heat.

Zhong Guo Ji Ben Zhong Chen Yao (Fundamentals of Chinese Prepared Medicines, 1988) includes *Xiang Fu, Chun Bai Pi, Ji Guan Hua, Bai Shao, Sha Ren, Bu Gu Zhi, Chuan Xiong,* and *Du Zhong* in its standardized formula for *Zhi Dai Wan.*

Wu Ji Bai Feng Wan †
烏雞白鳳丸
Black Chicken and White Phoenix Pills

12.12

Source: Shou Shi Bau Yuan *(Protection of Vital Energy for Long Life Book),* Ming Dynasty (1368-1644).

Primary Functions and Applications: **Wu Ji Bai Feng Wan** is among the most commonly used medicines in China for the adjustment of menstruation. Its special formulation strengthens qi and blood without producing stasis or stagnation and warms the yang without producing dryness. It is used to treat gynecological disorders that result from qi and blood depletion, and its use is indicated by such symptoms as irregular menstruation (early or late menses), hypermenorrhea or hypomenorrhea, pre-menstrual syndrome, dysmenorrhea or pain with ovulation, leukor-rhea, postpartum weakness, postpartum bleeding, fatigue, low back pain, feelings of weakness in the legs, poor appetite, and weight loss or weight gain problems.

It may also be used to treat general syndromes of qi and blood depletion, including cases of chronic hepatitis. Clinical research in China has shown this formula to decrease SGPT levels in the blood in chronic hepa-titis cases.

Format and Administration: **Wu Ji Bai Feng Wan** is produced by the Tientsin Drug Manufactory and by the Beijing Tong Ren Tang as *Wuchi Paifeng Wan.* Beijing Tong Ren Tang manufactures the formula as one large honey pill inside a wax ball. Tientsin produces a wax ball containing many small honey pills, as well as bottles of 120 pills. Boxes that contain miniature pills will have the words, *"Xiao Mi Wan'* or *"Xiao Li Wan"* ("small honey pill") printed on the package.

Recommended Dosage: One honey pill (the entire contents of wax ball) twice a day.

Contraindications: Zhong Guo Ji Ben Zhong Chen Yao (Fundamentals of Chinese Prepared Medicines, 1988) recommends not administering **Wu Ji Bai Feng Wan** during pregnancy.

Wu Ji Bai Feng Wan		
Constituent Substances		
Pinyin Name	**Pharmaceutical Name**	**% Composition**
Wu Ji	*Pullus cum Osse Nigro*	33.80
Ren Shen	*Radix Ginseng*	6.45
Huang Qi	*Radix Astragali*	1.63
Dang Gui	*Radix Angelicae Sinensis*	6.45
Bai Shao	*Radix Paeoniae Lactiflora*	6.45
Sheng Di Huang	*Radix Crudae Rehmanniae Glutinosae*	12.90
Shou Di Huang	*Radix Rehmannia Glutinosae*	12.90
Xiang Fu	*Rhizoma Cyperi Rotundi*	6.45
Shan Yao	*Radix Dioscoreae Oppositae*	6.45
Lu Jiao Jiao	*Gelatinum Cornu Cervi*	6.45

Composition and Rationale: Wu Ji strengthens the liver and kidney yin and supplements blood; *Ren Shen* supplements the qi and strengthens the spleen; *Huang Qi* strengthens the qi and controls daytime sweating. *Dang Gui* nourishes the blood, promotes blood circulation, and controls bleeding; *Bai Shao* nourishes the yin, strengthens the blood, relieves abdominal pain, and relaxes smooth muscles; *Sheng Di Huang* strengthens the yin and clears depletion heat; *Shou Di Huang* nourishes the yin and supplements the blood; *Xiang Fu* regulates qi and blood and relieves menstrual cramping; *Shan Yao* strengthens the spleen and controls leukorrhea; and *Lu Jiao* strengthens the kidney yang.

Zhong Guo Ji Ben Zhong Chen Yao (Fundamentals of Chinese Prepared Medicines, 1988) includes *Dang Shen, Bie Jia, Yin Chai Hu, Qian Shi, Sang Piao Xiao, Chuan Xiong, Gan Cao, Tian Men Dong, Mu Li* and *Lu Jiao Shuang* in its standardized formula for **Wu Ji Bai Feng Wan**. More recently, some manufactories have modified this formula, and have added such supplements as *Ren Shen (Radix Ginseng)* or *Lu Rong (Cornu Cervi Parvum)* to further nourish qi and blood, and, when *Lu Rong* is included, to warm kidney yang. Some of these altered formulae are available under the names **Shen Rong Bai Feng Wan [12.12a]** or **Zhen Zhu Bai Feng Wan [12.12b]**. These will often cost double or triple the original formula, **Wu Ji Bai Feng Wan**.

249

12.13   Wu Jin Wan †
烏金丸
Black Gold Pills

Source: Zhong Guo Yi Xue Da Ci Dian (Complete Glossary of Traditional Chinese Medicine), 1924.

Primary Functions and Applications: **Wu Jin Wan** promotes blood circulation, removes stagnant qi, regulates menstruation, and relieves pain. It is used to treat such symptoms of stagnant qi and blood stasis as sharp pain in the hypochondrium, dysmenorrhea, amenorrhea, or postpartum pain in the lower abdomen. Patients with such symptoms may also have a pale face, fatigue, low-grade afternoon fever, and dry skin.

Wu Jin Wan may be used to help expel a retained placenta, and to treat endometriosis when in the presence of the symptoms mentioned above.

Format and Administration: **Wu Jin Wan** is produced by the Chan Li Chai Medical Factory, Hong Kong, in honey pill format, 10 pills per box.

Recommended Dosage: One honey pill twice a day.

Contraindication: **Do not use Wu Jin Wan during pregnancy.** This formula contains strong herbs to move qi and blood.

Wu Jin Wan		
Constituent Substances		
Pinyin Name	**Pharmaceutical Name**	**% Composition**
Yi Mu Cao	*Herba Leonuri Artemisiae*	38.4
San Leng	*Rhizoma Sparganii*	2.4
E Zhu	*Rhizoma Zedoariae*	2.4
Xiang Fu	*Rhizoma Cyperi Rotundi*	14.4
Yan Hu Suo	*Tuber Corydalis Yanhusuo*	7.2
Wu Zhu Yu	*Fructus Evodiae*	2.4
Xiao Hui Xiang	*Fructus Foeniculi Vulgaris*	2.4
Mu Xiang	*Radix Saussureae seu Vladimiriae*	2.4
Bai Shao	*Radix Paeoniae Lactiflora*	7.2
Chuan Xiong	*Rhizoma Ligustici Wallichii*	7.2
Dang Gui	*Radix Angelicae Sinensis*	2.4
Shou Di Huang	*Radix Rehmannia Glutinosae*	2.4
Bu Gu Zhi	*Semen Psoralae Corytoliae*	2.4
Pu Huang	*Pollen Typhae*	2.4
Ai Ye Tan	*Folium Carbonisatum Artemisiae*	2.4

Compostition and Rationale: *Yi Mu Cao, San Leng,* and *E Zhu* promote blood circulation and disperse blood stasis; *Xiang Fu, Yan Hu Suo, Wu Zhu Yu, Xiao Hui Xiang,* and *Mu Xiang* course the liver and relieve pain; *Bai Shao, Chuan Xiong, Dang Gui,* and *Shou Di Huang* supplement and move and regulate menstruation; *Bu Gu Zhi* fortifies kidney yang and warms the spleen; and *Pu Huang* and *Ai Ye Tan* are menstruation regulating antihemorrhagics.

Zhong Guo Ji Ben Zhong Chen Yao (Fundamentals of Chinese Prepared Medicines, 1988) includes *Rou Gui* and *Jiang Can* in its standardized formula for **Wu Jin Wan**.

Manufactories in China produce different formulae of the same name. A formula manufactured in Hong Kong with a similar name, **Fu Ke Wu Jin Wan** (gynecology black gold pills), has twelve ingredients: *Liu Ji Nu, Xiang Fu, E Zhu, Qing Pi, Zhi Qiao, Ai Ye, Dang Gui, Huang Qin, Chi Gui (Rou Gui), Bai Zhu,* and *Gan Jiang.*

12.14 Dang Gui Su
當歸素
Angelica Sinensis Extract

Primary Functions and Applications: **Dang Gui Su** nourishes blood to regulate menstruation, promotes blood circulation, and relieves pain, and is used to treat blood depletion related to gynecological disorders. It regulates menstruation and relieves menstrual cramping (dysmenorrhea), and is indicated in the presence of the following symptoms: delayed menstruation, hypomenorrhea or hypermenorrhea with pale blood, or amenorrhea. In addition, it may be used to treat postpartum abdominal pain. It is indicated in heart blood depletion, with palpitations, poor memory, insomnia, uneasiness; in spleen blood depletion (with fatigue, pale face, poor appetite); and in liver blood depletion, with dizziness, vertigo, tinnitus, tremor. It is recommended in cases of sports injuries, chronic carbuncles that have failed to heal properly, anemia, and coronary artery disease. Laboratory research in China has observed that **Dang Gui Su** has been found to gradually increase the red blood cell count and gradually increase the blood supply to the heart.

Format and Administration: **Dang Gui Su** is produced by the Lanchow Chinese Medicine Works as *Tang Kui Su* in pill format, 100 per bottle.

Recommended Dosage: Six pills, 3 times a day.

Dang Gui Su		
Constituent Substances		
Pinyin Name	**Pharmaceutical Name**	**% Composition**
Dang Gui	*Radix Angelicae Sinensis*	100

Composition and Rationale: *Dang Gui* nourishes the blood and promotes blood circulation.

Fu Ke Zhong Zi Wan   12.15
婦科種子丸
Gynecological Seed-Planting Pills

Source: *Tong Shou Lu (Longevity Book)*, Qing Dynasty (1644-1911).

Primary Functions and Applications: **Fu Ke Zhong Zi Wan** regulates menstruation, supplements the blood, removes qi stagnation, and transforms static blood. It is used to treat such manifestations of abdominal blood stasis and qi stagnation as irregular menstruation (early or late), dysmenorrhea, menstrual bleeding with dark blood or clots; and feelings of fullness in the chest or abdomen. It is also used to treat uterine tumors, endometriosis, or infertility resulting from qi stagnation and blood stasis in the abdomen.

Format and Administration: **Fu Ke Zhong Zi Wan** is produced by the Lanchow Chinese Medicine Works, Lanchow, China, in bottles of 100 pills.

Recommended Dosage: Eight pills, 3 times a day.

Contraindication: **Do not use Fu Ke Zhong Zi Wan during pregnancy.**

Fu Ke Zhong Zi Wan		
Constituent Substances		
Pinyin Name	Pharmaceutical Name	% Composition
Yi Mu Cao	*Herba Leonuri Artemisiae*	50
Dang Gui	*Radix Angelicae Sinensis*	17
Bai Shao	*Radix Paeoniae Lactiflora*	17
Chai Hu	*Radix Bupleuri*	8
Mu Xiang	*Radix Saussureae seu Vladimiriae*	4
Chuan Xiong	*Rhizoma Ligustici Wallichii*	4

Composition and Rationale: *Yi Mu Cao* promotes blood circulation and transforms static blood. *Dang Gui* nourishes the blood, promotes blood circulation, and regulates menstruation; *Bai Shao* strengthens the yin, nourishes the blood, relieves abdominal pain, and relaxes smooth muscle spasms; *Chai Hu* moves stagnant liver qi; *Mu Xiang* moves stagnant qi in the abdomen, relieves pain, and disperses abdominal mass; and *Chuan Xiong* promotes blood circulation, transforms static blood, and relieves pain.

This formula is also called *Zhong Zi Wan* or, in *Zhong Guo Ji Ben Zhong Chen Yao (Fundamentals of Chinese Prepared Medicines) De Sheng Dan*, both of which are commonly mentioned in Chinese herbal medicine literature.

12.16   Bu Xue Tiao Jing Pian †
補血調經片
Blood-Nourishing Menses-Regulating Tablets

Primary Functions and Applications: **Bu Xue Tiao Jing Pian** nourishes the blood, regulates qi, and adjusts menstruation. It is used to treat menstrual disorders due to blood depletion, accompanied by the following symptoms: fatigue, pale face, pre-menstrual syndrome (signs including menstrual cramps, insomnia, headache, emotional imbalance), amenorrhea, hypomenorrhea, hypermenorrhea, or dysmenorrhea. It is also effective in the treatment of leukorrhea due to depletion of spleen qi and yang and retention of damp.

Format and Administration: **Bu Xue Tiao Jing Pian** is produced by the United Pharmaceutical Manufactory Guangzhou, China, as *Butiao Tablets*, 100 per bottle.

Recommended Dosage: Three tablets, twice or 3 times per day with warm water. Do not take during the early stage of common cold or flu when fever is present.

Bu Xue Tiao Jing Pian		
Constituent Substances		
Pinyin Name	**Pharmaceutical Name**	**% Composition**
Dang Shen	*Radix Codonopsis Pilosulae*	2.70
Gan Cao	*Radix Glycyrrhizae Uralensis*	0.90
Ji Xue Teng	*Radix Millettiae Reticulatae*	9.04
Sang Ji Sheng	*Ramus Visci Loranthi*	9.40
A Jiao	*Gelatinum Corii Asini*	0.54
Da Ji	*Herba Cirsii Japonici*	3.60
Rou Gui	*Cortex Cinnamomi Cassiae*	0.46
Gao Liang Jiang	*Rhizoma Alpiniae Officinari*	6.33
Ai Ye	*Folium Artemisiae Argyi*	4.52
Xiang Fu	*Rhizoma Cyperi Rotundi*	9.40
Yi Mu Cao	*Herba Leonuri Artemisiae*	6.33
Cang Zhu	*Radix Atractylodis*	2.30
Jin Ying Zi	*Fructus Rosae Laevigatae*	9.04

Composition and Rationale: *Dang Shen* and *Gan Cao* supplement the qi and strengthen the spleen; *Ji Xue Teng, Sang Ji Sheng, A Jiao* and *Da Ji* nourish the blood, regulate blood circulation, and control bleeding; *Rou Gui* strengthens the yang, warms the channels, expels cold, and relieves pain; *Gao Liang Jiang* and *Ai Ye* relieve pain; *Xiang Fu* and *Yi Mu Cao* regulate circulation of qi and blood, transform static blood, and regulate menstruation; and *Cang Zhu* and *Jin Ying Zi* dry dampness and control leucorrhea.

Zhong Guo Ji Ben Zhong Chen Yao (Fundamentals of Chinese Prepared Medicines, 1988) refers to this formula as *Bu Xue Tiao Jing Wan*, and includes *Gang Shen Zi, Wu Zhi, Mao Tao, Qian Jin Ba, Bai Bei Ye,* and *Dao Chi Jiang.*

13

Supplements

To supplement the qi and the blood	
13.1 Ling Zhi Feng Wang Jiang	13.9 Shen Jing Shuai Ruo Wang
13.2 Shi Quan Da Bu Wan	13.10 Fu Ke Ba Zhen Wan
13.3 Tai Pan Tang Yi Pian	13.11 Dang Gui Pian
13.4 Ge Jie Da Bu Wan	13.12 Shuang Bao Su
13.5 Ren Shen Yang Rong Wan	13.13 An Tai Wan
13.6 Bu Zhong Yi Qi Wan	13.14 Dang Gui Yang Xue Gao
13.7 Shen Ling Bai Zhu Wan	13.15 Ci Wu Jia Pian
13.8 Gui Pi Wan	13.16 Shen Qi Da Bu Wan

To supplement the yin and the yang	
13.17 He Che Da Zao Wan	13.25 Ge Jie Bu Shen Wan
13.18 Liu Wei Di Huang Wan	13.26 Kang Gu Zeng Sheng Pian
13.19 Hai Ma Bu Shen Wan	13.27 Shen Rong Hu Gu Wan
13.20 Ren Shen Lu Rong Wan	13.28 Er Ming Zuo Ci Wan
13.21 Ming Mu Di Huang Wan	13.29 Da Bu Yin Wan
13.22 Qi Ju Di Huang Wan	13.30 Quan Lu Wan
13.23 Shi Hu Ye Guang Wan	13.31 Yu Chuan Wan
13.24 Gui Ling Ji	13.32 Zhi Bao San Bian Wan

Pattern Identification and Formula Differentiation

Supplementation is generally associated with depletion patterns, and focuses on four primary objects: qi, blood, yin, and yang. Although there are cases for which generalized supplementation is appropriate (such as during recovery from a debilitating illness), treatment usually focuses on the supplementation of qi, blood, yin, or yang of specific organs, organ systems, and/or organic functions. Dual vacuity of yang and qi, blood and yin, and qi and blood, also occur, and are addressed in the structures of some formula (**Fu Ke Ba Zhen Wan [13.10]**, for example, addresses depletion of qi and blood).

The range of approaches to supplementation is evident in the terminology developed to differentiate between them. Consider the following excerpt from the glossary of *Fundamentals of Chinese Medicine*, p. 506, on the term *supplementation, bu fa*:

> "Supplementation of yin is often referred to as **nourishing, fostering,** or **enriching yin,** the last of these referring in particular to supplementation of kidney yin. **Strengthening yin** is a method of supplementing yin essence in patterns characterized by lumbar pain, seminal emission, copious urine, etc. **Emolliating** the liver is a method used to treat insufficiency of liver blood. **Engendering** liquid denotes supplementation of the fluids.

> "Supplementation of yang is often referred to as **reinforcing** yang. **Yang salvage,** or **yang restoration,** is the method used to treat yang collapse... Since yang depletion is characterized by pronounced cold signs, the method of **warming** is used. **Freeing yang** and **perfusing yang** refer to the method of eliminating yang qi flow stoppage. Supplementation of qi, usually referred to as **qi boosting,** uses agents that are less hot. **Fortification** is usually applied to the spleen or center. Fortifying the center and boosting qi is a method of treatment whereby qi is boosted by enhancing the assimilative function of the spleen. **Moving the spleen** refers to supplementation of the spleen to improve movement and transformation of water-damp. **Upraising center qi** is the method of fortifying the center to treat prolapse conditions. **Quieting the spirit** is a method of treating disquiet of the spirit-disposition, using supplementing agents, sometimes combined with heavy settlers."

As with all medicines, use supplements with care. Avoid the tendency to consider supplements "herbal vitamins," and the premise that "a little tonification can't hurt." Used excessively or inappropriately, supplements can stress the splenogastric system, and can produce unwanted heat and stasis.

We have included the following alphabetic summary of the supplements to aid in initial differentiation among the many formulae in this chapter.

Overview of Supplements	
Supplement	**Summary of Applications**
An Tai Wan [13.13] (Soothe Fetus Pills)	Obstetric formula, supplements qi and blood in the mother to calm the fetus, prevent miscarriage, arrest uterine hemorrhage.
Bu Zhong Yi Qi Wan [13.6] (Center-Supplementing, Qi-Boosting Pills)	Splenogastric tonic, whose special function is to clear heat from middle burner qi depletion. A representative blood and qi supplement, often prescribed for center qi fall.
Ci Wu Jia Pian [13.15] (Acanthopanax Root Tablets)	A single-constituent medicine to fortify central qi and supplement kidney jing. Preferred over ginseng for immune system enhancement.
Da Bu Yin Wan [13.29] (Great Yin-Supplementing Pills)	Used to enrich yin and downbear the fire effulgence that commonly occurs in yin depletion patterns.
Dang Gui Pian [13.11] (Angelica Tablets)	Blood and qi supplement used in cases of postpartum hemorrhage.
Dang Gui Yang Xue Gao [13.14] (Angelicae Blood-Nourishing Syrup)	General gynecological formula used to regulate menstruation and to treat blood depletion syndromes.
Er Ming Zuo Ci Wan [13.28] (Tinnitus Left-Supporting Pills)	Supplement designed to treat the specific symptom of tinnitus in cases of kidney yin depletion and liver yang hyperactivity. A *Liu Wei Di Huang Wan* variant, with *Ci Shi (Magnetitum)* and *Chai Hu (Radix Bupleuri)* added to address ascendent liver yang and to enrich liver yin.

Continued

Overview of Supplements *(Continued)*	
Supplement	**Summary of Applications**
Fu Ke Ba Zhen Wan [13.10] (Gynecology Eight Values Pills)	Popular gynecological formula used to treat dual depletions of qi and blood. A combination of the two classical formulae *Si Jun Zi Tang* and *Si Wu Tang* (*Four Nobles Decoction* and *Four Agents Decoction*).
Ge Jie Bu Shen Wan [13.25] (Gecko Kidney-Nourishing Pills)	Strengthens kidney yang and congenital jing, used as a general rejuvenant during recuperation from a long illness. Supplements both lung and kidney for cases of "kidney not grasping the qi" ("lung and kidney not communicating").
Ge Jie Da Bu Wan [13.4] (Gecko Great Supplement Pills)	Common geriatric formula, used as a general tonic, and for the treatment of rheumatism.
Gui Ling Ji [13.24] (Turtle Age Gather-Up)	Twenty-ingredient wide-spectrum kidney yang tonic, specifically appropriate in the treatment of chronic asthma.
Gui Pi Wan [13.8] (Angelica Splenic Pills)	Gynecological formula used to address blood depletion as it effects the spleen and the heart, indicated in the presence of menstrual irregularities and spirit disorders (particularly the "preoccupied" state evident of splenic involvement).
Hai Ma Bu Shen Wan [13.19] (Sea Horse Supplementing Pills)	Used to nourish both kidney yin and kidney yang, specifically in cases of impotence and spermatorrhea.
He Che Da Zao Wan [13.17] (Human Placenta Great Nourishment Pills)	Used in cases of yin depletion (especially of kidney and liver), for spermatorrhea.
Kang Gu Zeng Sheng Pian [13.26] (Anti Bone-Hyperplasia Tablets)	Specific for joint pain, especially with over-exertion or exposure to wind-cold.
Ling Zhi Feng Wang Jiang [13.1] (Ganoderma Royal Jelly)	A general blood and qi supplement, used during recovery from a long illness.
Liu Wei Di Huang Wan [13.18] (Six Flavor Rehmannia Pills)	A basic and representative formula to enrich kidney yin in accordance with the principle "invigorate the governor of water to counteract the brilliance of yang." (*Fundamentals of Chinese Medicine*, p.376).
Ming Mu Di Huang Wan [13.21] (Bright Eyes Rehmannia Pills)	A liver and kidney yin enricher, especially beneficial for the eyes and vision.

Continued

Overview of Supplements *(Continued)*	
Supplement	**Summary of Applications**
Qi Ju Di Huang Wan [13.22] (Lycium, Chrysanthemum, and Rehmannia Pills)	*Liu Wei Di Huang Wan [13.18]* with chrysanthemum and lycium for the blurred vision and dizziness.
Quan Lu Wan [13.30] (Complete Deer Pills)	A large (25-ingredient) formula employing deer meat, gelatin, horn, and testicles, used to fortify the kidney and in cases of spermatorrhea and impotence.
Ren Shen Lu Rong Wan [13.20] (Ginseng Deer Antler Pills)	Used to supplement qi and strengthen yang.
Ren Shen Yang Rong Wan [13.5] (Ginseng Support Pills)	Used in cases of heart-spleen depletion (blood and qi depletion).
Shen Jing Shuai Ruo Wan[13.9] (Ruo Wan Nerve Weakness Pills)	For cardiorenal depletion, used to calm the spirit.
Shen Ling Bai Zhu Wan [13.7] (Codonopsis, Poria, and Atractylodes Pills)	A gentle, general splenogastric tonic, often used for diarrhea in children.
Shen Qi Da Bu Wan [13.16] (Codonopsis and Astragalus Great Supplementing Pills)	A two-ingredient central qi (splenogastric) fortifier, especially recommended for diabetes mellitis.
Shen Rong Hu Gu Wan [13.27] (Ginseng, Deer Antler, and Tiger Bone Pills)	Used for numbness and pain in the limbs, including arthritic pain.
Shi Chuan Da Bu Wan [13.2] (Complete Great Supplement Pills)	Used to treat central qi depletion, in cases of post-illness recovery, and for excessive bleeding during menses.
Shi Hu Ye Guang Wan [13.23] (Dendrobium Night Light Pills)	Used to treat eye diseases due to liver and kidney yin depletion, in the presence of heat signs.
Shuang Bao Su [13.12] (Double Precious Extract)	General supplement for weakness, and for chronic diseases.
Tai Pan Tang Yi Pian [13.3] (Placenta Sugar-Coated Tablets)	Strengthens essence and kidney yang, used to treat debility from long illness.
Yu Chuan Wan [13.31] (Jade Stone Fountain Pills)	Addresses the thirst that results from the dryness of kidney yin deficiency, clears depletion heat, and relieves diabetic thirst.
Zhi Bao San Bian Wan [13.32] (Crown Jewels Penis Trio Pills)	Used in cases of kidney yang depletion

13.1   Ling Zhi Feng Wang Jiang
靈芝蜂王漿
Ganoderma Royal Jelly

Primary Functions and Applications: **Ling Zhi Feng Wang Jiang** is used as a general tonic to strengthen qi and blood. It is recommended post-partum, for patients recovering from a long illness, and in cases of neurasthenia, weakness associated with aging, malnutrition in children, diabetes, and gastric ulcer. It may also be used as an assistant medicine to help strengthen the body in consumptive diseases such as chronic hepatitis, chronic tuberculosis, and cancer.

Format and Administration: **Ling Zhi Feng Wang Jiang** is available in boxes of ten 10 ml vials.

Recommended Dosage: One 10 ml vial of liquid per day, taken in the morning upon arising. This medicine can be taken indefinitely.

Ling Zhi Feng Wang Jiang		
Constituent Substances		
Pinyin Name	**Pharmaceutical Name**	**% Composition**
Ling Zhi	*Fructificatio Ganodermatus*	—
Feng Wang Jiang	*Royal Jelly*	—
Dang Shen	*Radix Codonopsis Pilosulae*	—
Gou Qi Zi	*Fructus Lycii Chinensis*	—

Composition and Rationale: *Ling Zhi* supplements qi and blood, nourishes the heart, and calms the spirit; *Feng Wang Jiang* supplements qi and blood and fortifies the liver and spleen; *Dang Shen* supplements qi; and *Gou Qi Zi* fortifies the liver and kidney.

Royal jelly forms the basis for several related products:

Ren Shen Feng Wang Jiang [13.1a], produced by the China National Import and Export Corporation in 10 ml vials, contains royal jelly, honey, and ginseng, and is especially good for patients with a depletion of qi and yang.

Feng Ru Jiang [13.1b], also appropriate for patients with qi and yang depletion, contains royal jelly with *Huang Qi (Radix Astragali)* and *Dang Shen (Radix Codonopsis Pilosulae)*, and is available in liquid or capsule form.

Lu Wie Ba Jiang [13.1c] contains royal jelly and the testes and penis of deer. Its effect is similar to that of **Ling Zhi Feng Wang Jiang**, though it emphasizes kidney yang supplementation as it relates to the treatment of impotence. It is produced by the Changchun Chinese Medicines and Drug Manufactory in 10 ml vials.

Bei Jing Feng Wang Jiang [13.1d], composed of royal jelly only, is used to supplement qi and blood and to strengthen the liver and spleen. Produced by the Peiking Dietetic Preparation Manufactory, it is available in 10 ml vials.

Shi Chuan Da Bu Wan †   13.2
十全大補丸
Perfect Major Supplementation Pills

Source: *Tai Ping Hui Min He Ji Ju Fang (Formularies of the People's Welfare Pharmacies)*, Song Dynasty (960-1279).

Primary Functions and Applications: According to classical Chinese medical theory, all chronic disease eventually leads to qi depletion (evidenced by facial palor, weariness, shortness of breath, cold limbs) and blood depletion (indicated by palpitations, insomnia and dizziness). **Shi Chuan Da Bu Wan** supplements both qi and blood, and is used to treat depletion of central qi, and in cases of general debility following surgery or a long illness.

Shi Chuan Da Bu Wan is indicated when blood insufficiency and the inability of the qi to contain the blood causes excessive menstrual bleeding. Combine with **Wu Ji Bai Feng Wan [12.12]** if clinical results from **Shi Chuan Da Bu Wan** alone are unsatisfactory. **Shi Chuan Da Bu Wan** is not indicated in cases of excessive menstrual bleeding when caused by heat.

Shi Chuan Da Bu Wan may be used to treat spermatorrhea caused by qi and blood depletion, and to treat chronic subcutaneous ulcer, which may be deep rooted, and of a year or more duration.

Format and Administration: **Shi Chuan Da Bu Wan** is available in the U.S. in bottles of 200 pills produced by the Lanzhou Fo Ci Pharmaceutical Company, and in China as 9-gram honey pills.

Recommended Dosage: One honey pill twice a day, or 8 smaller pills, 3 times a day. Temporarily suspended for 1 week after every three months of use. Once the desired effect has been obtained, reduce dosage or discontinue use.

Shi Chuan Da Bu Wan		
Constituent Substances		
Pinyin Name	**Pharmaceutical Name**	**% Composition**
Ren Shen	*Radix Codonopsis Pilosulae*	10.54
Huang Qi	*Radix Astragali*	10.53
Bai Shao	*Radix Paeoniae Albae*	10.53
Bai Zhu	*Rhizoma Atractylodis Macrocephalae*	10.53
Fu Ling	*Sclerotium Poriae Cocus*	10.53
Shou Di Huang	*Radix Rehmannia Glutinosae*	15.78
Dang Gui	*Radix Angelicae Sinensis*	15.78
Rou Gui	*Cortex Cinnamomi Cassiae*	5.26
Chuan Xiong	*Rhizoma Ligustici Wallichii*	5.26
Gan Cao	*Radix Glycyrrhizae Uralensis*	5.26

Composition and Rationale: *Dang Shen* strengthens the qi and the spleen; *Huang Qi* supplements the qi and treats chronic carbuncles; *Bai Shao* nourishes the yin, builds the blood, and relieves abdominal pain; *Bai Zhu* strengthens the spleen and eliminates dampness; *Fu Ling* strengthens the spleen, promotes urination, and calms the spirit; *Shou Di Huang* nourishes the yin and strengthens the blood; *Dang Gui* supplements the blood; *Rou Gui* warms the yang; *Chuan Xiong* promotes blood circulation; and *Gan Cao* strengthens the qi of the middle burner.

Tai Pan Tang Yi Pian
胎盤糖衣片
Sugar-Coated Placenta Tablets

13.3

Primary Functions and Applications: **Tai Pan Tang Yi Pian** supplements congenital jing and kidney yang, and builds blood and qi. It is used to treat kidney yang depletion, with accompanying symptoms such as infertility, impotence, spermatorrhea, tinnitus, dizziness, and cold extremities. This formula is recommended in cases of general debility, fatigue, and weakness following long illnesses, particularly respiratory.

Tai Pan Tang Yi Pian is effective in cases of spleen depletion syndromes, with poor appetite and loose stools, and for nursing mothers with an insufficient supply of milk. In such cases this formula may be combined with other supplementing or spleen strengthening medicines.

It is also indicated in cases of pulmonary tuberculosis when accompanied by syndromes of lung qi depletion — difficulty breathing, weak cough, neurasthenia, and anemia.

Format and Administration: **Tai Pan Tang Yi Pian** is produced by the Central Medical Manufactory Company as *Placenta Sugar Coated Tablets* in bottles of 100.

Recommended Dosage: Five tablets, 3 times a day.

Tai Pan Tang Yi Pian		
Constituent Substances		
Pinyin Name	**Pharmaceutical Name**	**% Composition**
Tai Pan	*Placenta Hominis*	100

Composition and Rationale: *Tai Pan* fortifies congenital jing and kidney yang. Placenta contains ovarian hormone, luteal hormone, acetylglucosamine ($C_6H_{14}O_5N$), mannitose, and amino acids.

The processing of fresh placenta at home may be of some interest to both practitioners and mothers, and is thus offered below.

Preparation of Placenta	
Step 1:	After the umbilicus has been cut, wash the placenta and remove the blood.
Step 2:	Soak the cleaned placenta in fresh water at least three times, until no "fish" odor is left.
Step 3:	Put the placenta in a non-metal (glass or clay) pot, cover it with water, and boil it until the placenta floats to the top.
Step 4:	Remove the placenta from the pot, and lay it out on a baking sheet.
Step 5:	Bake the placenta in an oven, at very low heat (the lower, the better) until thoroughly dry (the placenta may be dried overnight).
Step 6:	Grind the placenta into a powder, and store in a dry place until ready to use.

Recommended Dosage: Three to 4 grams, twice to 3 times a day. In cases of hypoplastic anemia, 6-9 grams, 3 times a day.

13.4 Ge Jie Da Bu Wan
蛤蚧大補丸
Gecko Major Supplementation Pills

Primary Functions and Applications: **Ge Jie Da Bu Wan** fortifies the kidney, liver, and spleen, and treats chronic rheumatism. It is used as a general tonic, and is often recommended in cases of weakness associated with chronic illnesses. It is commonly used by the elderly to help maintain good health, and to treat kidney, liver, and/or spleen depletion syndromes. Guiding symptoms include weakness, shortness of breath, fatigue, dizziness, vertigo, tinnitus, frequent urination, lumbago, cold limbs, pain and stiffness in joints or limbs, problems walking, and poor appetite.

Ge Jie Da Bu Wan is effective in cases of anemia, chronic rheumatism, neurasthenia and Meniere's Disease. Since this formula will both enrich kidney yin and supplement kidney yang, neither kidney yin nor kidney yang depletion should be predominant in the symptom pattern.

Format and Administration: **Ge Jie Da Bu Wan** is produced by the Yulin Drug Manufactory as *Gejie Da Bu Wan*, in bottles of 50 capsules.

Recommended Dosage: Three to 5 capsules, twice a day after meals.

Ge Jie Da Bu Wan		
Constituent Substances		
Pinyin Name	**Pharmaceutical Name**	**% Composition**
Ge Jie	*Gecko*	21.5
Dang Shen	*Radix Codonopsis Pilosulae*	4.3
Huang Qi	*Radix Astragali*	4.3
Gou Qi Zi	*Fructus Lycii Chinensis*	4.1
Dang Gui	*Radix Angelicae Sinensis*	3.8
Fu Ling	*Sclerotium Poriae Cocus*	5.0
Shou Di Huang	*Radix Rehmannia Glutinosae*	6.8
Nu Zhen Zi	*Fructus Ligustri Lucidi*	5.2
Gan Cao	*Radix Glycyrrhizae Uralensis*	2.8
Shan Yao	*Radix Dioscoreae*	5.3
Mu Gua	*Fructus Chaenomelis Lagenariae*	4.7
Gou Qi Zi	*Fructus Lycii Chinensis*	4.8
Ba Ji Tian	*Radix Morindae Officinalis*	4.3
Bai Zhi	*Radix Angelicae*	4.3
Xu Duan	*Radix Dispaci*	4.8
Du Zhong	*Cortex Eucommiae Ulmoidis*	4.3
Huang Jing	*Rhizoma Polygonati*	5.7
Gu Sui Bu	*Rhizoma Drynariae*	4.0

Composition and Rationale: *Ge Jie* supplements kidney yang and lung yin; *Dang Shen* supplements qi and fortifies the spleen; *Huang Qi* fortifies the yang; *Gou Qi Zi* fortifies liver yang; *Dang Gui* supplements and moves the blood; *Fu Ling* fortifies the spleen and removes damp; *Shou Di Huang* nourishes the yin and supplements the blood; *Nu Zhen Zi* fortifies the kidney; *Gan Cao* warms the middle burner and fortifies the spleen; *Shan Yao* fortifies the splenogastric function; *Mu Gua* nourishes the liver and kidney and fortifies the spleen; *Gou Qi Zi* supplements the liver and kidney and strengthens the bones; *Ba Ji Tian* fortifies the kidneys; *Bai Zhi* supplements the spleen and dries damp; *Xu Duan* supplements the liver and kidney and strengthens the sinews and bones; *Du Zhong* supplements the liver and kidney, treats lumbago, and fortifies the limbs; *Huang Jing* nourishes the yin and fortifies the spleen and lung; and *Gu Sui Bu* facilitates the healing of broken bones.

13.5 Ren Shen Yang Rong Wan †
人參養榮丸
Ginseng Contruction-Nourishing Pills

Primary Functions and Applications: **Ren Shen Yang Rong Wan** fortifies the qi and blood, calms the spirit, and sharpens the memory. It is used to treat cardiosplenic depletion syndromes (blood and qi depletion), with such symptoms as fatigue, low energy, poor appetite, loose stool, poor memory, palpitations, excessive daytime sweating, shortness of breath, and general weakness following long or chronic illnesses. It is also indicated in cases of spleen or kidney yang depletion. Symptoms in such cases include chills, cold limbs, early morning diarrhea, lumbago, and weakness in the knees. **Ren Shen Yang Rong Wan** is effective in cases of anemia, hypothyroidism, muscle spasms due to hypocalcemia (including leg cramps at night), and boils or skin ulcers that have not healed (use internally for these symptoms) when accompanied by qi and blood depletion symptomology.

Format and Administration: **Ren Shen Yang Rong Wan** is produced as *Yang Rong Wan* by the Lanzhou Fo Ci Pharmaceutical Factory in both 200-pill bottles, and as a 9-gram honey pill.

Recommended Dosage: One honey pill, twice a day, or six small pills three times a day.

Ren Shen Yang Rong Wan

Constituent Substances

Pinyin Name	Pharmaceutical Name	% Composition
Ren Shen	*Radix Ginseng*	9.0
Bai Zhu	*Rhizoma Atractylodis Macrocephalae*	9.0
Huang Qi	*Radix Astragali*	9.0
Chen Pi	*Pericarpium Citri Reticulatae*	9.0
Shou Di Huang	*Radix Rehmannia Glutinosae*	7.0
Wu Wei Zi	*Fructus Schizandra Chinensis*	7.0
Fu Ling	*Sclerotium Poriae Cocus*	7.0
Da Zao	*Fructus Zizyphi Jujubae*	13.5
Bai Shao	*Radix Paeoniae Albae*	9.0
Yuan Zhi	*Radix Polygalae Tenuifoliae*	4.5
Rou Gui	*Cortex Cinnamomi Cassiae*	2.5
Sheng Jiang	*Rhizoma Recens Zingiberis Officinalis*	4.5
Gan Cao	*Radix Glycyrrhizae Uralensis*	9

Composition and Rationale: *Ren Shen* supplements the qi and fortifies the spleen; *Bai Zhu* fortifies the spleen and eliminates damp; *Huang Qi* fortifies the qi, controls sweating and heals boils on the skin; *Chen Pi* fortifies the spleen, moves stagnant spleen qi, and dries damp; *Shou Di Huang* enriches the yin and supplements the blood; *Wu Wei Zi* supplements the qi, fortifies the kidney, nourishes the heart, and controls sweating; *Fu Ling* fortifies the spleen, promotes urination, and calms the spirit; *Da Zao* fortifies the spleen, nourishes the blood, and calms the spirit; *Bai Shao* nourishes the yin, fortifies the blood, and relieves abdominal pain and muscle spasms (smooth or striated muscle); *Yuan Zhi* calms the spirit and pacifies the heart; *Rou Gui* fortifies the yang, warms the middle burner, expels cold, and relieves pain; *Sheng Jiang* warms the stomach and controls vomiting; and *Gan Cao* warms the middle burner and harmonizes the other herbs.

Zhong Guo Ji Ben Zhong Chen Yao (Fundamentals of Chinese Prepared Medicines, 1988) includes *Dang Gui* and omits *Da Zao* and *Shen Jiang* in its standardized formula for **Ren Shen Yang Rong Wan**.

Ren Shen Yang Ying Wan [13.5a] is similar in name, clinical application, and ingredients. Since it does not contain the warming herbs *Rou Gui, Sheng Jiang* or *Gan Cao*, **Ren Shen Yang Ying Wan [13.5a]** is not as effective in treating cold limbs and cold sensation as **Ren Shen Yang Rong Wan**.

13.6   Bu Zhong Yi Qi Wan †
補中益氣丸
Center-Supplementing Qi-Boosting Pills

Source: Pi Wei Lun (Treatise on the Spleen and Stomach), Li Gao, 1249.

Primary Functions and Applications: **Bu Zhong Yi Qi Wan** fortifies the qi, causes yang qi to ascend, and regulates the function of the splenogastric system. It is used to raise middle burner vital qi and to treat organ prolapse. Symptoms indicating its use include fatigue, shortness of breath, headache, general feeling of coldness and sensitivity to cold, desire to drink warm liquids, daytime sweating, poor appetite, and chronic diarrhea or loose stools.

Bu Zhong Yi Qi Wan is also used to clear heat in the special circumstance where the heat is due to qi depletion in the middle burner. In addition to the qi depletion symptoms listed above, symptoms in such cases will include chronic low-grade fever and thirst with a desire to drink warm liquids (a primary indicator that fever is due to middle burner qi depletion). It is interesting to note the use in such cases of warming, sweet herbs, rather than cooling, bitter herbs to clear heat.

In the presence of middle burner qi depletion, **Bu Zhong Yi Qi Wan** may be used to treat chronic gastroenteritis, chronic diarrhea, chronic dysentery, and such organ prolapses as gastroptosis, anal prolapse, and uterine prolapse; drooping of the upper eyelids; and hypomenorrhea or hypermenorrhea (each can be due to spleen qi depletion). In the book, *Zhong Yao Cheng Yao Xue (A Textbook of Patent Medicine) by Liu De-Yi (Tianjing, 1984), this herbal formula is listed as being used in cases of myasthenia gravis.*

Format and Administration: **Bu Zhong Yi Qi Wan** is produced by the Lanzhou Fo Ci Pharmaceutical Factory in 100-pill bottles.

Recommended Dosage: Eight pills, 3 times a day.

Bu Zhong Yi Qi Wan		
Constituent Substances		
Pinyin Name	Pharmaceutical Name	% Composition
Huang Qi	Radix Astragali	27.78
Dang Shen	Radix Codonopsis Pilosulae	8.33
Gan Cao	Radix Glycyrrhizae Uralensis	13.89
Bai Zhu	Rhizoma Atractylodis Macrocephalae	8.33
Dang Gui	Radix Angelicae Sinensis	8.33
Chen Pi	Pericarpium Citri Reticulatae	8.33
Sheng Ma	Rhizoma Cimicifugae	8.33
Chai Hu	Radix Bupleuri	8.33
Sheng Jiang	Rhizoma Recens Zingiberis Officinalis	2.78
Da Zao	Fructus Zizyphi Jujubae	5.57

Composition and Rationale: *Huang Qi* supplements the qi; *Dang Shen* supplements the qi and fortifies the spleen; *Gan Cao* warms the middle burner and harmonizes the other herbs; *Bai Zhu* fortifies the spleen; *Dang Gui* supplements the blood and promotes blood circulation; *Chen Pi* fortifies the spleen, moves static spleen qi, and dries damp; *Sheng Ma* causes the yang qi to ascend and treats prolapse; *Chai Hu* causes yang qi to ascend and smoothes liver qi; *Sheng Jiang* warms the middle burner and relieves nausea and vomiting; and *Da Zao* fortifies the spleen and nourishes the blood.

The original formula (as well as the formulae listed in *Zhong Guo Ji Ben Zhong Chen Yao [Fundamentals of Chinese Prepared Medicines, 1988]*) contains neither *Sheng Jiang* nor *Da Zao*.

A study of 103 cases of gastroptosis treated with **Bu Zhong Yi Qi Wan** was reported in China in 1974. The diagnosis of gastroptosis was made using barium X-ray. **Bu Zhong Yi Qi Wan** was administered in herbal decoction form rather than pill form. Prior to treatment, patients had symptoms such as nausea, poor appetite, stomachache, and constipation. After treatment, 54 cases recovered, 25 cases had obvious improvement, and 22 cases had some improvement. Twenty-one of the 54 cases with recovery were followed for two years. None of these cases had recurrence of the gastroptosis (*Xin Yi Yao Xue Za Zhi* 1974, no. 11).

A second study was reported in China in 1960, in which 23 cases of uterine prolapse were treated with a decoction of **Bu Zhong Yi Qi Wan**. Prior to treatment, patients showed fatigue, shortness of breath, low back pain, sensation of pulling down in the lower abdomen, and thin and empty pulses. The patients took the herbal tea every day for two weeks. Two patients did not complete the first two-week course. Of the remaining 21 cases, 76.2% recovered, 6.5% improved; and 14.3% showed no response (*Tian Jin Yi Yao Za Zhi*, Jan. 1980).

13.7   Shen Ling Bai Zhu Wan
參苓白朮丸
Codonopsis, Poria and Atractylodes Pills

Source: *Tai Ping Hui Min He Ji Ju Fang (The Formularies of the People's Welfare Pharmacies)*, Song Dynasty (960-1279).

Primary Functions and Applications: **Shen Ling Bai Zhu Wan** fortifies and supplements the splenogastric system, and eliminates damp. The herbs used in this formula are warming without being drying. It is a commonly used and popular formula, particularly gentle for the treatment of digestive disorders, even in children. Symptoms indicating its use include fatigue, indigestion, nausea, a full sensation in the chest or middle burner, loose stools or diarrhea, facial palor. The tongue will be pale in color, and the pulse empty. It may be used in cases of chronic gastroenteritis, anemia, pulmonary tuberculosis, and chronic nephritis when accompanied by gastrointestinal disorders.

Shen Ling Bai Zhu Wan is commonly used in the treatment of children with diarrhea accompanying passage of undigested food. It is especially indicated for children showing signs of underweight and malnourishment, with abdominal pain that is relieved somewhat when the abdomen is touched (an indication that the pain is depletion-type).

Format and Administration: **Shen Ling Bai Zhu Pian** is produced by the Sian Chinese Drug Factory, Xian, in bottles of 150 pills.

Recommended Dosage: Adults, 12 pills, twice a day before meals, with warm water or *Dao Zao (Fructus Ziziphi Jujubae)* broth to strengthen the spleen and to supplement the blood. To make 1 cup of broth, halve 10 *Da Zao* and simmer in 1½ cups of water until 1 cup remains. Strain, and squeeze the fruit. Drink while it is still warm. Children: 5-12 years old: 5 pills, twice a day. Children under age 5: 3 pills, 2 times a day. Dissolve the pills in warm water, if necessary. The pills do not have a bitter taste.

Shen Ling Bai Zhu Wan		
Constituent Substances		
Pinyin Name	**Pharmaceutical Name**	**% Composition**
Dang Shen	*Radix Codonopsis Pilosulae*	11.22
Fu Ling	*Sclerotium Poriae Cocus*	11.22
Bai Zhu	*Rhizoma Atractylodis Macrocephalae*	11.22
Jie Geng	*Radix Platycodonis Grandiflori*	6.12
Shan Yao	*Radix Dioscoreae*	11.22
Chen Pi	*Pericarpium Citri Reticulatae*	11.22
Sha Ren	*Semen et Pericarpium Amomi*	6.12
Lian Zi Rou	*Semen Nelumbinis*	6.12
Bai Bian Dou	*Semen Dolichoris Lablab*	8.17
Yi Yi Ren	*Semen Coicis Lachryma-Jobi*	6.12
Gan Cao (cooked)	*Radix Glycyrrhizae Uralensis*	11.22

Composition and Rationale: *Dang Shen* fortifies the spleen and supplements the qi; *Fu Ling* fortifies the spleen, controls diarrhea, and eliminates damp; *Bai Zhu* fortifies the spleen and eliminates damp; *Jie Geng* opens the lung and guides the other herbs upward; *Shan Yao* fortifies the spleen; *Chen Pi* fortifies the spleen, moves stagnant spleen qi, and dries damp; *Sha Ren* moves the middle burner qi, fortifies the stomach, transforms damp, and controls vomiting; *Lian Zi Rou* and *Bai Bian Dou* strengthen the spleen and stop diarrhea; *Yi Yi Ren* fortifies the spleen, controls diarrhea, eliminates damp, and promotes urination; and *Gan Cao* warms the middle burner and harmonizes the other herbs.

Zhong Guo Ji Ben Zhong Chen Yao (Fundamentals of Chinese Prepared Medicines, 1988) includes *Da Zao* in its standardized formula for **Shen Ling Bai Zhu Wan**.

13.8

Gui Pi Wan †
歸脾丸
Angelica Splenic Pills

Source: Ji Sheng Fang *(Treatment Formulas to Promote Life)*, Song Dynasty, (960-1279).

Primary Functions and Applications: **Gui Pi Wan** fortifies the qi, supplements the blood, fortifies the spleen, and nourishes the heart. It is used to treat cardiosplenic depletion syndromes caused by mental preoccupation, with such symptoms as insomnia, poor memory, nightmares, palpitations, restlessness, agitation, dizziness, depletion-type headache, tiredness, facial palor, and poor appetite. The tongue in such cases will be pale, with thin white moss, and the pulse will be empty (thin and weak).

Gui Pi Wan is also effective in the treatment of gynecological problems, particularly irregular menstrual cycles due to blood depletion, hypermenorrhea with light red blood due to spleen depletion, and leucorrhea due to spleen depletion. In addition, it is used to treat chronic bleeding, e.g., gastric ulcer, functional uterine bleeding, bleeding due to thrombocytopenia, and aplastic anemia.

These symptoms all may all be ascribed to blood depletion. In classical Chinese medical theory, the spleen governs the blood. Thus, blood depletion affects both the spleen and the heart. Preoccupation, a presenting symptom often accompanying such cases, will also limit the spleen's function to contain the blood in the blood vessels, causing bleeding problems. This in turn will cause an insufficient blood supply to the heart.

Format and Administration: **Gui Pi Wan**, also called **Ren Shen Gui Pi Wan [13.8a]**, is produced by the Lanzhou Fo Ci Pharmaceutical Factory as *Kwei Be Wan* in bottles of 200 pills.

Recommended Dosage: Eight to 10 pills, 3 times a day.

Gui Pi Wan		
Constituent Substances		
Pinyin Name	**Pharmaceutical Name**	**% Composition**
Dang Shen	*Radix Codonopsis Pilosulae*	13.8
Fu Shen	*Poria cum Radice Pini*	13.8
Suan Zao Ren	*Semen Zizyphi Spinosae*	13.8
Yuan Zhi	*Radix Polygalae Tenuifoliae*	6.9
Dang Gui	*Radix Angelicae Sinensis*	6.9
Mu Xiang	*Radix Muhsiang*	3.5
Bai Zhu	*Rhizoma Atractylodis Macrocephalae*	13.8
Gan Cao	*Radix Glycyrrhizae Uralensis*	3.5
Long Yan Rou	*Arillus Longanae*	13.8
Huang Qi	*Radix Astragali*	10.2

Composition and Rationale: **Dang Shen** fortifies the spleen and supplements the qi; *Fu Shen* calms the spirit; *Suan Zao Ren* nourishes the heart and calms the spirit; *Yuan Zhi* calms the spirit and pacifies the heart; *Dang Gui* nourishes the blood; *Mu Xiang* moves stagnant qi; *Bai Zhu* fortifies the spleen and eliminates dampness; *Gan Cao* fortifies the middle burner and harmonizes the other herbs; *Long Yan Rou* fortifies the heart and nourishes the blood; and *Huang Qi* fortifies the qi.

Zhong Guo Ji Ben Zhong Chen Yao (Fundamentals of Chinese Prepared Medicines, 1988) includes *Fu Ling* and *Da Zao* in its standardized formula for **Gui Pi Wan**.

Shen Jing Shuai Ruo Wan   13.9
神經衰弱丸
Neurasthenia Pills

Source: Dr. Shi Jinmo, one of the foremost doctors of traditional Chinese medicine of the 20th century.

Primary Functions and Applications: **Shen Jing Shuai Ruo Wan** fortifies the qi and the blood, improves mental disposition, fortifies kidney yin, and calms the spirit. It is used to treat depletion heart fire due to kidney yin and heart yin depletion. **Shen Jing Shuai Ruo Wan** extinguishes depletion heart fire by nourishing kidney yin, by nourishing heart blood (yin), and through its properties of coldness and bitterness. Symptoms in such cases include fatigue, insomnia, nightmares, night sweats, poor memory, poor concentration, dizziness, tinnitus, palpitations, restlessness, and agitation.

In the presence of these depletion heart fire symptoms, this formula may be used to treat neurosis, neurasthenia, and anxiety attacks, as well as other mental problems.

Format and Administration: **Shen Jing Shuai Ruo Wan** is produced by the Beijing Tong Ren Tang in bottles of 200 pills.

Recommended Dosage: Twenty pills, twice a day. Clinical results may not be evident for one to two weeks.

Shen Jing Shuai Ruo Wan		
Constituent Substances		
Pinyin Name	**Pharmaceutical Name**	**% Composition**
Dang Gui	*Radix Angelicae Sinensis*	3.0
Zi He Che	*Placenta Hominis*	12.0
Huang Lian	*Rhizoma Coptidis*	6.0
He Shou Wu	*Rhizoma Polygoni Multiflori*	6.0
Fu Ling	*Sclerotium Poriae Cocus*	3.0
Suan Zao Ren	*Semen Zizyphi Spinosae*	12.0
A Jiao	*Gelatinum Corii Asini*	6.0
Mai Men Dong	*Radix Ophiopogonis Japonici*	6.0
Ren Shen	*Radix Ginseng*	15.0
Bei Zi	*Concha Cypraeae*	6.0
Wu Wei Zi	*Fructus Schizandra Chinensis*	6.0
Huang Qi	*Radix Astragali*	19.0

Composition and Rationale: *Dang Gui* nourishes the heart blood; *Zi He Che* fortifies the kidney, supplements the qi, and nourishes the blood; *Huang Lian* clears heart heat; *He Shou Wu* supplements the kidney and fortifies the blood; *Fu Ling* and *Suan Zao Ren* nourish liver blood, tranquilize the heart, and calm the spirit; *A Jiao* nourishes the blood and yin; *Mai Men Dong* nourishes the heart yin and calms the spirit; *Ren Shen* fortifies the spleen qi and improves energy; *Zi Bei Chi* calms the spirit and tranquilizes; *Wu Wei Zi* nourishes the kidney and heart yin, calms the heart, and tranquilizes; and *Huang Qi* fortifies the qi and stops sweat.

Fu Ke Ba Zhen Wan
婦科八珍丸
Gynecology Eight-Jewel Pills

13.10

Source: *Rui Zhu Tang Jing Yan Fang (Rui Zho Tang Pharmacy's Formulas from Experience),* Yuan Dynasty (1279-1368).

Primary Functions and Applications: **Fu Ke Ba Zhen Wan** supplements qi and nourishes blood. It is used to treat gynecological disorders with qi and blood depletion, often the result of blood loss. Guiding symptoms include fatigue, pale face, dizziness, vertigo, shortness of breath, with irregular menstruation, and general pre- or post-partum depletion, including fatigue with low-grade fever *not* attributable to infection.

It is also effective in the treatment of qi and blood depletion due to spleen depletion, with such symptoms as fatigue, pale face, weight loss, dizziness, poor appetite, palpitations, and low-grade fever with uneasiness due to exhaustion. With these symptom patterns, **Fu Ke Ba Zhen Wan** may be used in cases of anemia, hypoglycemia, and optic atrophy. Finally, it is used to treat stubborn un-healed skin ulcers, with the area around the ulcer flat, not red or swollen.

Format and Administration: **Fu Ke Ba Zhen Wan** is produced by the Lanzhou Fo Ci Pharmaceutical Factory as *Ba Zhen Wan* (also as *Women's Precious Pills* or *Precious Pills*) in bottles of 200.

Recommended Dosage: Eight to 10 pills, 3 times a day.

Fu Ke Ba Zhen Wan		
Constituent Substances		
Pinyin Name	**Pharmaceutical Name**	**% Composition**
Dang Shen	*Radix Codonopsis Pilosulae*	12.12
Fu Ling	*Sclerotium Poriae Cocus*	12.12
Bai Zhu	*Rhizoma Atractylodis Macrocephalae*	12.12
Dang Gui	*Radix Angelicae Sinensis*	18.18
Chuan Xiong	*Rhizoma Ligustici Wallichii*	9.10
Bai Shao	*Radix Paeoniae Albae*	12.12
Shou Di Huang	*Radix Rehmannia Glutinosae*	18.18
Gan Cao	*Radix Glycyrrhizae Uralensis*	6.06

Composition and Rationale: *Dang Shen* fortifies the spleen and supplements the qi; *Fu Ling* and *Bai Zhu* strengthen the spleen and dry dampness; *Dang Gui* nourishes the blood and promotes blood circulation; *Chuan Xiong* promotes blood circulation, regulates qi, and adjusts menstruation; *Bai Shao* nourishes the blood and the yin, relieves pain, and relaxes smoothe muscle spasms; *Shou Di Huang* nourishes the yin and the blood; and *Gan Cao* warms the middle burner, fortifies the spleen, and harmonizes the other herbs.

Zhong Guo Ji Ben Zhong Chen Yao (Fundamentals of Chinese Prepared Medicines, 1988) lists this medicine as *Fu Ke Shi Zhen Wan*, adding *Xiang Fu* and *Da Zao* to its standardized formula.

Fu Ke Ba Zhen Wan is a combination of two basic formulae, *Si Jun Zi Tang (Four Gentlemen Soup)*, a basic formula to strengthen qi, and *Si Wu Tang (Four Agents Soup)*, a basic formula to strengthen blood. The principal treatment strategy in gynecological disorders is to supplement blood. However, classical Chinese medical theory states that blood is difficult to supplement directly because it is visible. Since the qi is the leader of the blood, and since the qi, by its invisibility, may be supplemented directly, it is necessary to supplement the qi and blood simultaneously.

Tai Shan Pan Shi San [13.10a], a modification of **Fu Ke Ba Zhen Wan** adds *Huang Qi*, *Xu Duan*, *Huang Qin*, and *Sha Ren*, and omits *Fu Ling*. This formula strengthens qi, supplements blood, and soothes the embryo. It is commonly used to treat excessive fetal movement, and to help prevent miscarriage in qi and blood depletion cases. It is not commonly available in prepared medicine form.

Dang Gui Ji Jin [13.10b], another related formulae, is produced by the United Pharmaceutical Manufactory as *Essence of Chicken with Tangkwei* in 70 gram bottles. **Dang Gui Ji Jin** contains chicken, and is especially nourishing for patients with qi and blood depletion. Stir one bottle into an equal amount of warm water, and sip throughout the day. **Ren Shen Ji Jin [13.10c]**, which replaces *Ren Shen (Radix Ginseng)* for *Dang Gui (Radix Angelicae)*, is especially effective for qi supplementation. **Ba Zhen Yi Mu Wan [13.10d]** adds *Yi Mu Cao* to move blood.

Dang Gui Pian 13.11
當歸片
Angelica Sinensis Tablets

Primary Functions and Applications: **Dang Gui Pian** nourishes the blood and supplements qi, and is used to treat post-partum blood depletion. Such conditions are often the result of either prior blood depletion syndromes, or excessive blood loss during childbirth. Symptoms in such cases include post-partum hemorrhage, facial palor, dizziness, vertigo, palpitations, spontaneous sweating (day or night), feeling of cold in the limbs, and an empty pulse.

Format and Administration: **Dang Gui Pian** is produced by the Lanchow Chinese Herb Works in bottles of 100 pills.

Recommended Dosage: Five tablets, 3 times a day.

Dang Gui Pian		
Constituent Substances		
Pinyin Name	**Pharmaceutical Name**	**% Composition**
Dang Gui	*Radix Angelicae Sinensis*	70
Chuan Xiong	*Rhizoma Ligustici Wallichii*	10
Bai Zhu	*Rhizoma Atractylodis Macrocephalae*	10
Da Zao	*Fructus Zizyphi Jujubae*	10

Composition and Rationale: *Dang Gui* nourishes the blood and promotes blood circulation; *Chuan Xiong* promotes blood circulation, moves stagnant qi, and relieves pain; *Bai Zhu* fortifies the spleen and dries damp; and *Da Zao* fortifies the spleen and nourishes blood that has become insufficient as a result of spleen qi and liver blood depletion.

13.12

Shuang Bao Su
雙寶素
Double Gem Extract

Primary Functions and Applications: **Shuang Bao Su** is used to strengthen vital qi, nourish the liver, and supplement the spleen. As such, it is a general tonic, used to treat generalized weakness. **Shuang Bao Su** is also useful as an assistant medicine in the treatment of such chronic diseases as coronary artery disease, chronic hepatitis, neurasthenia, rheumatoid arthritis, chronic gastritis, gastric or duodenal ulcer, hair loss due to weakness, and impotence.

Format and Administration: **Shuang Bao Su** is produced by the Hangzhou Second Traditional Chinese Pharmaceutical Works, Hangzhou, China, as *Shuangbaosu Oral Liquid, Ginseng Extract* and as *Fresh Royal Jelly Mixture.* It is available in 10 ml vials, 10 vials per box, and as capsules, 30 per bottle.

Recommended Dosage: One or 2 capsules, 3 times per day, or 1 vial, once a day in the morning.

Shuang Bao Su		
Constituent Substances		
Pinyin Name	**Pharmaceutical Name**	**% Composition**
Feng Wang Jing	*Royal Jelly*	—
Ren Shen	*Radix Ginseng*	—
Pu Tao Tang	*Glucose*	—

Composition and Rationale: All three ingredients supplement qi and blood.

An Tai Wan
安胎丸
Fetus-Quieting Pills

13.13

Source: **An Tai Wan** originally appeared as *Bao Chan Wu Yu Ying*, in the Ming Dynasty sourcebook *Chan Hou Bian*. Several modifications were eventually developed and manufactured as prepared medicines. Along with **An Tai Wan**, varieties of *Bao Chan Wu Yu Ying* included **Bao Tai Wan [13.13a]**, **Shi San Tai Bao Wan [13.13b]**, and **Bao Chan Wu Yu Wan [13.13c]**.

Primary Functions and Applications: **An Tai Wan** nourishes qi and blood, soothes the embryo, and regulates stomach qi. It is used to treat overactive movement of the embryo caused by qi and blood depletion in the mother. **An Tai Wan** may be used to help treat lumbago or leg pain in the mother, and to help prevent miscarriage or premature delivery by arresting uterine bleeding.

Format and Administration: **An Tai Wan** is produced by the United Pharmaceutical Manufactory, Guangzhou, in 100-pill bottles, and as 9 gram honey pills.

Recommended Dosage: One honey pill twice a day, or 7 pills, three times a day.

An Tai Wan		
Constituent Substances		
Pinyin Name	**Pharmaceutical Name**	**% Composition**
Dang Gui	*Radix Angelicae Sinensis*	8.5
Shou Di Huang	*Radix Rehmannia Glutinosae*	6.8
Bai Shao	*Radix Paeoniae Albae*	8.5
Chuang Xiong	*Radix Ligustici Wallichii*	6.8
Huang Qi	*Radix Astragali*	5.1
Bai Zhu	*Rhizoma Atractylodis Macrocephalae*	6.8
Gan Cao	*Radix Glycyrrhizae Uralensis*	5.1
Tu Si Zi	*Herba et Semen Cuscutae*	6.8
Ai Ye	*Folium Artemisiae Argyi*	4.3
Huang Qin	*Radix Scutellaria*	5.1
Sha Ren	*Semen et Pericarpium Amomi*	4.3
Qiang Huo	*Rhizoma et Radix Notopterygii*	2.6
Jing Jie	*Herba seu Flos Schizonepetae Tenuifoliae*	5.1
Zhi Qiao	*Fructus Citri seu Ponciri*	6.8
Hou Po	*Cortex Magnoliae Officinalis*	4.3
Chuan Bei Mu	*Bulbus Fritillariae Cirrhosae*	8.5

Composition and Rationale: *Dang Gui, Shou Di Huang, Bai Shao,* and *Chuang Xiong* strengthen the blood and nourish the yin; *Huang Qi, Bai Zhu,* and *Gan Cao* strengthen the qi; *Tu Si Zi* and *Ai Ye* strengthen the liver and kidney, arrest bleeding, and soothe the embryo; *Huang Qin* clears heat and soothes the embryo; *Sha Ren* regulates spleen qi and soothes the embryo; *Qiang Huo* and *Jing Jie* eliminate wind and relieve pain; *Zhi Qiao* and *Hou Po* regulate stomach qi and relieve pain; and *Chuan Bei Mu* clears heat and reduces phlegm.

Zhong Guo Ji Ben Zhong Chen Yao (Fundamentals of Chinese Prepared Medicines, 1988) lists a much simpler standardized formula for **An Tai Wan**, composed only of *Dang Gui, Bai Shao, Chuan Xiong, Bai Zhu,* and *Huang Qin.*

Dang Gui Yang Xue Gao   13.14
當歸養血膏
Angelicae Blood-Nourishing Syrup

Primary Functions and Applications: **Dang Gui Yang Xue Gao** nourishes qi and blood, and is used to treat syndromes of blood depletion, Guiding symptoms include dizziness, palpitations, poor memory, fatigue, and anemia. Guiding symptoms related to gynecological disorders include irregular menstruation with light-colored blood, amenorrhea or hypomenorrhea, and postpartum weakness due to excessive blood loss.

Format and Administration: **Dang Gui Yang Xue Gao** is produced by Zhong Lian Manufacturing Co., Wuhan, as *Tankwe Gin for Tea* in 150-ml bottles. It is also often known as *Dang Gui Jin Gao*.

Recommended Dosage: Two tbl. in warm water, twice a day.

Contraindication: Discontinue use during a cold or flu.

Dang Gui Yang Xue Gao		
Constituent Substances		
Pinyin Name	**Pharmaceutical Name**	**% Composition**
Dang Gui	*Radix Angelicae Sinensis*	69.0
Shou Di Huang	*Radix Rehmannia Glutinosae*	4.5
Bai Shao	*Radix Paeoniae Albae*	4.5
Dang Shen	*Radix Codonopsis Pilosulae*	4.5
Huang Qi	*Radix Astragali*	4.5
Fu Ling	*Sclerotium Poriae Cocus*	4.5
Gan Cao	*Radix Glycyrrhizae Uralensis*	2.0
Chuan Xiong	*Rhizoma Ligustici Wallichii*	2.0
A Jiao	*Gelatinum Corii Asini*	4.5

Composition and Rationale: *Dang Gui, Shou Di Huang,* and *Bai Shao* nourish the blood and the yin and regulate menstruation; *Dang Shen, Huang Qi, Fu Ling,* and *Gan Cao* strengthen the spleen and supplement the qi; *Chuan Xiong* fortifes the blood and protects against potential blood stasis from the blood supplementers by promoting blood circulation; *A Jiao* fortifies the blood, nourishes the yin, and arrests bleeding.

13.15

Ci Wu Jia Pian
刺五加片
Acanthopanax Root Tablets

Primary Functions and Applications: **Ci Wu Jia Pian** fortifies correct qi and supplements kidney essence, calms the spirit, and stimulates the brain. It is used to treat the symptoms of central qi depletion (including fatigue, dizziness, insomnia, poor appetite, and migraine headaches); and to treat sexual dysfunction, including spermatorrhea, impotence, and reduced sexual desire.

Research in China indicates that the herb *Radix Acanthopanax*, the sole ingredient of **Ci Wu Jia Pian**, is more effective than ginseng in simultaneously relieving fatigue and reducing anxiety. It also has been credited with enhancing the immune system, protecting the body from radiation, reducing inflammation, normalizing blood pressure (raising or lowering it as needed), increasing endocrine function (ovarian, testicular, adrenal and pancreatic, where insulin levels may be increased and high blood sugar levels decreased), promoting retention of vital body fluids, treating SSK sarcoma (in experiments with rats), and inhibiting metastasis (anthropanax is preferred over ginseng in the treatment of cancer in China).

Format and Administration: **Ci Wu Jia Pian** is produced by the Harbin Sixth Pharmacy Factory as *Cuwujia Tablet*, in bottles of 100 coated tablets.

Recommended Dosage: Three tablets, twice or 3 times a day.

Ci Wu Jia Pian		
Constituent Substances		
Pinyin Name	**Botanical Name**	**% Composition**
Ci Wu Jia	*Anthropanax Senticosus*	100

Shen Qi Da Bu Wan †
參耆大補丸
Astragalus and Codonopsis Major Supplementation Pills

13.16

Primary Functions and Applications: **Shen Qi Da Bu Wan** supplements the central qi and fortifies the spleen. It is used to treat central qi depletion resulting from long illness, blood loss, or post-partum illness. Guiding symptoms include spontaneous sweating (especially in the daytime), fatigue, thirst, poor appetite, and weight loss. It is also recommended in the treatment of diabetes mellitus.

Format and Administration: **Shen Qi Da Bu Wan** is produced by the Lanzhou Fo Ci Pharmaceutical Factory in bottles of 100 pills. It is also available in a sugar-coated tablet form called **Shen Qi Pian [13.16b]**. The original format was as a syrup, **Shen Qi Gao [13.16a]**, though this is not commonly available.

Recommended Dosage: Eight to ten pills or tablets, three times a day.

Shen Qi Da Bu Wan		
Constituent Substances		
Pinyin Name	**Pharmaceutical Name**	**% Composition**
Huang Qi	*Radix Astragali*	50%
Dang Shen	*Radix Codonopsis Pilosulae Pilosulae*	50%

Composition and Rationale: Both *Huang Qi* and *Dang Shen* are representative qi fortifiers and gastrosplenic fortifiers, acting together to supplement the qi of the spleen, the lung, and the heart.

13.17　He Che Da Zao Wan †
河車大造丸
Greatly Fortifying Placenta Pills

Source: Jing Yue Quan Shu (Jing Yue's Complete Works), Ming Dynasty (1368-1644).

Primary Functions and Applications: **He Che Da Zao Wan** nourishes the liver and kidney and enriches yin. Symptoms indicating its use include dizziness, tinnitus, weakness and tiredness of the legs, aching in the lower back or waist, fatigue, low-grade afternoon fever, red cheeks or hot flushed face, night sweats, and nocturnal emission. The spermatorrhea referred to here is the yin depletion type, semen loss usually occurring at night and accompanied by dreams.

He Che Da Zao Wan may be used in cases of yin depletion symptomology (headache, dizziness, restlessness etc.), in later stages of tuberculosis with yin depletion symptomology (dry cough, possibly with the expectoration of blood), and for any consumptive disease that manifests syndromes of yin depletion (cancer, chronic hepatitis, chronic hyperthyroidism, chronic diabetes, chronic nephritis, chronic bronchitis).

Format and Administration:

Recommended Dosage: Eight pills, 3 times a day. In China, patients with yin depletion symptomology have used this medicine for months or years as necessary, without adverse effects.

He Che Za Zao Wan		
Constituent Substances		
Pinyin Name	**Pharmaceutical Name**	**% Composition**
Gui Ban	*Plastrum Testudinis*	15.0
Shou Di Huang	*Radix Rehmannia Glutinosae*	15.0
Dang Shen	*Radix Codonopsis Pilosulae*	11.0
Huang Bai	*Cortex Phellodendri*	11.0
Du Zhong	*Cortex Eucommiae Ulmoidis*	11.0
Zi He Che	*Placenta Hominis*	8.0
Niu Xi	*Radix Achyranthes Bidentatae*	8.0
Tian Men Dong	*Tuber Asparagi Cochinensis*	8.0
Mai Men Dong	*Radix Ophiopogonis Japonici*	8.0
Fu Ling	*Sclerotium Poriae Cocus*	3.5
Sha Ren	*Semen et Pericarpium Amomi*	1.5

Composition and Rationale: *Gui Ban* supplements yin, settles yang and lowers depletion heat; *Shou Di Huang* supplements the blood and enriches the yin; *Dang Shen* supplements qi; *Huang Bai* settles ascending kidney fire; *Du Zhong* supplements liver and kidneys, fortifies the sinews and bones, and lowers blood pressure; *Zi He Che* supplements kidney qi and fortifies the blood; *Niu Xi* promotes blood circulation, eliminates blood stasis, induces downward movement of blood, lowers blood pressure, supplements the liver and kidneys, and fortifies the sinews and bones; *Tian Men Dong* nourishes yin, clears heat, and supplements kidney and lung yin; *Mai Men Dong* nourishes yin, clears heat, moistens the lung, fortifies stomach yin, tranquilizes the heart, and clears heat in the heart; *Fu Ling* fortifies the spleen and tranquilizes the heart and spirit; and *Sha Ren* regulates the stomach qi to prevent possible stagnation of qi in the stomach during therapy.

Zhong Guo Ji Ben Zhong Chen Yao (Fundamentals of Chinese Prepared Medicines, 1988) omits *Dang Shen, Fu Ling,* and *Bei Mu* in its standardized formula for **He Che Za Zao Wan.**

13.18   Liu Wei Di Huang Wan †
六味地黃丸
Rehmannia Six Pills

Source: *Xiao Er Yao Zheng Zhi Jue (Pediatric Pharmaceutics),* Song Dynasty (960-1279).

Primary Functions and Applications: Originally a pediatric formula, **Liu Wei Di Huang Wan** is now used by both adults and children to nourish the kidney and liver, and to clear depletion heat. It is the primary formula used to treat symptoms of yin depletion, especially of the liver. Symptoms indicating its use include headache, dizziness, tinnitus, hearing problems, debility of the lumbar area, weakness of the legs (difficulty remaining standing), "steaming bone tidal fever" (a term for afternoon fever and night sweating, symptoms of consumptive disease with extreme yin depletion), low-grade afternoon fever, difficult urination, diabetes, and nocturnal emission. The tongue in such cases will be red; the pulse, thin and rapid. From a modern biomedical perspective, **Liu Wei Di Huang Wan** is effective in the treatment of nephritis, yin depletion diabetes, tuberculosis, hyperthyroidism, and mild emotional disturbances.

Patient studies in China have shown that **Liu Wei Di Huang Wan** improves kidney function in cases of glomerulonephritis due to tonsillitis, and to decrease the mortality rate in patients with kidney infections. Its use can inhibit abnormal cell growth in the esophagus, thus indicating a potential for the treatment of epitheliosis, where cells may become potential cancer cells (*Xin Yi Yao Xue Za Zhi,* 1977, number 7).

Format and Administration: **Liu Wei Di Huang Wan** is produced by the Lanzhou Fo Ci Pharmaceutical Factory in 200-pill bottles, and as a 9-gram honey pill.

Recommended Dosage: One honey pill twice or 3 times a day, or 8-10 smaller pills, 3 times a day, both with warm water.

Liu Wei Di Huang Wan		
Constituent Substances		
Pinyin Name	Pharmaceutical Name	% Composition
Shou Di Huang	*Radix Rehmannia Glutinosae*	32
Shan Yao	*Radix Paeoniae Rubra*	16
Mu Dan Pi	*Cortex Radicis Mouton*	12
Fu Ling	*Sclerotium Poriae Cocus*	12
Shan Zhu Yu	*Fructus Corni Officinalis*	16
Ze Xie	*Buthus Martensi*	12

Composition and Rationale: Shou Di Huang nourishes the yin and strengthens blood; *Shan Yao* supplements the spleen and stomach; *Mu Dan Pi* clears blood heat and extinguishes liver fire; *Fu Ling* strengthens the spleen, discharges damp and promotes urination; *Shan Zhu Yu* strengthens liver and kidney yin, controls sweating and spermatorrhea; and *Ze Xie* promotes urination and drains kidney depletion heat.

Liu Wei Di Huang Wan is a basic formula for enriching yin and strengthening the kidneys. It is a unique combination of supplements and depletion-heat draining agents. There are several variations of this basic kidney-yin enriching formula used to treat disorders other than kidney yin depletion. **Zhi Bai Di Huang Wan[13.18a]** more effectively clears depletion heat; **Qi Ju Di Huang Wan[13.18b]** strengthens liver yin, calms internal wind, and brightens the eyes; **Gui Shao Di Huang Wan[13.18c]**, strengthens the blood and soothes the liver; and **Mai Wei Di Huang Wan [13.18d]**, also called **Ba Xian Chang Shou Wan [3.15]**, addresses yin depletion of both the lung and kidney.

Qian Yi, the author of the Song Dynasty text *Xiao Er Yao Zheng Zhi Jue (Pediatric Pharmaceutics)*, in which **Liu Wei Di Huang Wan** first appeared, used it for children who experienced any of the "five delays" — delay in standing up; delay in walking; delay in growth of hair on the head; delay in development of teeth; and delay in speech development.

13.19   Hai Ma Bu Shen Wan
海馬補腎丸
Seahorse Kidney-Supplementing Pills

Primary Functions and Applications: **Hai Ma Bu Shen Wan** nourishes kidney yin and kidney yang, strengthens the lumbar area, and stimulates the brain. It is used to treat symptoms caused by qi depletion, blood depletion, and kidney jing insufficiency, including low sperm count or weak sperm, impotence, spermatorrhea, debility of limbs, night sweat or day sweat, insomnia, palpitations, soreness and weakness in the lumbar area, poor eyesight (kidney yin depletion that has led to liver yin depletion), tinnitus, and weariness. This formula will both enrich yin and reinforce yang, though its emphasis is on yang reinforcement.

Hai Ma Bu Shen Wan may be used to treat neurasthenia and other psychological disorders with kidney yang depletion.

Format and Administration: **Hai Ma Bu Shen Wan** is produced by the Tientsin Drug Manufactory as *Sea Horse Genital Tonic Pills*, in bottles of 120.

Recommended Dosage: Ten pills, twice a day. In cases of impotence due to kidney depletion, it is better to avoid excessive sexual intercourse during therapy.

Hai Ma Bu Shen Wan		
Constituent Substances		
Pinyin Name	**Pharmaceutical Name**	**% Composition**
Hai Ma	*Hippocampus*	10
Ren Shen	*Radix Ginseng*	10
Long Gu	*Os Draconis*	5
Gou Qi Zi	*Fructus Lycii Chinensis*	5
Hei Lu Shen	*Testis et Penis Equus*	3
Bu Gu Zhi	*Semen Psoralae Coryfoliae*	3
Fu Ling	*Sclerotium Poriae Cocus*	3
Huang Qi	*Radix Astragali*	5
He Tao Ren	*Semen Juglandis Regiae*	3
Lu Rong	*Cornu Cervi Parvum*	6
Ge Jie	*Gecko*	6
Hai Gou Shen	*Testis et Penis Otariae*	5
Hua Lu Shen	*Penis Ettes Tiscervi*	5
Hu Gu	*Os Tigris*	6
Shan Zhu Yu	*Fructus Corni Officinalis*	3
Dang Gui	*Radix Angelicae Sinensis*	5
Ding Xiang	*Flos Caryophylli*	2
Shou Di Huang	*Radix Rehmannia Glutinosae*	5

Composition and Rationale: *Hai Ma*, *Lu Rong*, and *Bu Gu Zhi* warm the kidney yang; *Ren Shen* supplements the qi and fortifies the spleen; *Long Gu* controls spermatorrhea and calms the spirit; *Gou Qi Zi* strengthens the liver and kidney, builds the blood and brightens the eyes; *Hei Lu Shen*, *Hai Gou Shen*, and *Hua Lu Shen* strengthen kidney yang; *Fu Ling* fortifies the spleen, eliminates damp, and promotes urination; *Huang Qi* strengthens the qi and controls sweat; *Hu Tao Ren* supplements the kidney and liver; *Ge Jie* strengthens kidney yang and supplements the lungs; *Hu Gu* strengthens the bones and sinews; *Shan Zhu Yu* strengthens liver yin; *Dang Gui* supplements the blood; *Ding Xiang* warms the kidney yang and moves cold stagnation in the stomach; and *Shou Di Huang* nourishes yin and supplements the blood.

13.20 Ren Shen Lu Rong Wan †
人參鹿茸丸
Ginseng and Young Deer Antler Pills

Primary Functions and Applications: **Ren Shen Lu Rong Wan** supplements qi and strengthens yang, nourishes the blood, and promotes congenital jing. It is used effectively to treat both depletion of yin and depletion of yang, with such symptoms as fatigue, weariness, shortness of breath, poor hearing, and tinnitus; and as a general tonic for patients with weakness associated with long illness. It is indicated in the presence of leg weakness, palpitations, and insomnia, and for weakness of the kidney with accompanying impotence, spermatorrhea, frequent urination, cold feelings, and chills. It is also indicated in cases of gynecological disorders resulting from qi and blood depletion, such as amenorrhea, hypomenorrhea, hypermenorrhea and leukorrhea. Neurasthenia, anemia, and diabetes mellitus are also addressed.

Format and Administration: **Ren Shen Lu Rong Wan** is produced as a 9 gram honey pill and as smaller pills in 200-pill bottles.

Recommended Dosage: One honey pill or 5 smaller pills twice a day. Diabetic patients should use the smaller pills.

Ren Shen Lu Rong Wan		
Constituent Substances		
Pinyin Name	**Pharmaceutical Name**	**% Composition**
Ren Shen	*Radix Ginseng*	4.7
Du Zhong	*Cortex Eucommiae Ulmoidis*	9.0
Ba Ji Tian	*Radix Morindae Officinalis*	9.0
Huang Qi	*Radix Astragali*	9.0
Lu Rong	*Cornu Cervi Parvum*	3.8
Dang Gui	*Radix Angelicae Sinensis*	9.0
Niu Xi	*Radix Achyranthis Bidentatae*	9.0
Long Yan Rou	*Arillus Longanae*	9.0

Composition and Rationale: *Ren Shen* supplements qi and lowers blood sugar levels; *Du Zhong* and *Niu Xi* strengthen kidney yang, nourish the liver, and strengthen the sinews and bones; *Ba Ji Tian* strengthens kidney yang; *Huang Qi* strengthens qi; *Lu Rong* supplements kidney yang, strengthens blood, congenital jing, sinews and bones; *Dang Gui* strengthens blood and regulates menstruation; *Long Yan Rou* supplements the spleen and heart, nourishes the blood, and calms the spirit.

Zhong Guo Ji Ben Zhong Chen Yao (Fundamentals of Chinese Prepared Medicines, 1988) includes *Bu Gu Zhi, Dong Chong, Xia Cao, Tu Si Zi, Wu Wei Zi, Fu Ling, Huang Bai,* and *Xiang Fu* in its standardized formula for **Ren Shen Lu Rong Wan.**

Ming Mu Di Huang Wan †   13.21
明目地黃丸
Eye Brightener Rehmannia Pills

Source: *Wan Bing Hui Chun (Recovery of Ten Thousand Diseases)*, Ming Dynasty (1368-1644).

Primary Functions and Applications: **Ming Mu Di Huang Wan** nourishes liver and kidney yin and improves vision. It is used to treat eye disorders caused by liver and kidney yin depletion with depletion heat. Guiding symptoms include poor vision, vertigo, photophobia, excess tearing of the eyes, and night blindness. It is also indicated in other disorders associated with liver and kidney yin depletion, such as dizziness, dry mouth, dry throat, tinnitus, night sweat, and fatigue.

Ming Mu Di Huang Wan is recommended in cases of retinitis, optic neuritis, and vitreous opacity, though only when accompanied by symptoms of liver and kidney yin depletion. If fire is present, (swollen, red eyes, etc.), wind-heat expelling or liver-fire clearing formulae should be used instead of **Ming Mu Di Huang Wan.**

Format and Administration: **Ming Mu Di Huang Wan** is produce by the Lanzhou Fo Ci Pharmaceutical Company in 200-pill bottles.

Recommended Dosage: Ten pills, 3 times a day.

Ming Mu Di Huang Wan		
Constituent Substances		
Pinyin Name	**Pharmaceutical Name**	**% Composition**
Shou Di Huang	*Radix Rehmannia Glutinosae*	12.0
Shan Yao	*Radix Paeoniae Rubra*	6.0
Mu Dan Pi	*Cortex Radicis Mouton*	4.5
Fu Ling	*Sclerotium Poriae Cocus*	4.5
Shan Yu Rou	*Fructus Corni Officinalis*	6.0
Ze Xie	*Buthus Martensi*	4.5
Gou Qi Zi	*Fructus Lycii Chinensis*	25.0
Shi Jue Ming	*Concha Haliotidis*	12.5
Bai Ji Li	*Fructus Tribuli Terrestris*	12.5

Composition and Rationale: Shou Di Huang nourishes yin and supplements blood; *Shan Yao* strengthens the spleen and nourishes the kidney; *Mu Dan Pi* clears depletion heat and blood heat; *Fu Ling* strengthens the spleen; *Shan Yu Rou* strengthens kidney yin and smooths the liver; *Ze Xie* promotes urination and drains kidney fire; *Gou Qi Zi* strengthens the liver and kidney and nourishes the eyes; *Shi Jue Ming* calms liver fire as it affects the eyes; and *Bai Ji Li* extinguishes liver wind and brightens the eyes.

The original formula, and the standardized formula listed in *Zhong Guo Ji Ben Zhong Chen Yao (Fundamentals of Chinese Prepared Medicines,)* for **Ming Mu Di Huang Wan** contains *Dang Gui, Bai Shao,* and *Ju Hua*.

13.22   Qi Ju Di Huang Wan †
杞菊地黃丸
Lycium, Chrysanthemum, and Rehmannia Pills

Primary Functions and Applications: **Qi Ju Di Huang Wan** is used to treat liver and kidney yin depletion syndromes, especially when acompanied by dryness in the eyes and poor vision, and in the presence of dizziness, vertigo, and tinnitus. This formula is a modification of **Liu Wei Di Huang Wan[13.18]**, the basic formula for kidney yin nourishment.

Format and Administration: **Qi Ju Di Huang Wan** is produced by the Lanzhou Fo Ci Pharmaceutical Manufactory in 100-pill bottles as *Lycium-Rehmannia Pills.*

Recommended Dosage: Eight pills, 3 times a day.

Qi Ju Di Huang Wan		
Constituent Substances		
Pinyin Name	Pharmaceutical Name	% Composition
Shou Di Huang	*Radix Rehmannia Glutinosae*	27.90
Shan Yao	*Radix Paeoniae Rubra*	13.79
Mu Dan Pi	*Cortex Radicis Mouton*	10.35
Fu Ling	*Sclerotium Poriae Cocus*	10.35
Shan Yu Rou	*Fructus Corni Officinalis*	13.78
Ze Xie	*Buthus Martensi*	10.35
Gou Qi Zi	*Fructus Lycii Chinensis*	6.90
Ju Hua	*Flos Chrysanthemi Indicae Morifolii*	6.90

Composition and Rationale: Shou Di Huang nourishes yin and supplements blood; *Shan Yao* strengthens the spleen and nourishes the kidney; *Mu Dan Pi* clears depletion heat and blood heat; *Fu Ling* strengthens the spleen; *Shan Yu Rou* strengthens kidney yin and smooths the liver; *Ze Xie* promotes urination and drains kidney fire; *Gou Qi Zi* strengthens the liver and the kidney and nourishes the eyes; and *Ju Hua* expels wind-heat and brightens the eyes.

Shi Hu Ye Guang Wan †   13.23
石斛夜光丸
Dendrobium Night Vision Pills

Source: Rui Zhu Tang Jing Yan Fang (Formulas from Experience from the Rui Zhu Tang Pharmacy), Yuan Dynasty, 1279-1368. The formula is referred to here as *Ye Guang Wan*. After the Ming Dynasty (1368-1644), the name was changed to **Shi Hu Ye Guang Wan**.

Primary Functions and Applications: **Shi Hu Ye Guang Wan** nourishes yin to eliminate depletion heat and nourishes the liver to improve eyesight. It is used to treat eye diseases due to liver and kidney yin depletion with signs of depletion heat, including poor vision, photophobia, feelings of dryness in the eyes, and other general yin depletion signs (fatigue, lumbago, insomnia and night sweats). This formula may be used to treat cases of glaucoma, retinitis, choroiditis, and optic neuritis, though only when liver and kidney yin depletion signs with depletion heat are present.

Format and Administration: **Shi Hu Ye Guang Wan** is produced as 9-gram honey pills in boxes of 10.

Recommended Dosage: One honey pill, twice a day.

Shi Hu Ye Guang Wan		
Constituent Substances		
Pinyin Name	Pharmaceutical Name	% Composition
Ling Yang Jiao	*Cornu Antelopis*	4
Xi Jiao	*Cornu Rhinocerotis*	4
Shi Hu	*Herba Dendrobi*	4
Ren Shen	*Radix Ginseng*	16
Gou Qi Zi	*Fructus Lycii Chinensis*	6
Ju Hua	*Flos Chrysanthemi Indicae Morifolii*	6
Fang Feng	*Herba Ledebouriellae Sesloidis*	4
Chuan Xiong	*Rhizoma Ligustici Wallichii*	4
Mai Men Dong	*Radix Ophiopogonis Japonici*	8
Sheng Di Huang	*Radix Crudae Rehmanniae Glutinosae*	8
Jue Ming Zi	*Semen Cassiae Torae*	6
Rou Cong Rong	*Herba Cistanches*	4
Bai Ji Li	*Fructus Tribuli Terrestris*	4
Niu Xi	*Radix Achyranthis Bidentatae*	6
Wu Wei Zi	*Fructus Schizandra Chinensis*	4
Zhi Qiao	*Fructus Citri seu Ponciri*	4
Qing Xiang Zi	*Semen Celosiae*	4
Huang Lian	*Rhizoma Coptidis*	4

Composition and Rationale: *Ling Yang Jiao* clears liver heat; *Xi Jiao* clears heat in the heart; *Shi Hu* nourishes yin, clears heat, and promotes the production of body fluid; *Ren Shen* supplements qi and strengthens the spleen; *Gou Ji Zi* nourishes yin, strengthens the blood, soothes the liver, and improves eyesight; *Ju Hua* clears heat, expels wind-heat, and improves eyesight; *Fang Feng* expels wind; *Chuan Xiong* promotes blood circulation, moves stagnant qi, and relieves headache; *Mai Men Dong,* and *Sheng Di Huang* nourish yin and clear heat; *Jue Ming Zi* clears heat and improves vision; *Rou Cong Rong* supplements the kidney and strengthens the yang; *Bai Ji Li* extinguishes wind and brightens the eyes; *Niu Xi* nourishes the liver and kidney; *Wu Wei Zi* strengthens the kidney and nourishes the qi; *Zhi Qiao* and *Qing Xiang Zi* clear heat and improve vision; *Huang Lian* clears heat and resolves fire toxin.

Zhong Guo Ji Ben Zhong Chen Yao (Fundamentals of Chinese Prepared Medicines, 1988) includes *Fu Ling, Shou Di Huang, Shan Yao, Tu Si Zi, Xing Ren, Tian Men Dong* and *Gan Cao* in its standardized formula for **Shi Hu Ye Guang Wan.**

Gui Ling Ji †   13.24
龜靈集
Tortoise Age Conglomerate

Source: This formula originated in the Song Dynasty (960-1279), and was later listed in the book *Ji Yan Liang Fang (Collection of Effective Formulas).*

Primary Functions and Applications: **Gui Ling Ji** strengthens kidney yang, and is used to treat the following disorders associated with depletion of kidney yang:

Kidney yang depletion disorders with such symptoms as impotence, spermatorrhea, lumbago with feeling of coldness in lower lumbar area, frequent urination, and dizziness or tinnitus.

Liver disorder due to kidney yang depletion, with hypermenorrhea or amenorrhea.

Lung disorders due to kidney yang depletion with the following symptoms: chronic asthma (used to strengthen pulmorenal function, and thus reduce the severity of future asthma attacks), and chronic cough (weak cough with thin white phlegm).

Spleen disorders due to kidney yang depletion, indicated specifically by "fifth-watch" diarrhea *(wu geng jing xie),* and leukorrhea.

Heart disorders due to kidney yang depletion, as indicated by poor memory.

Gui Ling Ji is thus indicated in cases of sexual dysfunction associated with neurasthenia, problems associated with climacteric syndrome in men or women, and chronic nephritis when associated with kidney yang depletion.

Format and Administration: **Gui Ling Ji** is produced by the Shansi Drug Manufactory in bottles of 30 capsules.

Recommended Dosage: Two or 3 capsules, once a day.

Contraindications: **Do not use Gui Ling Ji during pregnancy or during an acute phase of attack by wind-cold or wind-heat pathogens.**

Gui Ling Ji		
Constituent Substances		
Pinyin Name	**Pharmaceutical Name**	**% Composition**
Ren Shen	*Radix Ginseng*	20
Lu Rong	*Cornu Cervi Parvum*	25
Hai Ma	*Hippocampus*	8
Gou Qi Zi	*Fructus Lycii Chinensis*	3
Shou Di Huang	*Radix Rehmannia Glutinosae*	6
Que Nao	*Cerebrum Passeris Montani Saturatis*	2
Niu Xi	*Radix Achyranthis Bidentatae*	3
Suo Yang	*Herba Cynomorri Songarici*	2
Ding Xiang	*Flos Caryophylli*	2
Sha Ren	*Semen et Pericarpium Amomi*	3
Du Zhong	*Cortex Eucommiae Ulmoidis*	2
Da Qing Yan	*Halitum*	2
Rou Cong Rong	*Herba Cistanches*	6
Chuan Shan Jia	*Squama Manitis*	6
Tu Si Zi	*Herba et Semen Cuscutae*	2
Bu Gu Zhi	*Semen Psoralae Coryfoliae*	2
Yin Yang Huo	*Herba Epimedii*	2
Gan Cao	*Radix Glycyrrhizae Uralensis*	2
Tian Men Dong	*Tuber Asparagi Cochinensis*	1
Shi Yan	*Fossilia Spirifera*	1

Composition and Rationale: *Ren Shen* supplements the qi and strengthens the spleen; *Lu Rong* warms the kidney yang; *Hai Ma* strengthens the yang; *Gou Qi Zi* strengthens the kidney and improves vision; *Shou Di Huang* nourishes the yin and strengthens the blood; *Que Nao* and *Suo Yang* treat impotence and spermatorrhea; *Niu Xi* promotes blood circulation; *Ding Xiang* warms the middle burner; *Sha Ren* moves stagnant qi, warms the spleen, and controls diarrhea; *Du Zhong* strengthens the kidney; *Da Qing Yan* directs the other herbs to the kidney through its salty taste; *Rou Cong Rong* strengthens the yang; *Chuan Shan Jia* promotes blood circulation; *Tu Si Zi* strengthens the jing; *Bu Gu Zhi* warms the kidney yang; *Yin Yang Huo* strengthens the bones and sinews; *Gan Cao* harmonizes the other herbs and strengthens the middle burner; *Tian Men Dong* nourishes the yin and moistens dryness that could develop from use of the several warm and dry herbs contained in this formula.

Zhong Guo Ji Ben Zhong Chen Yao (Fundamentals of Chinese Prepared Medicines, 1988) includes *Fu Zi, Lai Fu Zi, Huai Jiao, Ji Xing Zi, Hai Zhi Ma, Mo Han Lian, Dang Gui, Lian Zi Rou, Sheng Di, Ba Ji Tian, Di Gu Pi, Qing Pi,* and *Zhu Sha,* and omits *Sha Ren, Tu Su Zi, Du Zhong,* and *Yin Yang Huo* in its standardized formula for **Gui Ling Ji.**

Ge Jie Bu Shen Wan

13.25

蛤蚧補補丸
Gecko Kidney Nourishing Pills

Primary Functions and Applications: **Ge Jie Bu Shen Wan** has the special function of strengthening kidney yang and congenital jing. In addition, it supplements lung yin, qi, and blood. It is used to treat general weakness after a long illness or during a chronic disease; to treat lumbago arising from kidney and liver depletion; and to treat lung depletion syndrome due to kidney depletion (kidney not grasping the qi which has led to lung depletion). Symptoms indicating its use include difficult breathing, chronic cough with or without white thin phlegm; and kidney depletion type asthma with difficult breathing, especially on inhalation, but without wheezing.

Ge Jie Bu Shen Wan is also used to treat kidney yang depletion, indicated by the presence of impotence, spermatorrhea, premature ejaculation, frequent urination with clear copious urine (without heat signs).

Format and Administration: **Ge Jie Bu Shen Wan** is produced by the Yulin Drug Manufactory in 50-pill bottles.

Recommended Dosage: Three to 4 pills, twice to 3 times a day, at mealtime.

Contraindications: Do not use **Ge Jie Bu Shen Wan** in cases of repletetype asthma (indicated by the presence of thick yellow phlegm).

Ge Jie Bu Shen Wan		
Constituent Substances		
Pinyin Name	**Pharmaceutical Name**	**% Composition**
Ge Jie	*Gecko*	20
Lu Rong	*Cornu Cervi Parvum*	5
Ren Shen	*Radix Ginseng*	5
Huang Qi	*Radix Astragali*	10
Du Zhong	*Cortex Eucommiae Ulmoidis*	10
Gou Shen	*Testis et Penis Canis*	5
Dong Chong Xia Cao	*Sclerotium Cordycipitis Chinensis*	5
Gou Qi Zi	*Fructus Lycii Chinensis*	10
Fu Ling	*Sclerotium Poriae Cocus*	17
Bai Zhu	*Rhizoma Atractylodis Macrocephalae*	13

Composition and Rationale: *Ge Jie* supplements kidney yang and lung yin; *Lu Rong* supplements kidney yang; *Ren Shen* supplements qi, strengthens the spleen and lung, and strengthens the congenital jing; *Huang Qi* strengthens qi and yang; *Du Zhong* supplements the liver and kidney; *Gou Shen* and *Dong Chong Xia Cao* nourish kidney yin and yang and lung yin; *Gou Qi Zi* strengthens kidney and liver yang; *Fu Ling* fortifies spleen qi and eliminates damp; and *Bai Zhu* fortifies the spleen and dries damp.

Kang Gu Zeng Sheng Pian †   13.26
抗骨增生片
Hyperosteogenesis Tablets

Primary Functions and Applications: **Kang Gu Zeng Sheng Pian** strengthens the liver and kidneys, improves the function of the sinews and bones, promotes blood circulation, regulates qi, and relieves pain. It is used to treat joint pain (both large and small joints, including vertebrae) due to liver and kidney depletion. Most such cases will have bone hyperplasia. In classical Chinese medical theory, the liver controls the sinews and the kidney controls the bones. After middle-age, the liver blood and kidney jing begin to weaken and the qi and blood begin to become insufficient; the tendons and bones weaken, and joint pain becomes a significant problem, especially with over-exertion or exposure to exogenous wind-cold damp.

In some cases, the joint pain originates from chronic overexertion, rather than from liver and kidney depletion. However, continued overexertion and damage to the tendons and bones may in turn weaken the liver and kidneys.

Symptoms indicating its use include joint pain (dull, aching pain made worse temporarily when the patient initiates movement, such as getting out of bed in the morning); joint dysfunction; fatigue; pale face and feelings of coldness in the limbs. The pulse in such cases will be thin and deep; the tongue pale.

In patients over forty years of age with signs of depletion, this formula may be used in cases of spondylitis associated with bone hyperplasia, slipped or dislocated intervertebral disc after the disc has returned to the original position (to prevent future dislocation), and bone hyperplasia.

Format and Administration: **Kang Gu Zeng Sheng Pian** is produced by the United Pharmaceutical Company in bottles of 100 tablets.

Recommended Dosage: Six tablets, 3 times a day. This medicine may be taken for as long as 6 months.

Contraindications: Do not use **Kang Gu Zeng Sheng Pian** in the presence of fever, common cold, or flu.

Kang Gu Zeng Sheng Pian		
Constituent Substances		
Pinyin Name	**Pharmaceutical Name**	**% Composition**
Shou Di Huang	*Radix Rehmannia Glutinosae*	15
Lu Han Cao	*Herba Pyrolae*	10
Lu Lu Tong	*Fructus Liquidambaris Taiwanianae*	10
Chuan Shan Liang	*Radix Dioscoreae*	8.2
Lao Huan Cao	*Herba Geranii*	8
Rou Cong Rong	*Herba Cistanches*	12.5
Chang Chun Teng	*Caulis et Foilum Hederae*	10
Yin Yang Huo	*Herba Epimedii*	3.5
Hu Gu	*Os Tigris*	8

Composition and Rationale: *Shou Di Huang* nourishes the kidney yin and supplements the blood; *Lu Han Cao* and *Lao Guan Cao* are especially good for older patients, strengthening the sinews and bones and relieving pain; *Lu Lu Tong* clears the channels and relieves joint pain; *Chuan Shan Long* promotes blood circulation and relieves joint pain; *Rou Cong Rong* strengthens the liver and kidney; *Chang Chun Teng* is another herb that is especially good for older people, strengthening the tendons and bones and relieving joint pain; *Yin Yang Huo* strengthens the kidney yang and relieves leg pain; and *Hu Gu* strengthens the bones and relieves joint pain.

Zhong Guo Ji Ben Zhong Chen Yao (Fundamentals of Chinese Prepared Medicines, 1988) lists this medicine as *Kang Gu Zhi Zeng Wan*. It is comprised of *Shou Di, Rou Cong Rong, Yin Yang Huo, Gou Qi Zi, Niu Zhen Zi, Gu Sui Bu, Niu Xi, Ji Xue Teng,* and *Lai Fu Zi.*

13.27   Shen Rong Hu Gu Wan †
參茸虎骨丸
Ginseng, Young Deer Antler, and Tiger Bone Pills

Primary Functions and Applications: **Shen Rong Hu Gu Wan** strengthens qi, nourishes blood, strengthens tendons and bones, eliminates wind-cold and damp (bi syndrome), and relieves pain. It is used to treat weakness of the limbs and lumbar area from depletion of qi and blood and depletion of kidney yang, with such symptoms as numbness and pain in the limbs or lumbar area; feelings of cold, especially in the limbs or lumbar area, and fatigue. It is also used to treat chronic arthritis (rheumatoid arthritis or osteoarthritis) in cases that have reached the stage in which the sharp pain in the joints has become dull or non-existent, and where there is joint deformity and dysfunction.

Format and Administration: **Shen Rong Hu Gu Wan** is produced as pills, 100 per bottle.

Recommended Dosage: Adults, 4 to 6 pills, twice a day. Do not increase the dose to more than 8 pills, twice a day. Children: 9 to 11 years old, 1 to 2 pills, twice a day; 12 to 16 years old, 2 to 3 pills, twice a day. Do not increase these dosages.

Contraindications: **Do not use Shen Rong Hu Gu Wan** during pregnancy. Do not use when fever is present. Decrease the dose if a feeling of warmth in the chest, numbness in the limbs, or slight dizziness develops. Decrease the dosage for cardiac patients.

Shen Rong Hu Gu Wan		
Constituent Substances		
Pinyin Name	Pharmaceutical Name	% Composition
Ren Shen	*Radix Ginseng*	5
Lu Rong	*Cornu Cervi Parvum*	2
Dang Gui	*Radix Angelicae Sinensis*	30
Hu Gu	*Os Tigris*	5
Fang Ji	*Radix Aristolochae Fangji*	25
Fang Feng	*Herba Ledebouriellae Sesloidis*	33

Composition and Rationale: Ren Shen, Lu Rong, and *Dang Gui* strengthen the qi and blood, supplement the spleen, and strengthen the kidney yang; and *Hu Gu, Fang Ji,* and *Fang Feng* strengthen the tendons and bones, expel wind-damp, and relieve joint pain.

13.28   Er Ming Zuo Ci Wan †
耳鳴左慈丸
Tinnitus Left-Supporting Pills

Source: *Xiao Er Yao Zeng Zhi Jue (Pediatric Pharmaceutics),* Song Dynasty (960-1279).

Primary Functions and Applications: **Er Ming Zuo Ci Wan** nourishes yin and reduces ascendent liver yang. It is used to treat hearing disorders such as tinnitus and partial deafness (sensori-neural) arising from kidney yin depletion with relative replete yang. In addition, the patient may have such related symptoms as dizziness or vertigo. **Er Ming Zuo Ci Wan** may also be used to treat poor and blurred vision due to kidney yin and liver yin depletion.

Format and Administration: **Er Ming Zuo Ci Wan** is produced by the Lanchow Chinese Medicine Works, Lanchow, China, as *Tso-Tzu Otic Pills,* 200 pills per bottle.

This formula is manufactured with different names in different localities. In Wuhan, it is called *Chai Ci Di Huang Wan*; in Nanking, *Er Ming Wan.* The current official Chinese pharmacopoeia *Zhong Guo Ji Ben Zhong Chen Yao (Fundamentals of Chinese Prepared Medicines, 1988)* refers to this formula as *Er Long Zuo Ci Wan.*

Recommended Dosage: Eight pills, 3 times a day with warm water. Slightly salty water may be used as an herbal conductor (*yao yin*).

Er Ming Zuo Ci Wan		
Constituent Substances		
Pinyin Name	**Pharmaceutical Name**	**% Composition**
Shou Di Huang	*Radix Rehmannia Glutinosae*	.0
Shan Yao	*Radix Paeoniae Rubra*	15.0
Shan Zhu Yu	*Fructus Corni Officinalis*	15.0
Mu Dan Pi	*Cortex Radicis Mouton*	10.5
Fu Ling	*Sclerotium Poriae Cocus*	10.5
Ze Xie	*Buthus Martensi*	10.5
Ci Shi	*Magnetitum*	4.0
Chai Hu	*Radix Bupleuri*	4.5

Composition and Rationale: The word *Zuo* ("left") in the name of this formula refers to the left kidney and to its function of nourishing kidney yin. (*Ming men* [life gate] would refer to the right kidney, and to kidney yang).

The formula consists of **Liu Wei Di Huang Wan [13.8]** to which the herbs *Ci Shi* and *Chai Hu* have been added. *Shou Di Huang* nourishes the yin and strengthens blood; *Shan Yao* fortifies the spleen and stomach; *Mu Dan Pi* clears blood heat and extinguishes liver fire; *Fu Ling* strengthens the spleen, discharges damp, and promotes urination; *Shan Zhu Yu* strengthens liver and kidney yin, and controls sweating and spermatorrhea; *Ze Xie* promotes urination and drains kidney depletion heat; *Ci Shi* eliminates excess liver yang and improves hearing and vision; and *Chai Hu* smoothes the liver and moves stagnant liver qi.

Zhong Guo Ji Ben Zhong Chen Yao (Fundamentals of Chinese Prepared Medicines, 1988) includes *Shou Di, Tong Cao, Wu Wei Zi,* and *Ju Hua* in its standardized formula for **Er Long Zuo Ci Wan**.

13.29   Da Bu Yin Wan †
大補陰丸
Major Yin Supplementation Pills

Source: From the book, *Dan Xi Xin Fa III (The Teachings of Dr. Danxi Zhu's Treatment Methodology, vol.3)*, Yuan Dynasty (1279-1368).

Primary Functions and Applications: **Da Bu Yin Wan** nourishes kidney yin and reduces depletion heat. It is used to treat kidney and liver yin depletion syndromes, especially when the depletion of yin has caused depletion heat (depletion heat syndrome). It is indicated in the presence of hot flashes, night sweats, spermatorrhea, insomnia, nightmares, dizziness, tinnitus, lumbago, and weakness of the knees.

Da Bu Yin Wan is also indicated in the condition known as "yin depletion fails to balance the yang," which produces relative yang repletion and bleeding due to the relative excess heat. Thus, it is used when blood appears in the sputum or vomitus.

In the presence of the above symptoms, **Da Bu Yin Wan** is indicated in the treatment of hyperthyroidism, diabetes mellitus, and kidney, lung, or bone tuberculosis (acute or chronic).

Format and Administration: **Da Bu Yin Wan** is produced by the Szechuan Chengtu Chinese Medicine Works, Szechuan, China, as *Laryngitis Pills*. It is available in small pill format, 10 small pills per vial.

Recommended Dosage: Ten pills, 3 times a day.

Da Bu Yin Wan		
Constituent Substances		
Pinyin Name	**Pharmaceutical Name**	**Composition**
Shou Di Huang	*Radix Rehmannia Glutinosae*	—
Gui Ban	*Plastrum Testudinis*	—
Ju Ji Sui	*Pig Spinal Cord*	—
Zhi Mu	*Rhizoma Anemarrhenae Ashphodeloidis*	—
Huang Bai	*Cortex Phellodendri*	—

Composition and Rationale: *Shou Di Huang* nourishes and strengthens the kidney and nourishes the blood; *Gui Ban* and *Ju Ji Sui* nourish the yin, settle the yang, strengthen bones and marrow, and cool the blood; and *Zhi Mu* and *Huang Bai* eliminate depletion heat by their cold property, and protect body fluid against the depletion heat. Certain drug manufactories, such as the Tianjin Pharmaceutical Works, omit the pig spinal cord.

During the Yuan dynasty, when this medicine was developed, Dr. Zhu Danxi believed that yin was almost always deplete and that yang was almost always replete. He developed this formula as a model formula to treat yin depletion with relative yang repletion. Dr. Danxi Zhu headed his own successful medical school where this belief was prevalent.

Quan Lu Wan †   13.30
全鹿丸
Whole Deer Pills

Source: *Jing-Yue Quan Shu (Jing-Yue's Complete Book)*, Ming Dynasty (1368-1644).

Primary Functions and Applications: **Quan Lu Wan** strengthens kidney yang and yin, strengthens vital qi, and nourishes blood and is used to treat syndromes arising from both yang and yin depletion. Guiding symptoms include general weakness, fatigue, dizziness, tinnitus, low back pain, weak knees, poor appetite, weight loss, and spontaneous and night sweating. It is indicated in cases of spermatorrhea or impotence due to kidney yang or kidney yin depletion, and in cases of menstrual disorders, including irregular period, hyper- or hypomenorrhea, and leukorrhea. In addition, **Quan Lu Wan** may be used in cases of neurasthenia, adult-onset diabetes, pulmonary tuberculosis, and chronic nephritis in the presence of symptoms due to qi and blood depletion.

Format and Administration: **Quan Lu Rong** is produced as a 9-gram honey pill, and in bottles of 100 smaller pills.

Recommended Dosage: One honey pill, twice a day, or four smaller pills three times a day.

Quan Lu Wan		
Constituent Substances		
Pinyin Name	**Pharmaceutical Name**	**% Composition**
Lu Rou	*Caro Cervi*	39.95
Lu Rong	*Cornu Cervi Parvum*	0.50
Lu Wei	*Penis et Testis Cervi*	0.25
Lu Shen	*Renal Cervi*	0.37
Lu Jiao Jiao	*Gelatinum Cornu Cervi*	1.00
Ren Shen	*Radix Ginseng*	2.00
Bai Zhu	*Rhizoma Atractylodis Macrocephalae*	2.00
Fu Ling	*Sclerotium Poriae Cocus*	2.00
Gan Cao	*Radix Glycyrrhizae Uralensis*	2.00
Dang Gui	*Radix Angelicae Sinensis*	2.00
Chuang Xiong	*Radix Ligustici Wallichii*	2.00
Shou Di Huang	*Radix Rehmannia Glutinosae*	2.00
Huang Qi	*Radix Astragali*	2.00
Gou Qi Zi	*Fructus Lycii Chinensis*	2.00
Du Zhong	*Cortex Eucommiae Ulmoidis*	2.00
Niu Xi	*Radix Achyranthis Bidentatae*	2.00
Xu Duan	*Radix Dispaci*	2.00
Rou Cong Rong	*Herba Cistanches*	2.00
Suo Yang	*Herba Cynomorri Songarici*	2.00
Ba Ji Tian	*Radix Morindae Officinalis*	2.00
Tian Men Dong	*Tuber Asparagi Cochinensis*	2.00
Mai Men Dong	*Radix Ophiopogonis Japonici*	2.00
Wu Wei Zi	*Fructus Schizandra Chinensis*	2.00
Chen Xiang	*Lignum Aquilariae*	1.00
Chen Pi	*Pericarpium Citri Reticulatae*	2.00

Composition and Rationale: *Lu Rou, Lu Rong, Lu Wei, Lu Shen,* and *Lu Jiao Jiao* strengthen the yang and kidney jing and nourish the qi and blood.

Ren Shen, Bai Zhu, Fu Ling, Gan Cao, Dang Gui, Chuang Xiong, Shou Di, and *Huang Qi* function as a group to nourish the qi and blood. Together, they are equivalent to the formula **Fu Ke Ba Zhen Wan** [13.10], in which *Huang Qi* is substituted for *Bai Shao.*

Gou Qi Zi, Du Zhong, Niu Xi, and *Xu Duan* supplement the liver, kidney, tendons and bones; *Rou Cong Rong, Suo Yang,* and *Ba Ji Tian* strengthen kidney yang and control spermatorrhea; *Tian Men Dong, Mai Men Dong* and *Wu Wei Zi* moisten the yin and calm the spirit; and *Chen Xiang* and *Chen Pi* regulate the flow of qi in the middle burner.

The cervine basis of this medicine (deer meat, deer horn, deer penis and testicle and deer kidney) explains the formula's name, *Complete Deer Pills.* The use of this formula is similar to that of **Ren Shen Lu Rong Wan [13.28a]** which may be substituted when **Quan Lu Wan** is unavailable.

Shen Gui Lu Rong Wan [13.28b], a formula similar to **Quan Lu Rong,** is produced as two slightly different formulae, one from Henan, one from Jianxi. The formula produced in Henan is more effective for supplementation of kidney yang; the Jianxi version is better when the therapeutic target is supplementing constitutional qi, blood, and liver yin.

Zhong Guo Ji Ben Zhong Chen Yao (Fundamentals of Chinese Prepared Medicines, 1988) includes *Sheng Di, Tu Si Zi, Shan Yao, Bu Gu Zi, Fu Pen Zi, Qian Shi, Hua Jiu, Xiao Hui Xiang, Qing Yuan, Qiu Shi,* and *Hu Lu Ba* in its standardized formula for **Quan Lu Wan.**

Yu Quan Wan †
玉泉丸
Jade Spring Pills

13.31

Source: The formula is from the Qing Dynasty writings of Ye Tianshi.

Primary Functions and Applications: **Yu Chuan Wan** nourishes kidney yin, clears depletion heat, relieves thirst due to depleted kidney yin and promotes salivation. It is used to treat excess thirst due to yin depletion and damaged body fluids, and to treat mild to moderately severe cases of diabetes.

Format and Administration: **Yu Chuan Wan** is produced by the United Pharmaceutical Company in 120-gram bottles.

Recommended Dosage: Six grams, 4 times per day.

Yu Chuan Wan		
Constituent Substances		
Pinyin Name	**Pharmaceutical Name**	**% Composition**
Wu Wei Zi	*Fructus Schizandra Chinensis*	8.4
Sheng Di Huang	*Radix Crudae Rehmanniae Glutinosae*	29.8
Tian Hua Fen	*Radix Tricosanthis*	23.0
Ge Gen	*Radix Puerariae Lobetae*	28.8
Gan Cao	*Radix Glycyrrhizae Uralensis*	10.0

Composition and Rationale: *Wu Wei Zi* nourishes kidney yin, promotes salivation, and relieves thirst; *Sheng Di Huang* nourishes the yin, clears depletion heat, and increases body fluid; *Tian Hua Fen* moistens dryness in the lungs, promotes salivation, and relieves thirst; *Ge Gen* clears stomach heat, promotes salivation, and relieves thirst; and *Gan Cao* clears heat in the middle burner and harmonizes the other herbs.

The *Chinese Journal of Patent Medicines (Zhong Cheng Yao Yen Jiou)* indicated that this medicine helped reduce blood and urine glucose levels in diabetic patients (*Zhong Cheng Yao Yen Jiou*, 1980 number 6).

Zhong Guo Ji Ben Zhong Chen Yao (Fundamentals of Chinese Prepared Medicines, 1988) includes *Mai Men Dong* and *Nu Mi* in its standardized formula for **Yu Chuan Wan**.

13.32   Zhi Bao San Bian Wan
至寶三鞭丸
Supreme Gem Penis Trio Pills

Primary Functions and Applications: **Zhi Bao San Bian Wan** promotes congenital jing, nourishes blood, strengthens qi, and increases brain function. It is used to strengthen a generally weak patient with kidney depletion syndrome, with symptoms such as dizziness, tinnitus, palpitations, shortness of breath, poor memory, and signs of premature aging (including prematurely grey hair and the appearance of premature aging). In addition, it is effective in the treatment of impotence and spermatorrhea.

Format and Administration: **Zhi Bao San Bian Wan** is produced by the Yantai Pharmaceutical Works as *Tzep Ao Sanpien Pills* in boxes of 10 9-gram honey pills.

Recommended Dosage: One pill, once a day.

Zhi Bao San Bian Wan		
Constituent Substances		
Pinyin Name	Pharmaceutical Name	% Composition
Ren Shen	*Radix Ginseng*	—
Huang Qi	*Radix Astragali*	—
Lu Rong	*Cornu Cervi Parvum*	—
Hai Ma	*Hippocampus*	—
Rou Gui	*Cortex Cinnamomi Cassiae*	—
Chen Xiang	*Lignum Aquilariae*	—
Ba Ji Tian	*Radix Morindae Officinalis*	—
Yin Yang Huo	*Herba Epimedii*	—
Hai Gou Shen	*Testis et Penis Otariae*	—
Lu Bian	*Tests et Penis Cervi*	—
Guang Gou Bian	*Testis et Penis Canis*	—
Shan Zhu Yu	*Fructus Corni Officinalis*	—
He Shou Wu	*Rhizoma Polygoni Multiflori*	—

Composition and Rationale: *Ren Shen* and *Huang Qi* strengthen the qi and the spleen; *Lu Rong, Hai Ma, Rou Gui, Chen Xiang, Ba Ji Tian, Yin Yang Huo, Hai Gou Shen, Lu Bian,* and *Guang Gou Bian* strengthen the kidney yang; *Shan Zhu Yu* strengthens the kidney and relieves spermatorrhea; and *He Shou Wu* strengthens the kidney yin, nourishes the blood, and reverses greying of hair.

14

Heart-Nourishing, Spirit-Quieting Formulae

Pattern Identification and Formulae Differentiation

Heart-nourishing and spirit quieting require *settling*, whereby yang is subdued, wind is extinguished, and qi absorption is promoted through the use of heavy minerals, heart and spirit quietants, and blood nourishers.

Such common blood nourishing, spirit quieting agents as *Zao Ren (Semen Zizyphi Jujube)*, *Dang Shan (Radix Codonopsis Pilosulae)*, and *Long Yan (Arillus Euphoriae Longanae)*, and the heart and spirit quietants *Fu Shen (Poria cum Radice Pini)*, *Zhu Sha (Cinnabaris)*, and *Yuan Zhi (Radix Polygalae)* appear repeatedly throughout these medicines. *Bai Zi Ren (Semen Biotae)*, which nourishes heart yin, and *Dang Gui (Radix Angelicae)*, which supplements heart blood, are also common, and will be found in fully half the formulae in this section.

Many formulae in this section focus on the spirit disturbances that result from depletion of heart qi and yang. Since such depletions are often accompanied by simultaneous depletions of cardiorenal yang or cardiopulmonary qi, kidney and/or lung supplements are included in many of the formulations. **Bu Nao Wan [14.2]** and **Jian Nao Wan [14.2]** underscore kidney and essence nourishment with *Cong Ru (Herba Cistanches)* and *Gou Qi Zi (Fructus Lycii Chinesnsis)*, agents that replenish essence and boost marrow, enrich hepatorenal yin-blood, and generally supplement the liver and kidney. Both formulae include wind-phlegm dispelling in their strategies, though **Jian Nao Wan [14.2]** emphasizes liver wind calming and kidney yang warming (with spleen protection), while **Bu Nao Wan [14.1]** addresses heart yin and blood depletion and stasis.

Tian Wang Bu Xin Dan [14.5], with *Mai Dong (Radix Ophiopogonis Japonici)*, *Sheng Di (Radix Crudae Rehmanniae Glutinosae)*, and *Xuan Shen (Radix Scrophulariae Ningpoensis)* decidedly emphasizes yin nourishment as well as blood supplementation and spirit quieting, and is indicated where the heat signs of depletion yin syndromes are evident. **Ding Xin Wan [14.9]** is a similar, though simpler, medicine. **An Shen Bu Nao Pian [14.7]** also nourishes yin, here with the non-glutinous hepatorenal yin enrichers *Nu Zhen Zi (Fructus Ligustri Lucidi)* and *Han Lian Cao (Herba Ecliptae Prostratae)*. *Han Lian Cao* does double duty as a blood supplementer with *He Shou Wu (Radix Polygoni Multiflori)*.

The emphasis of **Bai Zi Yang Xin Wan [14.6]** is on heart blood depletion with signs of cold. It includes the blood mover *Chuan Xiong (Radix Ligusitci Wallichii)*, and the yang warmer *Rou Gui (Cortex*

Cinnamomi Cassiae). In addition, damp is disinhibited and dried through the addition of *Fu Ling (Sclerotium Poriae Cocus)* and *Ban Xia (Rhizoma Pinelliae Ternatae)*.

Ci Zhu Wan [14.11] is a representative formulae for settling fright and calming the spirit, utilizing two heavy settlers *(Zhu Sha [Cinnabaris]* and *Ci Shi [Magnetitum])*, and an agent to protect the spleen from those minerals *(Shen Qu [Massa Medica Fermentata])*.

14.1

Bu Nao Wan †
補腦丸
Brain-Supplementing Pills

Primary Functions and Applications: **Bu Nao Wan** supplements the blood, the heart, and the kidneys, nourishes the brain, and quiets the spirit. It is indicated in the presence of such symptoms of heart blood depletion as poor memory, uneasiness, palpitations, and insomnia; in the presence of such symptoms of liver blood depletion and internal wind as headache and dizziness; and in cases of neurasthenia, neurosis, anxiety, and panic attacks and phobias.

Format and Administration: **Bu Nao Wan** is produced by the Sian Chinese Drug Pharmaceutical Works as *Nourish Brain Pills* in 300-pill bottles.

Recommended Dosage: Ten pills, 3 times a day.

Bu Nao Wan		
Constituent Substances		
Pinyin Name	**Pharmaceutical Name**	**% Composition**
Dang Gui	*Radix Angelicae Sinensis*	10
Suan Zao Ren	*Semen Ziziphi Spinosae*	16
Rou Cong Rong	*Herba Cistanches*	8
Bai Zi Ren	*Semen Biotae Orientalis*	6
Yuan Zhi	*Radix Polygalae Tenuifoliae*	4
He Tao Ren	*Semen Juglandis Regiae*	8
Tian Nan Xing	*Tuber Arisaematis*	4
Chang Pu	*Rhizoma Acori Graminei*	4
Gou Qi Zi	*Fructus Lycii Chinensis*	8
Hu Po	*Succinum*	4
Long Chi	*Dens Draconis*	4
Wu Wei Zi	*Fructus Schizandra Chinensis*	20

Composition and Rationale: *Dang Gui* supplements the blood; *Suan Zao Ren* nourishes the heart and liver and quiets the spirit; *Rou Cong Rong* supplements the kidneys and strengthens kidney yang; *Bai Zi*

Ren nourishes the heart and quiets the spirit; *Tian Ma* and *Gou Qi Zi* soothe the liver and calm internal wind; *Yuan Zhi* quiets the spirit; *Hu Tao Ren* supplements the kidney; *Tian Nan Xing* expels wind phlegm; *Chang Pu* opens the portals and quiets the spirit; *Hu Po* and *Long Chi* tranquilize the spirit; and *Wu Wei Zi* strengthens kidney and heart qi and improves sleep and memory.

Zhong Guo Ji Ben Zhong Chen Yao (Fundamentals of Chinese Prepared Medicines, 1988) includes *Yi Zi Ren, Zhu Huang,* and *Tian Ma* in its standardized formula for **Bu Nao Wan.**

Jian Nao Wan †   14.2
健腦丸
Brain-Fortifying Pills

Primary Functions and Applications: **Jian Nao Wan** nourishes the heart, calms the spirit, and is said to benefit wisdom. It is used to treat depletion syndromes of the heart, kidney, and blood, often accompanied by depletion-heat signs, with such symptoms as poor memory, uneasiness, insomnia, palpitations, vertigo, and tinnitus. It is also recommended in cases of Meniere's syndrome (vertigo, tinnitus). Such cases usually indicate a cardiorenal imbalance in which the kidneys fail to balance the fire of the heart, in turn producing depletion heat.

Format and Administration: **Jian Nao Wan** is produced by the Tsingtao Medicine Works as *Health Brain Pills* in 300 pill bottles.

Recommended Dosage: Ten pills, 3 times a day.

Jian Nao Wan		
Constituent Substances		
Pinyin Name	Pharmaceutical Name	% Composition
Suan Zao Ren	*Semen Ziziphi Spinosae*	18
Shan Yao	*Radix Dioscoreae*	10
Rou Cong Rong	*Herba Cistanches*	8
Wu Wei Zi	*Fructus Schizandra Chinensis*	6
Hu Po	*Succinum*	4
Long Chi	*Dens Draconis*	4
Tian Ma	*Rhizoma Gastrodiae Elatae*	4
Ren Shen	*Radix Ginseng*	4
Dang Gui	*Radix Angelicae Sinensis*	12
Gou Qi Zi	*Fructus Lycii Chinensis*	8
Yi Zhi Ren	*Fructus Alpiniae Oxyphyllae*	6
Tian Zhu Huang	*Concretio Silicea Bambusae*	4
Jiu Jie Chang Pu	*Rhizoma Anemonis Altaicae*	4
Zhu Sha	*Cinnibaris*	4
Bai Zi Ren	*Semen Biotae Orientalis*	4

Composition and Rationale: Suan Zao Ren nourishes the heart and liver and quiets the spirit; *Shan Yao* is a securing astringent; *Rou Cong Rong* supplements the kidneys and strengthens kidney yang; *Wu Wei Zi* strengthens the kidney and heart qi, and improves sleep and memory; *Hu Po, Zhu Sha,* and *Long Chi* tranquilize the spirit; *Tian Ma* and *Gou Qi Zi* soothe the liver and calm internal wind; *Ren Shen* supplements qi; *Dang Gui* supplements blood; *Yi Zhi Ren* warms the kidney; *Tian Zhu Huang* clears heat and quiets the spirit; *Jiu Jie Chang Pu* opens the portals and quiets the spirit; and *Bai Zi Ren* nourishes the heart and quiets the spirit.

Zhong Guo Ji Ben Zhong Chen Yao (Fundamentals of Chinese Prepared Medicines, 1988) includes *Tian Nan Xing*, and omits *Shan Yao, Tian Ma, Ren Shen,* and *Tian Zhu Huang* in its standardized formula for **Jian Nao Wan.**

Tian Ma Mi Huan Jun Pian
天麻密環菌片
Gastrodia Tablets

Primary Functions and Applications: Tian Ma Mi Huan Jun, the sole agent in these tablets, begins as a parasitic fungus growing on the rhizome of the *Tian Ma (Gastrodiae Elatae)* plant. As the fungus matures, the host-parasite relationship reverses: the *Gastrodia* becomes dependent on the *Armillaria.* **Tian Ma Mi Huan Jun Pian,** the tablets made from the dried and powdered fungus, reduces liver wind, nourishes the liver, quiets the spirit, and tranquilizes. It is used to treat the dizziness caused by liver wind, which is often accompanied by tinnitus and insomnia. It is also effective in the treatment of numbness in the limbs and for epileptic seizures.

Format and Administration: Recommended Dosage: Three to 5 tablets, 3 times a day taken with warm water, for two ten-day courses. If there is no improvement after two courses, then discontinue the medicine. If improvement is apparent, the medicine may be continued for another course, or until recovery.

Tian Ma Mi Huan Jun Pian		
Constituent Substances		
Pinyin	Pharmaceutical	% Composition
Tian Ma Mi Huan Jun	*Armillariae Mellea*	100

Zhu Sha An Shen Wan †
硃砂安神丸
Cinnibar Spirit-Quieting Pills

Source: Shou Shi Bao Yuan (Book on Longevity and Protection of Health), Ming Dynasty (1368-1644).

Primary Functions and Applications: **Zhu Sha An Shen Wan** quiets the heart spirit, clears heat, and nourishes the blood. It is used to clear heart fire that has damaged that organ's blood and yin. Symptoms in such cases include palpitations, uneasiness, nausea, feelings of heat in the chest, insomnia, and nightmares. In such cases, the tongue will be red, and the pulse thin and irregular. In the presence of heart fire symptoms, **Zhu Sha An Shen Wan** may be used to treat neurasthenia, including poor memory, depression, and hysteria.

Format and Administration: **Zhu Sha An Shen Wan** is produced by the Lanzhou Fo Ci Pharmaceutical Factory as *Cinnabar Sedative Pill* in bottles of 100 pills.

Recommended Dosage: Six pills, 3 times a day with warm water after meals.

Contraindications: Although this formula is commonly used in China, because of the high concentration (17.4%) of *Zhu Sha (Cinnabaris - mercuric sulfide)*, it is not used for extended periods of time, and dosages never exceed recommended levels. Administration should be temporarily discontinued for one week after every two weeks of use. **Do not use Zhu Sha An Shen Wan during pregnancy.** Do not consume spicy, greasy foods during therapy.

Zhu Sha An Shen Wan		
Constituent Substances		
Pinyin Name	**Pharmaceutical Name**	**% Composition**
Zhu Sha	*Cinnabaris*	17.4
Huang Lian	*Rhizoma Coptidis*	8.8
Dang Gui	*Radix Angelicae Sinensis*	43.4
Sheng Di Huang	*Radix Crudae Rehmanniae Glutinosae*	26.1
Gan Cao	*Radix Glycyrrhizae Uralensis*	4.3

Composition and Rationale: *Zhu Sha* quiets the spirit and relieves agitation; *Huang Lian* clears heat in the heart; *Dang Gui* strengthens the blood in heart; *Sheng Di* clears heat in the heart and nourishes the yin; and *Sheng Gan Cao* clears heat in the heart.

Tian Wang Bu Xin Dan † 14.5
天王補心丹
Celestial Emperor Heart-Supplementing Elixir

Source: *Shi Yi De Xiao Fang (Effective Formulae Tested by Physicians for Generations),* Yuan Dynasty (1279-1368).

Primary Functions and Applications: **Tian Wang Bu Xin Dan** nourishes the yin, clears heat, supplements the heart, and quiets the spirit. It is used to treat depletion heat due to kidney and heart yin depletion. Such depletion heat will have disturbed the heart and given rise to palpitations, restlessness, uneasiness, insomnia, poor memory, short attention span, poor concentration, constipation, and ulcers in the tongue and mouth. The tongue will be red with little or no coating. The pulse will be thin and rapid. In the presence of such depletion heat symptoms due to kidney and heart yin depletion, **Tian Wang Bu Xin Dan** is indicated in cases of rheumatic valvular heart disease, hyperthyroidism, neurasthenia, and menopausal symptoms.

Format and Administration: **Tian Wang Bu Xin Dan** is produced by the Lanzhou Fo Ci Pharmaceutical Company as *Tien Wang Pu Hsin Tan* in bottles of 200 pills.

Recommended Dosage: Eight pills, 3 times a day.

Tian Wang Bu Xin Dan		
Constituent Substances		
Pinyin Name	Pharmaceutical Name	% Composition
Sheng Di Huang	*Radix Crudae Rehmanniae Glutinosae*	29.63
Dang Gui	*Radix Angelicae Sinensis*	7.41
Wu Wei Zi	*Fructus Schizandra Chinensis*	7.41
Suan Zao Ren	*Semen Ziziphi Spinosae*	7.41
Bai Zi Ren	*Semen Biotae Orientalis*	7.41
Tian Men Dong	*Tuber Asparagi Cochinensis*	7.41
Mai Men Dong	*Radix Ophiopogonis Japonici*	7.41
Xuan Shen	*Radix Scrophulariae Ningpoensis*	7.41
Dan Shen	*Radix Salviae Miltiorrhizae*	3.7
Fu Ling	*Sclerotium Poriae Cocus*	3.7
Jie Geng	*Radix Platycodonis Grandiflori*	3.7
Yuan Zhi	*Radix Polygalae Tenuifoliae*	3.7

Composition and Rationale: Sheng Di Huang nourishes yin and clears heart and kidney heat; *Dang Gui* nourishes the blood and strengthens the heart; *Wu Wei Zi* nourishes the heart and strengthens the kidney; *Suan Zao Ren* and *Bai Zi Ren* nourish the heart and calm the spirit; *Tian Men Dong* nourishes yin and clears depletion heat. *Mai Men Dong* nourishes yin and clears heat in the heart; *Xuan Shen* nourishes yin and clears heat; *Dan Shen* strengthens the spleen and supplements the qi; *Fu Ling* strengthens the spleen and quiets the heart and spirit; *Jie Geng* guides the other herbs to the upper warmer; *Yuan Zhi* quiets the spirit and pacifies the heart.

Some brands of **Tian Wang Bu Xin Dan** may contain *Zhu Sha* and *Shi Chang Pu*.

Zhong Guo Ji Ben Zhong Chen Yao (Fundamentals of Chinese Prepared Medicines, 1988) includes *Chang Po, Zhu Sha,* and *Gan Cao* in its standardized formula for **Tian Wang Bu Xin Dan**.

14.6   Bai Zi Yang Xin Wan †
柏子養心散
Biota Seed Heart-Nourishing Pills

Source: Zheng Zhi Zhun Sheng (Standards for Diagnosis and Treatment), Ming Dynasty (1368-1644).

Primary Functions and Applications: **Bai Zi Yang Xin Wan** nourishes the blood, strengthens the heart, supplements qi, and quiets the spirit. It is used to treat heart depletion syndromes resulting from insufficiency of blood, with such symptoms as low energy, chills, cold limbs, palpitations, insomnia, headache, dizziness, poor memory, agitation, nightmares, and facial palor. It is also indicated in cases of neurasthenia when accompanied by the above symptoms.

Format and Administration: **Bai Zi Yang Xin Wan** is produced by the Lanzhou Fo Ci Pharmaceutical Works as *Pai Tzu Yang Hsin Wan* in 200 pill bottles.

Recommended Dosage: Eight to 10 pills, twice a day.

Bai Zi Yang Xin Wan		
Constituent Substances		
Pinyin Name	Pharmaceutical Name	% Composition
Dang Shen	*Radix Codonopsis Pilosulae*	13.10
Chuan Xiong	*Radix Ligustici Wallichii*	2.58
Rou Gui	*Cortex Cinnamomi Cassiae*	3.14
Fu Ling	*Sclerotium Poriae Cocus*	25.16
Yuan Zhi	*Radix Polygalae Tenuifoliae*	3.14
Wu Wei Zi	*Fructus Schizandra Chinensis*	3.14
Gan Cao	*Radix Glycyrrhizae Uralensis*	1.26
Huang Qi	*Radix Astragali*	12.58
Dang Gui	*Radix Angelicae Sinensis*	12.58
Ban Xia	*Rhizoma Pinelliae Ternatae*	12.58
Suan Zao Ren	*Semen Ziziphi Spinosae*	3.80
Bai Zi Ren	*Semen Biotae Orientalis*	3.14
Zhu Sha	*Cinnibaris*	3.80

Composition and Rationale: *Dang Shen* supplements the qi and strengthens the spleen; *Chuang Xiong* promotes blood circulation, moves stagnant qi, and relieves headaches; *Rou Gui* strengthens the yang, warms the middle burner, expels cold, and relieves pain; *Fu Ling* strengthens the spleen, promotes urination, and tranquilizes; *Yuan Zhi* quiets the spirit and pacifies the heart; *Wu Wei Zi* strengthens the qi, supplements the kidneys, nourishes the heart, and controls sweating; *Gan Cao* warms the middle warmer and harmonizes the other herbs; *Huang Qi* strengthens the qi and controls sweating; *Dang Gui* supplements the blood and promotes blood circulation; *Ban Xia Qu* dries damp and strengthens the spleen; *Suan Zao Ren* nourishes the heart, strengthens the blood, and quiets the spirit; *Bai Zi Ren* nourishes the heart and quiets the spirit; and *Zhu Sha* clears heat in the heart and calms the spirit.

14.7   An Shen Bu Nao Pian
安神補腦片
Spirit-Quieting Brain-Supplementing Tablets

Primary Functions and Applications: **An Shen Bu Nao Pian** calms the spirit, supplements the heart, nourishes the kidney and liver yin, and supplements the blood. It is used to treat blood depletion that has led specifically to liver blood or heart blood depletion. In classical Chinese medical theory, a depletion of liver blood will often produce upwardly rising liver wind, and symptoms that affect the head (headache, dizziness, and tinnitus).

In the treatment of heart blood depletion, the following symptoms will be prominent: palpitations, insomnia, poor memory, and uneasiness. In classical Chinese medical theory, when the blood (yin) cannot adequately nourish the heart, the relative excess of yang will disturb the heart. When such liver or heart blood syndromes are present, **An Shen Bu Nao Pian** may be used to treat neurasthenia, Meniere's disease, and hyperthyroidism.

Format and Administration: **An Shen Bu Nao Pian** is produced by the Chung Lien Drug Works as *Ansenpunaw Tablets* in bottles of 100 tablets.

Recommended Dosage: Four tablets, 3 times a day.

An Shen Bu Nao Pian		
Constituent Substances		
Pinyin Name	**Pharmaceutical Name**	**% Composition**
Huang Jing	*Rhizoma Polygonati*	36.0
Nu Zhen Zi	*Fructus Ligustri Lucidi*	36.0
Dang Gui	*Radix Angelicae Sinensis*	27.4
He Huan Pi	*Cortex Albizziae Julibrissim*	27.4
Han Lian Cao	*Herba Ecliptae Prostratae*	18.2
Suan Zao Ren	*Semen Ziziphi Spinosae*	18.2
Fu Ling	*Sclerotium Poriae Cocus*	11.5
He Shou Wu	*Radix Polygoni Multiflori*	11.5
Zhu Sha	*Cinnibaris*	6.9
Yuan Zhi	*Radix Polygalae Tenuifoliae*	6.9

Composition and Rationale: Huang Jing strengthens the blood and nourishes the yin; *Nu Zhen Zi* and *Han Lian Cao* nourish liver and kidney yin and extinguish liver wind; *Dang Gui* strengthens the blood and promotes blood circulation; *He Huan Pi* quiets the spirit and smoothes the liver; *Suan Zao Ren* nourishes the heart and liver yin and quiets the spirit; *Fu Ling* strengthens the spleen and tranquilizes the spirit; *He Shou Wu* strengthens the liver and kidney; *Zhu Sha* calms the spirit and clears heat in the heart; and *Yuan Zhi* quiets the heart spirit.

Suan Zao Ren Tang Pian
酸棗仁湯片
Zizyphus Spinosa Decocted Tablets

14.8

Source: Jin Gui Yao Lue (Synopsis of the Golden Chamber), Zhang Zhongjing, 219 A.D.

Primary Functions and Applications: **Suan Zao Ren Tang Pian** nourishes the blood, calms the spirit, clears heat, and relieves uneasiness. It strengthens liver blood, and is thus used to treat the depletion heat caused by liver blood depletion that has interfered with the heart spirit. Guiding symptoms include uneasiness, insomnia, palpitations, nightmares, night sweats, dizziness, vertigo, and dry mouth. The pulse in such cases will be wiry and thin, or thin and rapid. When the above symptoms of depletion-fire and depletion of liver blood are present, this formula may be used to treat neurasthenia and climacteric or menopausal syndromes.

Format and Administration: **Suan Zao Ren Tang Pian** is produced by the Sing-kyn Drug House as *Tabellae Suan Zao Ren Tang* in bottles of 48.

Recommended Dosage: Two to 3 pills, 3 times a day.

Suan Zao Ren Tang Pian		
Constituent Substances		
Pinyin Name	**Pharmaceutical Name**	**% Composition**
Suan Zao Ren	*Semen Ziziphi Spinosae*	50.0
Chuan Xiong	*Radix Ligustici*	8.3
Fu Ling	*Sclerotium Poriae Cocus*	17.0
Zhi Mu	*Rhizoma Anemarrhenae Ashphodeloidis*	17.0
Gan Cao	*Radix Glycyrrhizae Uralensis*	8.3

Composition and Rationale: *Suan Zao Ren* nourishes the liver blood, calms the heart, and quiets the spirit; *Chuan Xiong* promotes blood, qi, and circulation, and soothes the liver; *Fu Ling* calms the heart; *Zhi Mu* nourishes the yin, clears heat, and calms anxiety; and *Gan Cao* clears heat and harmonizes the other herbs.

14.9 Ding Xin Wan
定心丸
Heart-Stabilizing Pills

Primary Functions and Applications: **Ding Xin Wan** nourishes the blood, calms the spirit, and quiets the heart. Guiding symptoms include palpitations, insomnia, poor memory, dizziness, vertigo, hot flashes, dry mouth, and restlessness. When symptoms of heart depletion are present, **Ding Xin Wan** may be used to treat sinus tachycardia, neurasthenia with headache, insomnia, pre-menstrual syndrome, and climacteric or involutional psychosis.

Format and Administration: **Ding Xin Wan** is produced by the Min-Kang Drug Manufactory in bottles of 100 pills.

Recommended Dosage: Six pills, twice or 3 times a day.

Ding Xin Wan		
Constituent Substances		
Pinyin Name	**Pharmaceutical Name**	**% Composition**
Dang Shen	*Radix Codonopsis Pilosulae*	4.6
Dang Gui	*Radix Angelicae Sinensis*	9.1
Fu Shen	*Poria cum Radice Pini*	9.1
Yuan Zhi	*Radix Polygalae Tenuifoliae*	9.1
Suan Zao Ren	*Semen Ziziphi Spinosae*	9.1
Bai Zi Ren	*Semen Biotae Orientalis*	13.7
Mai Men Dong	*Radix Ophiopogonis Japonici*	9,1
Hu Po	*Succinum*	2.3

Composition and Rationale: *Dang Shen* strengthens the qi and nourishes the spleen; *Dang Gui* supplements the blood and promotes blood circulation; *Fu Shen* quiets the heart; *Yuan Zhi* quiets the spirit; *Suan Zao Ren* quiets the spirit and calms the heart; *Bai Zi Ren* nourishes the heart and quiets the spirit; *Huang Qin* clears the heart; *Mai Men Dong* nourishes the yin, clears heat, and increases body fluid; and *Hu Po* quiets the spirit.

An Mian Pian
安眠片
Sleeping Tablets

14.10

Primary Functions and Applications: **An Mian Pian** quiets the spirit, clears heat in the heart, tranquilizes, and strengthens the liver. It is used to treat heart yin depletion with depletion heat that has disturbed the spirit and caused insomnia. It is also used to treat symptoms such as agitation, anxiety, overthinking, excessive dreaming, and poor memory, all due to heart yin depletion. In the presence of such heart yin depletion signs, **An Mian Pian** may also be used to treat neurasthenia, panic attacks, and depression.

Format and Administration: **An Mien Pian** is produced by the Hebei branch of the China National Native Produce and Animal By-Products Import and Export Corporation in bottles of 60 pills.

Recommended Dosage: Four tablets, 3 times per day, with warm boiled water.

An Mian Pian		
Constituent Substances		
Pinyin Name	**Pharmaceutical Name**	**% Composition**
Suan Zao Ren	*Semen Ziziphi Spinosae*	—
Yuan Zhi	*Radix Polygalae Tenuifoliae Tenuifoliae*	—
Fu Ling	*Sclerotium Poriae Cocus*	—
Shan Zhi Zi	*Fructus Gardeniae Jasminoidis*	—
Shen Qu	*Massa Medica Fermentata*	—
Quan Xie	*Buthus Martensi*	—
Gan Cao	*Radix Glycyrrhizae Uralensis*	—

Composition and Rationale: *Suan Zao Ren, Yuan Zhi,* and *Fu Ling* nourish the blood, sootheing liver qi, and calm the spirit; *Quan Xie* and *Shan Zhi Zi* clear heat in the heart and calm the spirit; *Quan Xie* and *Shen Qu* supplement the spleen and regulate digestion; and *Quan Xie* and *Gan Cao* harmonize and supplement the spleen.

Ci Zhu Wan † 14.11
磁朱丸
Magnetite and Cinnibar Pills

Source: Qian Jin Yao Fang *(Priceless Prescriptions)*, Tang Dynasty (618-907).

Primary Functions and Applications: **Ci Zhu Wan** quiets the spirit and improves vision. It is used to treat patients with kidney/heart yin imbalance, with symptoms such as palpitations, insomnia, dizziness, tinnitus, deafness, blurred vision, cataracts, photophobia, restlessness, and agitation. In addition, **Ci Zhu Wan** makes a good secondary medication in the treatment of epilepsy. Its effectiveness may be increased in such cases if it is combined with other medicines, such as agents that reduce liver wind (*Tian Ma Wan*, for example) or calm the spirit and expel phlegm (such as **Bu Nao Wan [14.2]**).

Format and Administration: **Ci Zhu Wan** is produced by the Kwangchow Pharmaceutical Industry as *Tze Zhu Pills* in bottles of 120 pills.

Recommended Dosage: Four to 5 pills, three times a day.

Ci Zhu Wan		
Constituent Substances		
Pinyin Name	**Pharmaceutical Name**	**% Composition**
Ci Shi	*Magnetitum*	28.8
Zhu Sha	*Cinnabaris*	14.4
Shen Qu	*Massa Medica Fermentata*	56.8

Composition and Rationale: Ci Shi quiets the spirit, nourishes yin, reduces replete yang and improves vision; *Zhu Sha* clears heat in the heart and quiets the spirit; and *Shen Qu* strengthens the spleen, regulates digestion, prevents damage to the stomach qi from the minerals in the formula, and generally functions as a binder.

329

15

Astringent Formulae

To retain the sperm
15.1   Jin Suo Gu Jing Wan

Pattern Identification and Formula Differentiation

Securing astriction is employed as a method to prevent and to stem the draining of qi, blood, and fluids. It is used to constrain perspiration; to constrain the lungs (through the use of antitussives); to stem the flow of persistent diarrhea and to correct the resultant rectal prolapse and efflux desertion; to secure the menses; to check vaginal discharge; to arrest hemorrhage; and to reduce urine flow.

The single formula in this chapter targets a further application of astriction: securing essence. **Jin Suo Gu Jin Wan [15.1]** is a representative formula for cases of seminal emission due to depletion. It combines a number of essence securers with the kidney supplementer *Sha Yuan Ji Li (Semen Astragalis)*.

15.1   Jin Suo Gu Jing Wan †
金鎖固精丸
Golden Lock Essence-Securing Pills

Source: *Yi Fang Ji Jie (Explanation of Prescription)*, Qing Dynasty (1644-1911).

Primary Functions and Applications: **Jin Suo Gu Jing Wan** strengthens the kidneys and, through the use of astringents, stems nocturnal emissions due to kidney and liver depletion. Symptoms of nocturnal emission due to kidney depletion include nocturnal emission without dreams, accompanied by weariness, tiredness, lumbago, and tinnitus. The tongue in such cases will be pale, with thin white moss or no moss. The pulse will be thin and empty.

Format and Administration: **Jin Sou Gu Chin Wan** is produced by the Lanzhou Fo Ci Pharmaceutical Factory as *Chin So Ku Ching Wan* in 100-pill bottles.

Recommended Dosage: Fifteen pills, 3 times a day.

If the depletion-type nocturnal emission is accompanied by such spleen depletion symptoms as diarrhea and poor digestion, herbal medicines that fortify spleen and kidney yang, such as *Si Shen Wan*, or medicines that supplement spleen yang alone, such as **Bu Zhong Yi Qi Wan [13.6]** or **Shen Ling Bai Zhu Wan [13.7]** should be added.

If the deplete kidney nocturnal emission is accompanied by impotence and lumbago, therapy should include an herbal medicine to strengthen kidney yang, such as **Ren Shen Lu Rong Wan [13.20]**.

Contraindications: **Jin Suo Gu Jing Wan** is not recommended for cases of seminal emission due to kidney fire. In such cases, **Zhi Bai Di Huang Wan [13.18a]**, containing some cooling agents, would be the medicine of choice. It is important to differentiate between nocturnal emission due to heat (which is usually accompanied by dreams) and nocturnal emission due to depletion (which is not dream dependent).

Jin Sou Gu Jing Wan		
Constituent Substances		
Pinyin Name	**Pharmaceutical Name**	**% Composition**
Qian Shi	*Semen Euryales*	16.60
Lian Xu	*Stamen Nelumbinis Nuciferae*	16.60
Duan Long Gu	*Os Draconis (calcined)*	8.33
Duan Mu Li	*Concha Ostrae (calcined)*	8.33
Lian Zi	*Semen Nelumbinis*	33.33
Sha Yuan Ji Li	*Semen Astragalis*	16.67

Composition and Rationale: *Qian Shi* is an astringent herb that strengthens the kidney and spleen and stems nocturnal emission; *Lian Xu* stabilizes the kidney and controls nocturnal emissions; *Duan Mu Li* and *Duan Long Gu* are astringent herbs that control nocturnal emission, control frequent urination and reduce sweat; *Lian Zi* strengthens the kidney and spleen and controls nocturnal emission; and *Sha Yuan Ji Li* supplements the kidney, nourishes the sperm, and controls nocturnal emission.

Bibliography

Chinese Sources

Academy of Traditional Chinese Medicine, Institute of Chinese Materia Medica. *Zhong Yao Zhi Ji Shou Ci* (Handbook of Traditional Chinese Patent Medicine Formulae). Beijing: People's Medical Publishing House, 1975.

Beijing Academy of Traditional Chinese Medicine. *Zhong Yi Da Ci Dian* (Dictionary of Traditional Chinese Medicine). Beijing: People's Medical Publishing House, 1982.

——————. *Zhong Yi Ming Ci Shu Yu Xuan Shi* (Explanation of Traditional Chinese Medical Terminology). Beijing: People's Medical Publishing House, 1978.

Beijing College of Traditional Chinese Medicine. *Zhong Cao Yao Jiao Xue Can Kao Zi Liao* (The Teacher's Guide for Traditional Chinese Medicine). Beijing: Beijing College of Traditional Chinese Medicine, 1982.

Beijing Public Health Bureau. *Beijing Shi Zhong Yao Cheng Feng Xuan Ji* (The Beijing Selection of Traditional Chinese Patent Medicine Formulae). Beijing: Beijing Science and Technology Press, 1959.

——————. *Beijing Shi Zhong Yao Tiao Ji Gui Cheng* (Rules for the Preparation of Traditional Chinese Formulae in Beijing). Beijing: The Beijing Health Bureau Publishing Office, 1983.

——————. *Beijing Shi Zhong Yao Zhi Ji Xuan Bian* (The Selection of Traditional Chinese Patent Formulae in Beijing). Beijing: The People's Medical Publishing House, 1973.

Chen Zhong-rui, She Ji-lin. *Xiao Er Chang Yong Zhong Cheng Yao* (Common Traditional Chinese Patent Medicine for Children). Beijing: Intellectual Publishing House, 1983.

Chengdu College of Traditional Chinese Medicine. *Zhong Yao Xue* (Textbook of Chinese Medicine). Shanghai: Shanghai Science and Technology Press, 1978.

Guangzhou College of Traditional Chinese Medicine. *Fang Ji Xue* (Textbook of Traditional Chinese Medicine Formulae). Shanghai: Shanghai Science and Technology Press, 1979.

_____. *Wai Ke Xue* (Traditional Chinese Medical Textbook of Surgery). Shanghai: Shanghai Science and Technology Press, 1983.

_____. *Zhong Yi Shang Ke Xue* (Traditional Chinese Medical Textbook for Treating Trauma). Shanghai: Shanghai Science and Technology Press, 1981.

Hubei College of Traditional Chinese Medicine. *Zhong Yi Fu Ke Xue* (Traditional Chinese Medical Text for Gynecology). Shanghai Science and Technology Press, 1984.

Jin Shi-yuan. *Zhong Cheng Yao De He Li Ying Yong* (The Proper Use of Traditional Chinese Patent Medicine). Beijing: The People's Medical Publishing House, 1984.

Liu De-yi. *Zhong Yao Cheng Yao Xue* (Traditional Chinese Patent Medicine Text). Tianjin: Tianjin Science and Technology Press, 1984.

Shanghai College of Traditional Chinese Medicine. *Nei Ke Xue* (Traditional Chinese Medicine Textbook of Internal Medicine). Shanghai: Shanghai Science and Technology Press, 1979.

_____. *Zhong Yi Er Ke Xue* (Textbook of Traditional Chinese Medicine of Pediatrics). Shanghai: Shanghai Science and Technology Press, 1984.

Song Lian-zhu, Tau Nai-gui. *Shi Yong Zong Cheng Yao Shou Ce* (Practical Handbook of Chinese Patent Medicine). Jinan, Shendong Province: Shendong Science and Technology Press, 1985.

Yie Xian-chun. *Chang Yong Zhong Cheng Yao* (Common Traditional Chinese Patent Medicines). Shanghai: The Shanghai People's Publishing House, 1976.

Zhongshan Medical College. *Zhong Yao Lin Chuang Ying Yong* (The Clinical Use of Traditional Chinese Medicine). Guangdong: People's Publishing House, 1975.

Zhu Mei. *Lao Zhong Ti Zhu Mei Jing Yen Fang* (Effective Traditional Chinese Medicinal Formulae of Dr. Mei Zhu). Unpublished.

English Sources

Beijing Medical College. *A Concise Chinese-English Dictionary of Medicine.* Beijing: People's Medical Publishing House, 1982.

Bensky, Dan, and Andrew Gamble. *Chinese Herbal Medicine Materia Medica.* Seattle: Eastland Press, 1986.

Berkow, Robert, and John H. Talbott, eds. *The Merck Manual of Diagnosis and Therapy.* Rahway, New Jersey: Merk Sharp & Dohme Research Laboratories, 1977.

Huang Xiao-Kai, et al, eds. *English-Chinese Glossary of Basic Medical Terms.* Beijing: People's Medical Publishing House, 1975.

Kaptchuk, Ted. *The Web That Has No Weaver, Understanding Chinese Medicine.* New York: Congden and Weed, 1983.

Unschuld, Paul U. *Medicine in China: A History of Pharmaceutics.* Berkeley, California: University of California Press, 1986.

Wiseman, Nigel, Andrew Ellis, and Paul Zmiewski, trans. and eds. *Fundamentals of Chinese Medicine.* Brookline, Massachusetts: Paradigm Publications, 1985.

Wiseman, Nigel. *Glossary of Chinese Medicine.* 3 vols. Brookline, Massachusetts: Paradigm Publications, 1989-.

Index